Anecdotes of the Manners and Customs of London during the Eighteenth Century

Including the Fashions, Festivities, Dresses, and Amusements etc.

James Peller Malcolm

Alpha Editions

This edition published in 2024

ISBN : 9789366382784

Design and Setting By
Alpha Editions
www.alphaedis.com
Email - info@alphaedis.com

As per information held with us this book is in Public Domain.
This book is a reproduction of an important historical work. Alpha Editions uses the best technology to reproduce historical work in the same manner it was first published to preserve its original nature. Any marks or number seen are left intentionally to preserve its true form.

Contents

VOL. 1 ....- 1 -
PREFACE. ....- 3 -
CHAPTER. I. STATE OF PARISH CHILDREN—ANECDOTES OF VARIOUS DESCRIPTIONS OF CHARITY EXERCISED IN LONDON, BETWEEN THE YEARS 1700 AND 1800. ....- 17 -
CHAPTER. II. ANECDOTES OF DEPRAVITY, FROM 1700 TO 1800. ....- 63 -
CHAPTER. III. MANNERS AND CUSTOMS OF THE INHABITANTS OF LONDON FROM 1700 TO 1800. ....- 135 -
CHAPTER. IV. ANECDOTES OF ECCENTRICITY. ....- 223 -

VOL. 1

PREFACE.

I beg leave to return my sincere thanks to the community, for the flattering reception with which this undertaking has been honoured:—A more convincing proof of that approbation which every Author most ardently desires seldom occurs, and still more seldom is expressed in so short a period as between the dates of the first appearance of the book and the present preface (March 1808 and May 1809.)

It had been my intention, from the moment I thought of tracing the habits of the residents of our Metropolis, to give a history of them from the earliest ages to the close of the last century: those early ages should certainly have been noticed first; but the length of time required for collecting materials, and the heavy expences attending printing, made it imperiously necessary that I should offer to the publick the least difficult portion of my labours, in order to ascertain whether I might proceed in safety with the remainder. The result has surpassed my hopes, and roused me to redoubled exertion in preparing for the press a volume including Anecdotes of Manners and Customs from the Roman Invasion to 1700, in which will be found most of the *apparent omissions* discoverable in this; but I shall ever reserve a right to myself of saying nothing on a subject of which I have an imperfect knowledge, through impediments not always to be explained without a charge of prolixity. This circumstance, and the impossibility of knowing how the work would be received, compelled me to give a retrospective view, at the commencement of some chapters, that should contribute to render them satisfactory, provided the early portion never appeared. The readers of the Quarto edition of the History of the Eighteenth Century will therefore have the goodness to excuse the retrospective sketches in it; and those of the present will perceive the sketches alluded to are omitted, in order to confine each event to its proper æra in the work when completed.

It will be observed that I address myself in the above sentence solely to the liberal reader for information and amusement, and by no means to the invisible censors of the age, who kindly and charitably supply the place of Inquisitors without receiving their appointment either from the Church, the State, or the Publick. *A person* who honours this publication with his notice in the Eclectic Review remarks, "*We* should have thought the progress of learning, and the novelties in the trade of books, during the last century, well intitled to some regard; and, as Mr. M. has 'been indebted to his worthy friend Mr. Nichols for the inspection of his matchless collection of periodical publications, from which great part of his materials have been selected,' we wonder not a little how the very institution of periodical publications could escape his notice." The history of literature did not escape my recollection as connected with that of the manners of the Metropolis; but *you*, Gentlemen

Reviewers, *being literary men*, ought to have been aware that the very worthy friend you have mentioned had nearly printed his *Literary Anecdotes of the same century*, which would have appeared at the moment my Anecdotes were published, had not one general conflagration destroyed the whole of the impression, and a considerable number of my own books, and compelled the benevolent sufferer to recommence his labours. "Perhaps," continue the Reviewers, "Mr. M. did not know that the voracity of the publick for scandal demanded *four* editions, comprising 19,000 copies of the Town and Country Magazine, on its first appearance." I did know the prevailing voracity for scandal, and that it was *partly* supplied by *Reviews*. I do not mean by any particular work so termed, but by individual articles in many publications of that description.

Knowing the mischievous consequences to authors, of perversion, misquotation, and misrepresentation, before the *nature* of Reviews was fully understood, the enlightened and excellent Dr. Blair, whose Sermons do his head and heart so much honour, wrote thus to Mr. Bruce, the celebrated Abyssinian Traveller: "I do not get the Monthly Review, and never saw that article in it which has been so injurious to you. Indeed, I seldom see any Reviews, unless what is called The Analytical one, which a friend of mine takes, and commonly sends to me; and that Review appears abundantly favourable to you. But I entirely agree with Dr. Douglas, that the Reviews are beneath your notice. They are always guided by the interest of some booksellers; and it is not on their opinions that the reputation of books and authors will depend. I am so much of this mind, that though I lately published a volume of Sermons, I never gave myself the smallest trouble to enquire what the several Reviewers said of it, or whether they took any notice of it at all[viii:A]."

It is well known that Dr. Blair had established a reputation which it was impossible to undermine by secret attacks: hence he naturally held those who aimed them at others in sovereign contempt. There are authors, however, who are endeavouring by every laudable exertion in their power to establish a similar reputation; and would frequently accomplish it, did not the secret envious Reviewer annihilate their hopes by exciting terrors in their minds, and by this means destroy all their vigour, substituting hesitation for energy, and trepidation for modest confidence in their abilities. Worthy and enviable pursuit, to wound the feelings of a man we never saw, and rob him not only of fame, but of that remuneration which the risk of his property in some degree demands from the publick he endeavours to please!

When an author so far forgets his moral obligations as to publish to the world sentiments or narratives dangerous to the beautiful order and simplicity of social life, it becomes the province of a Reviewer to expose his intentions, and lash him into a sense of his duty; nor should arrogance and presumptuous folly escape the reprehension of a *gentleman* from the same source: but, when a work appears which demonstrates great labour and diligence in the compilation or invention, and contains nothing offensive to honour and morality, envy and malice, and the restless spirit termed *ill-nature*, should really be subdued in the breast of the Censor, so far as to permit him not to *expose himself*, and the Review *his individual article* disgraces. Besides, both the writer and publisher should reflect, that when *they* have almost forgotten the article which leaves a deep and a malignant sting, the party suffering from it lingers in hopeless melancholy; and in more than one instance even life is said to have been wasted in the decay produced by a malicious Review.

I should here apologize to the reader for having omitted the portrait of an incompetent and splenetic Reviewer in the first edition of this work; but, as it is never too late to amend, and I cannot violate my own sense of the injustice of giving information in a new edition withheld in the first, by noticing so common a character, I shall here proceed to shew him in his true colours, as part of the grand aggregate I have attempted to describe; merely observing, as a further excuse, in the words of the Critical Review on these Anecdotes: I am "more pleased with faithful delineations of general nature, than with the account of any anomalous productions." Unfortunately for the majority of authors, and most fortunately for the Reviewer, it too often happens that second editions of works are not called for; through this circumstance *Reviews* of *Reviewers* are rarely to be met with, and pamphlets refuting their strictures seldom answer any purpose, owing to their confined sale. Happily for myself, an opportunity offers which must have full effect, as the reader of these pages will judge for himself on their merits, and between the assertions of certain Reviewers, and what I have to offer in opposition to them.

These self-important *unknown* persons will find me combating on the side of injured authors, not only on my own account, but on that of other individuals severely and unjustly condemned. I certainly despise them with Dr. Blair; that I do not fear them in my literary pursuits, and have no cause for so doing, my own words, and the approbation of the publick, sufficiently demonstrate. I shall be highly gratified if the following investigation leads one man to judge for himself hereafter, when he finds Reviews of a similar description connected with others of liberality and moderation.

We may venture to attribute the introduction of Modern Reviews to Edward Cave eventually; for, although the Gentleman's Magazine never assumed that exclusive character, it certainly suggested the hint of issuing *monthly* anonymous strictures on new publications[ix;A]. All have since professed to commence their career with good humour, talents, liberality, candour, justice, mercy, and, in short, with the exercise of every virtue. Had they *all* strictly adhered to their professions, Literature would indeed have flourished under the moderate corrections of Criticism, which is necessary to raise a perfect stock for the great demand of England; but, instead of those tempered [xi]reproofs, we are often surprised by floods or torrents of censure, which beat to the earth, and completely destroy, every thing within their scope. It is the authors of those torrents that I combat: the impartial and candid Reviewer I honour and admire, in proportion to the dangers and difficulties of his office.

The Critical Review for May 1808—versus "*Anecdotes of the Manners and Customs of London.*" The writer of this article says: "The following sketch of the contents of this performance will convince the reader that he may expect much information and amusement in the perusal." This is extremely well for a preliminary assertion; and yet we shall find him contradicting it almost from page 1 to 15, where the Review terminates. The contents are then given, and the Reviewer continues: "Such is the bill of fare which Mr. M. has prepared: in which, perhaps, the generality will find many *agreeable dishes* and *savoury ingredients*. It is, however, rather a *confused medley*, than a well assorted or *nicely selected* entertainment." Here we have a simile warm from the Crown and Anchor or London Tavern. "Mr. M. has very industriously perused the public papers, periodical works, &c. of the last century; and from these he has *culled as much matter* as, with his *own head and tail* pieces of remark, explanation, and *connection*, compose an ample quarto of 490 pages."—"In *traversing* the pages of this *bulky volume*, we have sometimes been instructed, and often amused; but on the whole we have experienced sensations of tediousness and languor, which the author will perhaps impute to our *squeamishness of appetite* or apathy of temperament; but which *we* are more willing to ascribe to the prolixity of the work. When the reader has taken the trouble *to go through the book, we* shall leave him to determine whether *the critic* be insensible, or the author occasionally dull." This sneering *critic* (for he at length appears in the singular case, speaking grammatically) affects to be unwilling to accuse me of practising the art of book-making, and of inserting every piece of information which came in my way relative to the manners of London; but really "*we* would willingly have dispensed with many of his details, in which there is nothing either to edify or amuse."

The single critic, or congregated critics, which the reader pleases, next introduces the following quotation: "Then, says Mr. Malcolm, (meaning before the invasion of Cæsar) the hardy native stood erect in the full dignity and grace of nature, perfect from the hands of the Creator, and tinted with those pure colours which vary with the internal feelings. Cæsar, doubtless, found the males muscular and full of energy, the females graceful in their forms, and both wild and unrestrained in his estimation of manners; though probably they were such as we now admire in the Savage, sincerity unpolished and kindness roughly demonstrated."

I shall make no comments on this passage, which the reader of the Review is requested by the *critic* to take as a "specimen of that *affected, stiff,* and *verbose style* in which Mr. M. *sometimes* thinks proper to indulge, and on which the critic or critics would fail in *their* duty to the publick if *they* did not fix the seal of *their* utter reprobation."—"Perspicuity and ease are among those constituent principles of good writing, which we should be unwilling to sacrifice for any of the *starched refinements* and *elaborate perplexities* of modern composition."—"When Mr. M. *tells us* that Cæsar found the Aborigines of Britain 'tinted with those pure colours which vary with the internal feelings,' he seems to have forgotten that Cæsar himself *tells us* (B. G. lib. v.) that he found these 'hardy natives' *bedizened* with a coat of paint. And *we leave* our modern fine ladies to inform Mr. M. whether this artificial discoloration were likely to *serve as a mirror* for the varying emotions of the breast."

It may be presumed that he who undertakes to criticise the language of another should himself be perfect in the arrangement of his ideas, and of words to express them, and capable of composing similes that shall bear some reference to the subject illustrated. Whether the author of the Review in question is qualified for the employment he has undertaken, will appear in the elegant extracts which follow: "agreeable dishes," "savoury ingredients," "confused medley," "nicely selected," "culled as much matter," "his own head and tail pieces," "traversing the pages," "bulky volume," "squeamishness of appetite," "to go through the book," "affected, stiff," "starched refinements," "elaborate perplexities," "bedizened," and "*discoloration* were likely to serve as a *mirror*." Surely, if he asserts my style to be affected, stiff, and starched, I may venture to pronounce his extremely vulgar, incorrect, and confused.

I had not forgotten that Cæsar found the natives of England stained with the juices of plants, and partially covered with coloured earths; still I maintain that Nature had perfected her work, and given the fluids that due circulation, improved by exercise and temperance, which renders the complexion florid and beautiful. Extraneous matter at times defaced her operations; but luxury, disease, and enervation, had not dried the channels of the blood of the Aborigines, as it has those of the fine lady I am referred to, whose *discoloration* is to serve as a *mirror* to show my own folly.

"In p. 4. Mr. M. *tells us* what we suppose he discovered *after many nights of sleepless meditation,* that, 'There are in every human circle persons whose patriotism may be lulled; [the words between *lulled* and *and,* "such may be taught by invaders to execrate their chiefs or governors" are shamefully omitted by the Reviewer as well as the beginning of the first sentence] and glittering ornaments of dress, and indolence, soon produce unfavourable comparison between the former and a naked limb, and the exertions of what is termed savage and the more refined conceptions of quiet life.' *Without staying* to make any remarks on the phraseology or the structure of this sentence, we shall proceed to shew Mr. M. as a collector of curious anecdotes and amusing details, in which he appears to much more advantage than as a philosopher or a rhetorician."

Is it possible that an author can feel himself injured by such absurd and ridiculous spleen as those four lines and an half produced in the breast of this miserable Reviewer?

Contemptible and futile as my information is considered by the writer, he has deigned to compress nearly the whole matter of my Anecdotes of Charity for his own purposes; and, although he denies me any share of *his charity*, he is delighted with the instances of it *I have introduced to his notice* of that of others. For once he agrees with me in opinion as to the general improvement of manners; and occupies from the 3d to the 9th page in contradicting himself in almost all the positions he has endeavoured to establish as to my incompetency for the present undertaking.

"Mr. M's 4th chapter is intituled 'Eccentricity proved to be sometimes injurious, though often inoffensive.' We could willingly have spared Mr. Malcolm the necessity of exhibiting any proofs on this occasion; most of the Anecdotes *which he has scraped* together are destitute of interest." The writer has been much my friend in this instance, though certainly without intending it; for he could not have more effectually convinced the publick of his incapability. Can he suppose it possible that, in describing the Manners of the Metropolis, the eccentricities of its inhabitants should be omitted? It is as impossible as that any person should agree with him in all his absurdities. As to exciting of interest, the very nature of eccentricity is such, that pity alone must predominate in the breast of the considerate reader. The sneer that my specimens of eccentricity will make the Anecdotes "a favourite *of the* Circulating Libraries," came from the same hand that could write "*a bushel* of coals" instead of *a chaldron* of coals allowed by James Austin to boil his pudding fourteen days.

The *loyal* reader shall comment for himself on the following extract from this admirable Review: "In 1736, a laudable attempt was made to suppress the excessive use of Gin; and the resentment of the populace became so very turbulent, that they even presumed to exclaim in the streets, 'No Gin, no King.' *Whatever respect we may have for the exclamation, 'No Bishop, no King,' we do not think* that *either monarchy or any other government needs* the *support* of this, pernicious distillation." This is what the Reviewer 'tells us,' and *I* suppose the discovery was made "after many nights of sleepless meditation;" indeed the same degree of intense thought seems to have produced another sapient piece of philosophy or rhetoric, which is offered to our consideration in p. 11 of the Review. "When a bull *gives permission* to a greater brute than himself to bait him to death with dogs, we will allow that something like a sanction *is given* to the sport." Surely these specimens of deep cogitation are almost equal to my "*novel* observation that 'partnerships too frequently produce dissention and a struggle for individual power';" and the Reviewer's own words, "Mr. M. might have *added* to the spirit and interest of his work by *omitting* such superfluous details." These superfluous details, good reader, relate to the disputes between Messrs. Harris and Colman in 1768, which, having excited great interest amongst those who frequented the Theatre, could not, and ought not to be omitted to gratify an *invisible individual*, who is perhaps too much of a Philosopher to be pleased with Dramatic Entertainments.

The spleen of the Reviewer, having increased by indulgence, attains its *acmè* of virulence at the close of the article: "In his 12th Chapter Mr. M. professes to exhibit a Sketch of the present State of Society in London; in which we do not meet with much *sagacity of remark*, or *novelty of information*. Take an instance of his *common-place details*: 'The reader must recollect, that when a family is without visitors, it is governed by greater regularity. Many Merchants and rich Tradesmen pass much of their leisure time at Coffee-houses; and dinners are commonly given at those places'."

Now, what but blind and indiscriminating acrimony could dictate the above remarks? What sagacity was required to narrate facts as clear as noon-day? Or, what *novelty of information* could arise from describing the domestic occurrences of families in general? The Reviewer dared not say I have falsified a single article; perhaps he would rather I had drawn a *fancied picture* of present customs, that he might have added a charge of deeper dye against me. The Review of my performance, which has enabled him to earn a dinner, could not have been written if *similar common-place details had not appeared during the last century*. Good Sir, because *you know* how we *all live at present*, are we not to inform those who succeed us how *we have lived*? Taking the *conclusion* of sentences as a specimen of the *whole*, is peculiar to a certain description of Reviewers. Now, by referring to the page whence the extract is taken, it will be found I had been describing a family as entertaining their visitors, and naturally concluded by saying, "when alone, it was governed with greater regularity." For once we have an attempt at wit, which originates from my having asserted that the dissipation common *in high life*, and late hours, rendered eating of *breakfast* a "*languid operation*."—"We do not believe that there is, *in general*, so much *languor* in *this* operation of eating, as Mr. M. seems to suppose. But, perhaps, Mr. M. will think that we judge of the morning appetite of others by our own; and that we Reviewers have appetites like wolves, and are ready to *devour mountains of toast*, when they come in our way."—*Mountains of toast*—admirable metaphor! Surely this cannot be called affected, stiff, starched, verbose, or elevated language; it is familiar enough, and will be understood perfectly by the cook or house-maid, when the article which contains it reaches the Kitchen as waste paper.

"The author ends his *smooth-papered volume* (*a fault* I must transfer to the paper-maker, as I have not had it hot-pressed) with the following sentence: 'Such are the follies of many; but, thanks to Heaven! there are numbers of our nobility and gentry who live and act for the general benefit of mankind. And now, *Vale Londinium!*—We will add, *Vale* Mr. M. We have been indebted to you for some information and amusement; but should have been more gratified with the perusal of your work, if you had exhibited more judgment in the selection of the materials, and had not swelled the bulk by a number of futile, irrelevant, and incongruous details."

The readers of the first edition of this work, amounting perhaps to some thousands, have completely and decidedly contradicted the objections brought by the Reviewer in *general* terms, and supported by cavils upon four or six sentences selected from 490 pages. The readers of the present are offered all those cavils for their consideration, and will *judge for themselves* of their justice.

With due allowance for a small degree of asperity, for which the writer can have no good excuse, the Anti-Jacobin Review of December last contains some argumentative strictures on the arrangement of this work, as it appeared in the first edition. When a book is offered to the world, it cannot be expected that every fact in it, and the method, should meet the approbation of all descriptions of persons; as taste and opinions are acknowledged to be as various as the features of the face. That the publick at large have not disapproved of the progressive chronological manner adopted, I have the most positive evidence by the rapid sale of the work; and this I shall retain. However, as objections have been raised by individuals who act as Public Censors, I have adopted their suggestions in part, and given the Anecdotes a more connected form, by removing the breaks between each. But, while I submit to their decision in the above instance, I beg leave to deny that *any* of the materials are too trivial for insertion. I was to give the habits and manners of the Londoners as I found them. If their conduct was even infantile in some cases, the fault lay with them, not with me; if part of their conduct resembles that of all the rest of the world, it is still a part of their conduct, and requires notice as much as their peculiarities; and it is mere wanton contradiction to assert the contrary.

The Reviewer next discovers, that periodical publications are not the best authorities for ascertaining the manners of the times. This I utterly deny; and I challenge the Reviewer to point out the cases where falsehood and inaccuracy are discoverable, in the use I have made of them. In truth, they are almost the only vehicles by which we obtain any thing like a correct account of the foibles of the day—nay, any account at all. What does he say to the Spectator, the Tatler, the World, the Rambler, the Guardian, the Observator, the Female Tatler? Were they not periodical publications? Do they abound in "*shameful lies*" (the gross words of the Reviewer)? or are they not considered as faithful sketches of those customs which escape the notice of the Historian?

Every Newspaper may contain misrepresentations and falsehoods; but those are generally confined to politics and artifices of trade: when any indifferent circumstance is to be related, there is no inducement to *wilful* falsehood. Besides, our ingenuous Reviewer must have allowed me to have had sufficient discernment to reject articles of that description.—Were I to act with the same candour towards him as he has evinced towards "Newspapers, Intelligencers, and Magazines" (observe, *Reviews* are omitted) in his rejection of them as authorities, I should charge him with declaring a deliberate falsehood in informing his readers that my excellent friend Mr. Nichols had lost his matchless collection of periodical publications in the late burning of his warehouse and printing-office. A statement of this nature need not rest upon "*we believe*." London is extensive, but surely within the compass of a Reviewer's walk, who dogmatically substitutes *we believe* for the simple question at Mr. Nichols's door, "Have you lost your collection?"

I shall now follow this candid gentleman's example—he damns in the Theatrical term the whole of my book, by endeavouring to mislead the publick into a belief that it contains not a word of truth; and then a high-sounding apology in these words: "That Mr. M. would *intentionally* pervert a single fact, or make one statement that he *believed* to be erroneous, we certainly have not the most distant idea of intimating; he possesses too high a sense of honour, too great a feeling of manly integrity, even to permit the supposition." Pray, good Sir, who would willingly consider me rather as a fool than as a liar, apply your own words to yourself; and let me add, I am convinced you *believed* Mr. Nichols's collection to have been consumed by fire, though it certainly was not.

Further let me repeat your words, "Thus have I done, and *I challenge* contradiction:—mine are the *best authorities*."—Yes, they are the best authorities; such as the Journals of the House of Commons, the Gentleman's Magazine, official publications of Charities, and various institutions, under the signatures of their Secretaries, Reports of Coroners on Inquests, the Statements of G. A. Wachsel, Sir John Fielding's official reports, Mr. Howard's letters, Acts of Parliament, Dr. Hawes's information to the Author, Advertisements from different Speculators, the official statements of the Society for Reformation of Manners, Report of the Committee of Magistrates 1725, Letter from Secretary of State 1728, Proclamations by the

King and the Lord Mayor, original Letters of Richard Smith 1732, the Police Act, Evidence before the Committee of the House of Commons 1750, Address from Justice Fielding 1759, Narrative relating to the Cock-lane Ghost, Evidence of Physicians relating to Mad-houses 1762, Examinations before Committee of Commons respecting Robberies 1770, Sir J. Fielding's Address to Grand Jury 1773, official statement of Society for suppressing Vice; Quacks' own advertisements; Addison, from the Lover; London Gazette, ceremonial for receiving George I.; Royal Proclamation, 1721, confirming the existence of scandalous Clubs, Mackay's Journey through England 1724, Switterda's Advertisements, Act for suppressing Private Balls, Report of Committee of Common Council 1761, Charge by Sir J. Fielding respecting Profane Swearing 1763, original letters between the Bishop of Bristol and his Parishioners 1768, Grosley's Tour to London, Advertisements by C. Weedon, Esq. Life of Sacheverell, Henley's Advertisements, presentment of the Grand Jury relating to him 1728, Lady E. Hamilton's advertisements, Lord Viscount Vane's advertisement, original advertisements of Lotteries and Benefit Societies, Queen Anne's communication to the Lord Mayor respecting Riots 1709, Abstract of Wild's indictment 1725, official parish letter of Christ-church Surrey 1757, Minutes of Coroners Inquest 1763, Wilkes's letter 1768, Trial of Donald M'Lane, King's Proclamation 1768, that of Harley, Mayor, same period, Trial of J. Grainger, &c. 1768, Petition of W. Allen 1768, Presentment of Grand Jury 1701, that of Middlesex 1703; London Gazette, reformation of the Stage; the Presentment of Middlesex Grand Jury 1723, Advertisements of Figg and others, masters of defence, Notice from Wilks, &c. and Cibber's answer 1733, Notice from the Proprietor of Vauxhall-gardens, proposal from same 1738, Life of Handel, original letter from Mrs. Clive, Statements by Mr. Garrick and Mr. Beard, Letters of Messrs. Harris and Colman, Macklin's narrative, Plan of the Regatta 1775, Foote's letter to the Lord Chamberlain, Advertisements of Clothing lost, Peruke-makers' petition 1763, Sir William Davenant, original docquet to Mr. Cole for globe lamps, Act for improving London 1760, Notice from Commissioners for paving,—AND, LASTLY, PERIODICAL PUBLICATIONS.

My words in the Introduction are: "It gives me pleasure to acknowledge I have been indebted to my worthy friend Mr. Nichols for the inspection of his matchless collection of periodical publications, *from which great part of my materials* have been selected." Whether they were the sole sources of my Anecdotes let the above list of authorities testify, which the reader may verify by turning over the following pages. If the Reviewer *has read* this work, I charge him on his conscience to say why he asserts my information depends wholly upon lying newspapers, &c. Where, *alas!* has the "full spirit of moral honesty" evaporated which he so calmly professes?

Two sentences more, and I have done with the Anti-Jacobin. I am treated with the utmost superciliousness for attempting to prove that many male and female figures are to be found in London equal to the celebrated statues of the Venus de Medicis and the Apollo Belvidere, which were alluded to by the words *Grecian Apollos* and *Venuses*.—What, am I to be told that my powers of discrimination "are far *above par*," because I assert the British human form is equal to the conceptions of the antient Grecians? This "Grey-beard," as he calls himself, must have studied the Arts in a Mercantile way indeed, or he would have pronounced my powers were *below par* in saying they were only *equal*, as, upon a moment's consideration, I am convinced there are hundreds of persons in London whose forms in general, and the swells of their muscles, as far surpass the statues in question, excellent as they may be, as the works of God ever did and ever must exceed those of man. Indeed, the best Artists invariably acknowledge with humility and regret how very inferior their works are to the common productions of Nature. Then how extremely ridiculous are these words of the Reviewer: "That the Metropolis can furnish many beautiful figures both male and female, from the *millions* of its inhabitants, we readily allow; but that perfection of form and *character* which *characterises* an Apollo and a Venus, has *but few*, very *few resemblances*." I am almost tempted to say the latter part of this paragraph is impious: The most complicated, wonderful, and beautiful specimen of the powers of the *Creator*, exceeded by the works of the *created*; nay, so far exceeded as to leave but few even of resemblances!!! Has the Reviewer read that indefatigable and accurate author Keysler? Hear what he says of the Venus de Medicis, after paying it the just tribute due to superior excellence: "The head is by most Connoisseurs considered as too small in proportion to the rest of the body, particularly the hips; some censure the nose as too large; and possibly the furrow along the vertebræ of the back is something too deep, especially as the object represents a soft plump female; and both the bend of the arms and inclination of the body jointly conspire to lessen the depth of this furrow, if not totally to obliterate it. The fingers are remarkably long, and all, except the little finger of the left hand, destitute of joints; but this should not affect the reputation of the Artist, as it is sufficiently evident, that the *hands* had not received his last touches." It has often been asserted that the English Jacobin cordially hates his own countrymen, and endeavours to exalt the perfections of their enemies: the above fact seems to prove decidedly that an *Anti-Jacobin* treats an author with contempt, because he wished to say the truth of the Reviewer's countrymen. If the reverse was the case, and the British form was less perfect, I ought to have escaped censure merely for my *amor patriæ*.

It was to deprecate such criticism as the preceding, which I expected, through the experience of others, that I prescribed an Antidote in the Preface of the first edition.

And now I shall leave these two wise Reviewers "*to chew the cud in their own way*," according to the elegant expression of the Anti-Jacobin.

The Eclectic Review, in noticing this work, has confined itself to such observations as were highly proper, supposing the volume intended to form a *complete* history of the century. I have already explained the reasons why I offered it to the publick as it appeared, and shall not therefore repeat them; but I cannot avoid adding, I feel myself indebted for the offered suggestions, though they were anticipated. When gentlemanly reproof is tempered with praise, he must be an arrogant and presumptuous writer indeed who feels offended at the recital of his real or supposed errors. I shall give some commendatory extracts, and the Reviewer will permit me to refute one of his suppositions.

"We certainly approve Mr. M's choice of a subject; and highly should we have congratulated ourselves if collectors of equal diligence had performed the same task for the 17th and many preceding centuries which he has undertaken for the last."—"Mr. M. with equal modesty and prudence, intitles his volume *Anecdotes*."—"It presents some of the principal features of the times, and will afford amusement and knowledge to the present generation, and still more to future generations, who cannot by recollection compare the portrait with the original."—"Whoever desires to form a just estimate of the manners of the English in the 18th century will derive great assistance from Mr. M's collections."

After what has been said, I am sorry to be obliged to censure any part of this Review of my Anecdotes. Speaking of my prints of Dress, the Reviewer says, I should have consulted several works which he has named, particularly Hogarth's labours, or family pictures, and adds: "We are very much afraid Mr. M's prints on this subject have been made up *memoriter*." The above sentence must be considered by every impartial person as perfectly unjustifiable, and insulting to my moral character. This instance sufficiently proves that I am personally unknown to the Reviewer, or he would also have known deceit and baseness form no part of my composition. It now remains for me to give my authorities for the sketches of dress, which are full as authentic as any the Reviewer has mentioned; and to his surprize and regret he will learn that *the very Hogarth he blames me for neglecting is one of them.*

Dress 1690-1715, is from a print published immediately after the coronation of William and Mary representing that event, offered to the world by one of the Heralds at Arms. Dress 1721 is from a wooden cut in a newspaper exhibiting the young beau of the day. Dress 1735 is three figures grouped from Hogarth's plates. Dress 1738 is the old maid in Covent-garden from Hogarth, the position of the figure altered. Dress 1745 from Hogarth, the attitudes different. Dress 1752, attitudes altered from a large print of

Vauxhall-gardens. Dress 1766 from Rooker's view of Covent-garden Church. Dress 1773 from a Mezzotinto, figures altered. Dress 1779 the hint taken from Miss Burney's Evelina. Dress 1785 from a large Aquatinta of the interior of the Pantheon, Oxford-street, figures newly grouped. The two last the *Reviewer knows to be correct.*—In concluding this subject, I cannot do better than quote the words of the Reviewer of my work in the European Magazine for June 1808. Speaking of the Anecdotes of Dress, he could not omit noticing "a Chapter" that "has in a manner fixed these fleeting meteors of public absurdity, by a series of prints, that at once serve as embellishments and elucidations of the work."—"These prints we really wish our readers could see, because they are, in many instances, extremely curious, and also because, on subjects of this nature, an artist with a few strokes of his pencil can convey ideas in a much stronger manner to the mind than an author in pages of laboured description."

As I have candidly given the reader *all* that the preceding Reviewers have said *against me*, he will indulge me in adding a *few words* from those who *praise me*. Were all Reviews formed on the liberal plan which distinguishes the article concerning my Anecdotes in the European Magazine, every author must be gratified with the prospect of having his work fairly analysed, and receiving explanatory notices for a future edition, and rejoice that Reviews are published. In proceeding through the contents of my book this worthy critic has given explanations of such passages as his knowledge of London enabled him to illustrate, which I have inserted in the form of notes in their proper places in the present edition; and in this pursuit he has, to his great credit, never once indulged in captious exceptions against particular sentences, or spoken of every thing omitted and nothing inserted. The conclusion is extremely grateful to my feelings: "When we consider the labour which Mr. M. must have undergone in collecting such a variety of materials from such a number of volumes, pamphlets, and papers, as he must have perused (some of which are no longer accessible but to the curious) we are of opinion that he deserves great praise for his industry. As a body of information respecting the morals, the manners, the foibles, and follies of our ancestors, we think this work very useful; as a book of reference, still more so. As an amusement, therefore, to the idle, and an assistant to the industrious readers, we unequivocally recommend it to the publick."

It may, perhaps, be said this praise is venal; on the contrary, I most solemnly declare I know neither my bitter Censors nor my Panegyrists. As some other Reviews have praised the work, I shall refer the reader to the Gentleman's Magazine, the Annual Review, &c.

J. P. MALCOLM.

May 1809.

FOOTNOTES:

[viii:A] Murray's Life of Bruce, p. 281.

[x:A] The previous attempts of individuals, which never exceeded a few volumes, I do not consider as cases in point.

CHAPTER. I.
STATE OF PARISH CHILDREN—ANECDOTES OF VARIOUS DESCRIPTIONS OF CHARITY EXERCISED IN LONDON, BETWEEN THE YEARS 1700 AND 1800.

There is something in the composition of the British atmosphere highly congenial to human and animal life: the clouded air and frequent humidity, and consequent coolness, prevent the violent perspirations the natives of finer climates experience; hence the fluids remain in full effect, and expand every part of the frame to its full proportion.

The habits and manner of living at various periods of our history had great influence on the exteriors of our ancestors: when men were forced into armies to repel invaders from Saxony and Denmark, the whole race of Englishmen became either hardened into almost supernatural exertion and strength, or were victims to those chronic diseases which deform the body and destroy the regularity of features; then the youth of each sex experienced privations incident to war, and the whole population must have suffered in the gracefulness of their persons. It required many years of quiet to restore the disorders of the body politic; and those of individuals recovered in the same slow proportion. In the reign of Edward III. Englishmen had again expanded into full military vigour; they marched with the front of Hercules against their enemies, and they maintained their strength and courage beyond the period of our Henry V.

After that reign, I should imagine, their stature diminished, and their countenances assumed a less pleasing form; and we find them bending under the most profligate despotism through the reigns of Henry VII. and VIII. Elizabeth, possessed of equal power, but inclined to use it for the benefit of her subjects, as far as the confined ideas of the time permitted, raised the people nearer to manhood; and her young soldiers waited for the enemy on their coasts, not yet as *volunteers*, but as defenders of their metropolis for a virtuous arbitrary Monarch.

The sentiments imbibed during this auspicious period, contributed to render domestic life more cheerful than it had hitherto been; the person was enlarged, and became more graceful; discontent fled from the features; and the Londoner, still nearer perfection, at last accomplished those two Revolutions which have for ever banished Despotism, and secured his home—nay made it his *castle*. See the consequences in the myriads of beautiful infants that smile on every side of him, with the regular and placid lines that mark their faces, and the strait and truly proportioned limbs that distinguish vast numbers of all ranks of people of both sexes.

Still the deformed and pallid are numerous; but deformity and disease in London generally proceed from causes which *may be prevented*; very confined residences destroy the health of parents and their offspring; the lowest class of inhabitants drink away their comforts, and suffer their children to *crawl* into manhood.

The highest classes sometimes trust infants to mercenaries; crooked legs and injured spines are too often the consequence: yet we find thousands of males and females, who appear to have been nursed by the Graces, and as far surpass the celebrated statues of the Venus de Medicis and the Apollo Belvidere, as the works of the Creator ever will those of man. When a female of high rank emerges from the controul of her governess, and receives the last polish, I pronounce her an ornament to any Court in Europe.

Those favoured with an opportunity of seeing the 30,000 volunteers assembled at Hyde-park in 1804, determined to fight for their homes, must agree with me that no nation ever produced an equal number together so finely proportioned and handsome.

In confirmation of my assertion that part of the deformity observable in the lower class of people might be prevented, I shall insert a Parliamentary report concerning their children, and show how numbers taken from parents have been disposed of.

"Mr. Whitworth reported from the Committee appointed to inquire into the state of the parish poor infants, under the age of 14 years, within the bills of mortality, and to report their opinion to the House; that the Committee had inquired accordingly, and had come to several resolutions which they had directed him to report to the House. The said Report was read, and is as follows:

"The Committee having examined the registers of the several parishes referred to them by the House, have collected from them the state of the parish infant poor; and find, that taking the children born in workhouses or parish houses, or received of and under 12 months old in the year 1763, and following the same into 1764 and 1765, *only seven in one hundred* appeared to have survived this short period.

"That having called for the registers of the years 1754, 1755, 1761, 1762, of the children placed out apprentices by the parishes within the bills of mortality, it appears that there have been apprenticed out the number of 1419; but, upon examining the ages at which the said children so placed out were received in the seven years from 1741 till they grew up to be placed out, it appears that only 19 of those born in the workhouses, or received into them under 12 months old, compose any part of the 1419; and even of those received as far as three years old, only 36 appear to have survived in the hands of the said parishes to be placed out apprentices. It appears that the children are kept in the several workhouses in town, or in the hands of parish nurses in town, only a small portion of them being sent into the country to be nursed, and the price of 3*s.* and 2*s.* 6*d.* per week first paid, is often reduced so low as 1*s.* 6*d.* and 1*s.* per week; that it cannot be presumed to be equal to the necessary care of infants.

"Your Committee find the conduct of parish nurses was taken notice of by Parliament in the year 1715; and upon examining also into the recent facts above related, it doth not appear to your Committee that the evil is or can be remedied, unless proper regulations are established by legislative authority. It appears from the evidence of the parish officers of St. Andrew, Holborn (called within the City liberties), and also from Mr. Hutton, a principal inhabitant of that parish, that the sum of 2*s.* 6*d.* a week for the article of nursing, is as little as a child can be nursed at to have justice done it; but at the same time, they being sensible of the good conduct and management of the Hospital for the maintenance and education of exposed and deserted young children, they have proposed to the governors and guardians thereof, to receive their infant parish poor at a certain rate, which, by the minutes of the general court of the said Hospital, dated Feb. 18, 1767, which was produced to your Committee and read, the said governors and guardians are ready to comply with, and likewise to forward any general purpose the Legislature may think proper to direct, in relation to the preservation of the infant parish poor within the bills of mortality.

"It appears upon the examination of Saunders Welch, esq. that great inconveniences have been found from parish boys being placed out apprentice so long as till the age of 24; and upon reading the clause in the 43d of Elizabeth, cap. 2, intituled, 'An Act for the relief of the Poor,' in the 5th section thereof it is said, 'Parish officers are to bind their man child to the age of 24, but the woman child to the age of 21, or time of marriage.' This, your Committee thinks, checks marriage, and discourages industry. It appears to your Committee, that the usual sum given by parishes with apprentices, has been generally from 20 to 40*s.* only, which your Committee think inadequate to the procuring good masters.

"It appears that the register directed to be made out by the Act of the 2d of His present Majesty, intituled, 'An Act for keeping a regular, uniform, and annual register of all parish poor infants under a certain age, within the bills of mortality,' is deficient, by not setting forth how children are disposed of after the age of four years.

"Upon the whole, your Committee came to the following resolutions: That it is the opinion of this Committee, that the parish infant poor, within the bills of mortality, should be sent into the country to be nursed, at a distance not less than a certain number of miles from any part of the town: That it is the opinion of this Committee, that the parish officers should allow and pay a certain sum for nursing each child: That it is the opinion of this Committee, that a proper number of principal inhabitants should be chosen in every parish respectively, under the denomination of Guardians of the parish infant poor, to inspect into the treatment of the said children nursed as above: That it is the opinion of this Committee, that the parish officers, governors, and directors of the poor, should have the alternative of sending such children to the Hospital, for the maintenance and education of exposed and deserted young children; and the governors and guardians thereof be permitted to take them at a certain sum, and to be paid by the said officers for nursing such children out of the parish rates: That it is the opinion of this Committee, that parish children should be placed out apprentice for a shorter time than is by law prescribed: That it is the opinion of this Committee, that a proper sum should be given as apprentice fees with the said parish children: That it is the opinion of this Committee, that the register of infant poor under four years of age, should be continued on till the children are in the same manner disposed of in the world.

"These resolutions were agreed to by the House, and a bill ordered."

It appears from a return inserted in the Journals of the House of Commons, 1778, that, in the preceding eleven years, the following was the state of the reception and discharge of parish children in the parishes mentioned, from which an accurate estimate may be formed for the rest of London.

	Children under 6 years old.	Died.	Returned to their parents.	Apprenticed.
St. Giles in the Fields, and St. George Bloomsbury	1479	177	956	319
St. Margaret and St. John, Westminster	1109	181	766	172
St. Anne, Westminster	324	100	152	76
St. James, Westminster	861	215	250	243
St. Clement Danes	257	113	84	89

St. Andrew, Holborn, and St. George Martyr	756	137	308	207
Saffron Hill	231	30	82	95
St. James, Clerkenwell	701	104	456	116
St. Mary, Whitechapel	449	69	102	286
St. Saviour's, Southwark	539	105	205	187
St. Leonard, Shoreditch	586	99	178	185
St. John, Southwark	154	48	65	127
St. Luke, Old-street	421	103	103	234
St. Botolph, Aldgate	297	90	130	101
St. Martin in the Fields	1512	463	736	321
St. Paul, Covent-garden	51	8	27	36
	9727	2042	4600	2794

Children, nursed as the above authentic documents prove they were, cannot but have been checked in their growth; and perhaps many of them are at this moment part of the miserable objects we daily see in the streets. The exercise of a little humanity may prevent similar evils in future.

There is an admirable example, which has long been established for our imitation, where the offspring of vice and humble virtue, equally innocent, are received and nurtured with the utmost care, and where human nature is rescued from debasement, corporeal and mental. Let the reader reflect on the thousands originally preserved, and their descendants rendered happy, through the god-like benevolence of Captain Coram; and he will immediately recollect the *Foundling Hospital*.

In consequence of that worthy man's petition, George II. granted a Charter of incorporation, which authorised Charles duke of Richmond, and several other eminent persons, to purchase lands, &c. in mortmain, to the annual amount of 4000*l.* to be applied to the maintenance and education of exposed and deserted infants.

The first quarterly general meeting of the Corporation was held December 26, 1739, when subscription-books were ordered to be opened at the Bank of England and various bankers, for inserting the names of annual contributors. The governors and guardians then amounted to near 400, who unanimously determined to vote their thanks to Captain Coram; but he declined them, and modestly requested they might be transferred to those ladies whose subscriptions had enabled him to procure the Charter. This proposal was acceded to, and the benevolent Captain deputed to convey them.

Montague house, now the British Museum, had been thought by the governors in 1740, an eligible receptacle for the objects of the intended charity; but Messrs. Fazakerly, and the Attorney and Solicitor Generals, to whom the matter was referred, gave it as their opinion that the expence of obtaining those extensive premises would be too great. The governors resolved, in consequence, to open subscriptions for the purchase of land on which to erect an hospital, and in the mean time to receive sixty children in a temporary receptacle.

They accomplished their wishes in the following December, by obtaining 56 acres North of Ormond-street, of the earl of Salisbury, for 7000*l.* the present site of the Foundling hospital, Guildford-street, &c. On the 25th of March, 1741, 19 male and 11 female infants were received, all of whom were less than two months old; their baptism took place the ensuing Sunday, when two were honoured with the names of Thomas and Eunice Coram; others of robust frames and apparently calculated for future seamen, were called Drake, Blake, and Norris.

John Milner, esq. vice-president of the corporation, assisted by many governors, laid the first stone of the new hospital in 1742, when a copper plate, secured between two pieces of milled-lead, was deposited in a cavity; the plate is thus inscribed: "The foundation of this hospital for the relief of exposed and deserted young children, was laid 16th September, 16 George II. 1742."

The Corporation, laudably attentive to the future happiness of the orphans committed to their care, determined to have them inoculated for the small-pox in 1744; a process then as much condemned as vaccination is at present.

The first stone of the Chapel was deposited by —— Jacobson, esq. and contains the following inscription: "The foundation of this Chapel was laid the 1st day of May, A. D. 1747, and in the 20th year of his most sacred Majesty King George II." At the same time a successful attempt to obtain farther pecuniary assistance was made, by a public breakfast for ladies, at 2*s.* 6*d.* per ticket, when a collection for the Chapel amounted to 596*l.* 13*s.* and another for the hospital produced 110*l.* 9*s.* 6*d.*

The Prince and Princess of Wales honoured the governors with their presence at the Chapel, Saturday, May 27, 1749, to hear one of Handel's compositions performed for the benefit of the hospital; the audience is said to have consisted of 1000 persons, who each paid 10*s*. 6*d*. for their tickets. The King sent 2000*l*. and an unknown benefactor 50*l*.

The worthy and veteran Coram died March 29, 1751, aged 83, and was buried April 2d, in the vault beneath the chapel of *his* hospital. The honours due to this excellent philanthropist were paid by the Corporation to the utmost extent; and the choirs of St. Paul's and St. Peter's Westminster chaunted Dr. Boyce's funeral service over the body, which was covered by a pall borne by many persons of distinction, followed by the charter of the foundation carried on a velvet cushion; and the infants preserved by his exertions closed the procession. The present governors, fully sensible of the public debt of gratitude still in arrears, have recently given his name to Great and Little Coram streets, erected on the surplus ground belonging to the charity[13:A].

Frequent repetitions of Handel's music, and contributions of every description, enabled the governors to receive 1240 children from 1742 to 1754. They, however, thought proper to petition the legislature for assistance two years afterwards, and obtained 10,000*l*. to be applied for the reception of infants under two months old. On the 2d June, 1756, 117 were admitted[13:B].

The governors found it necessary to publish the following notice on this occasion: "The governors and guardians of this Hospital thinking it incumbent on them to expose the falsity of what has been propagated in several newspapers, that out of 10,000*l*. granted by Parliament to this Corporation, 1200*l*. was deducted in several offices for fees; do hereby assure the publick, that all fees whatsoever were charitably remitted by all the noblemen and gentlemen through whose offices the proper warrants pass, so that the clear sum of 10,000*l*. was paid into the Bank of England on account of the Hospital. By order of the general Committee,

J. COLLINGWOOD, *Sec.*"

Sept. 7, 1757.

In 1757, the House of Commons granted the enormous sum of 20,000*l*. to enable the governors to take all children under six months of age, brought to them before Jan. 1, 1758.

A general statement of the proceedings published in 1758, declared, that from the opening of the Hospital, March 25, 1741, to Dec. 31, 1757, 6894 children had been received, 5510 of whom were taken from the 1st of June, 1756, in consequence of the grant of 10,000*l*. The number of deaths to the 31st of Dec. 1757, was 2821. The sums presented to the charity in 1757, including 30,000*l*. from the legislature, amounted to 38,002*l*. 1*s*. 2*d*.; 2806*l*. 10*s*. 3*d*. of which was bequeathed to the Hospital, 508*l*. 4*s*. 6*d*. given in annual benefactions, and 96*l*. 14*s*. 6*d*. benefactions towards the charges of the Chapel.

The expences of this eventful year, in the annals of the charity, was 33,832*l*. 13*s*. 2*d*.; 502*l*. 4*s*. 6*d*. of which was paid in fees, when passing the warrants for 20,000*l*. the *second* grant from Parliament.

In 1797, there were 357 children on the establishment, 175 in the house, and 182 at nurse, principally received from the metropolis. From 1770 to 1797, 1684 were received, of which number, 482 died under the age of twelve months; their age when received is generally under two months, and the limitation is twelve months, unless in particular cases or when 100*l*. is sent with the child, and except the children of soldiers or sailors in the service of their country. Children are admitted on petition, and the mother is examined as to the truth of her statements, who is placed, if practicable, in a proper situation to obtain a livelihood[15:A].

WELSH CHARITY SCHOOL.

This school was established in 1718 for the reception, maintenance, education, and apprenticing poor children of Welsh parents, born in and near London, who have no settlement; the school was originally held at the Hat, Shire-lane, then on Clerkenwell-green; but the trustees finding it insufficient for the purpose, and it having been patronized by the Prince of Wales, and enriched by the donations of the publick, the governors were enabled in 1772, to purchase the piece of freehold ground in Gray's-inn lane, where the school is now situated; on which and other buildings for the reception of 42 boys and 14 girls, they expended 3695*l*. From the foundation to 1779, 642 boys were entered upon the establishment, of whom, 511 were apprenticed to captains of vessels and various trades[15:B].

Such have been part of the proceedings of the inhabitants of London, in endeavouring to preserve the lives of infants; to which might be added many collateral means, particularly those which adopt the offspring of criminals, and thus render them useful members of society.

The subject might now be spread into various ramifications; but as brevity should be preferred when practicable, I shall confine my information and observations to the *last century*, and present the reader with the most material occurrences in the still greater work of preserving the population of London from degenerating in every point of view, and even from starvation, during their progress to maturity, and in the decline of life.

The commencement of the century was remarkable for a grand effort of charity, not the passing charity which provides for temporary wants of the body, that may recur almost immediately upon the disposal of the gift, nor that which removes the possibility of penury from the residents of alms and workhouses; but that which rendered the infant mind the seat of innocence, morality, and knowledge. The reader will fully appreciate the importance of this event, when I mention the schools established by one divine impulse in every quarter of the metropolis, and when he compares the chaos of ideas which must have composed the minds of the poorest classes of children, previous to the existence of these institutions, with the instructed infant comfortably cloathed, clean, and regular in attending divine worship.

The next general act of beneficence originated from a forcible appeal to the feelings of the Londoners, who beheld many hundreds of deluded Germans or Palatines, deserted by those who had promised to convey them to America, houseless, and without food, and relieved them from the pressure of those evils.

Cavendish Weedon, esq. issued the following advertisement in 1701, which does him immortal honour: "His Majesty having been pleased by his late most gracious proclamation to signify his desires for the encouraging of piety and morality and suppression of vice, Mr. Weedon of Lincoln's-Inn, for the better promoting the honour of God and such his pious intentions, hath established a monthly entertainment of Divine Musick at Stationers-hall, on Monday, the 5th day of January next, and intended to be kept and continued there every first Monday in every month, excepting the Lent season, and the months of July, August, and September. The same to consist of Anthems, Orations, and Poems, in honour and praise of God, religion, and virtue, one day; and in discouragement of irreligion, vice, and immorality, the other, alternately: to be performed by the best masters in each faculty; for which purpose all ingenious persons skilled in those qualifications that shall think fit to send in any composition in prose or verse to Mr. Playford, bookseller in the Temple-change in Fleet-street, free from all manner of reflections on parties and persons in particular, such as shall be approved of, Mr. Playford shall have orders to gratify the authors, and to return the others with thanks for the Author's kind intentions. The performance to begin exactly at eleven of the clock in the morning; and tickets to be had at Mr. Playford's, Garraway's, the Rainbow, and at most of the chief coffee-houses in town. The benefit of the Tickets, being only 5*s*. a-piece, the common price of other Musick-tickets, is to be disposed of amongst decayed gentry, and the maintenance of a school for educating of children in Religion, Musick, and Accompts."

Mr. Weedon advertised in the Gazette of May 4, 1702, that his Musical and other entertainments would be performed at Stationers-hall on the 7th with Anthems by Dr. Blow, an Oration by Mr. Collier, and Poems by Mr. Tate, her Majesty's Poet Laureat, in praise of Religion and Virtue. The receipts to be applied as before-mentioned.

In 1711, British charity extended beyond the bounds of the realm, through an application from the Society for the propagation of the Gospel in foreign parts to her Majesty, who was pleased, in consequence, to permit a collection to be made from house to house in all the parishes and precincts within the bills of mortality, to be applied to the purposes of the institution; which was announced from the reading-desks on Trinity Sunday.

Exclusive of the annual meetings of the charity children, there were opportunities taken to impress the publick with a due sense of the value of the institutions.

In 1713, they were assembled in the Artillery-ground, where the duke d'Aumont the French resident, and other distinguished characters attended to inspect them; the ambassador evinced his approbation by handsome presents of money to buy them books, &c. And on the thanksgiving day 4000 of these youths were seated upon elevated benches, which extended 600 feet in the Strand, where they saluted the two Houses of Parliament and the great officers of state, with hymns sung in unison.

The trustees adopted a plan in 1713, that seems well worth imitation at present, which was a Sermon preached by the Rev. Dr. Waugh, at St. Bride's, from the 12th verse of the 27th Psalm, "When my father and my mother forsake me, the Lord taketh me up," before 1400 of those children, of 2250 who had been placed with persons as apprentices and servants. An impressive discourse addressed to young persons, under such circumstances, must be attended with the best effects.

The gifts of private individuals to the poor cannot often be ascertained, but, that they are generally considerable, may be accidentally collected through the death of common beggars: one of those who lived in Barbican, died in

October, 1713, when 80 years of age, and seems to have perished through the chill occasioned by some sour beer given to her in Smithfield; her pockets contained eight farthings, but the rags that covered her concealed 150 broad pieces and guineas.

In 1714, the King gave the Sheriffs 1000*l.* for the relief and discharge of poor prisoners for debt.

Mr. Feast, brewer, of Whitecross-street, set a most brilliant example of charity in the dreadful winter of 1715-16, by purchasing 400 chaldrons of coals, which he distributed to such poor persons as were deprived of work by the severity of the winter.

In the following year 4400 persons formed a Society for insurance upon Lives, with a monthly dividend; but that which distinguished this association, and rendered it a proper subject for this Chapter, was, their requesting the rectors, vicars, and wardens of St. Martin in the Fields, St. James, St. Margaret's, St. Giles, St. Andrew's Holborn, and St. Clement Danes, "to recommend two boys out of each parish to the Society, which shall be put forthwith to school, cloathed, and 10*l.* given to put them out apprentices; and as the Society receives encouragement, the same method will be used to the great parishes, within the bills of mortality, that are overburthened with poor; and that a monthly stock is kept, and security given to the trustees for the security of the stock, to put several hundred children apprentices, and the 10*l.* charity. Each subscriber pays only 1*s.* per week; and if the person dies in a month after entrance, you are entitled to a dividend of 500 months to be made; but, if your life should continue one year, you are entitled to 15*l.* to put out a child apprentice, or 10*l.* to be disposed of to charitable uses as you shall judge proper; and 125*l.* per month laid by as a stock to sink your weekly payments," &c. &c.[23:A]

4800 children attended the anniversary of the charity-schools in 1716, at St. Sepulchre's church; on which occasion the bishop of Lincoln preached from Dan. iii. 12. The number of schools of this description had increased from the reign of king William III. in England and Ireland to 1221, and near 30,000 children received the benefit of instruction, and in many instances food and cloathing; those of London were 124, the number of boys educated in them 3131, the girls 1789; the children apprenticed from them, boys 2513, girls 1056[24:A].

A most dreadful fire occurred at Limehouse in the month of December, 1716, by which near 200 houses were destroyed, and infinite distress occasioned; the Prince Regent, agitated with strong sentiments of compassion, ordered the sum of 1000*l.* to be distributed immediately to the most pitiable objects; which laudable example was promptly followed by others to a considerable amount. A more disinterested charity was prosecuting at the same period for the Episcopal Protestants of Poland; towards which, 60*l.* was obtained in the inconsiderable parish of St. Helen's, Bishopsgate[24:B].

The Prince of Wales, actuated by the same impulse which now operates in the Society for the relief of prisoners confined for Small Debts, sent 350*l.* at Christmas, for the discharge of those at Ludgate and the two Compters.

In the year following a person, unknown, sent a 50*l.* note to the treasurer and trustees of the Blue-coat school, near Tothill-fields, the receipt of which was acknowledged in an advertisement, stating the agreeable fact, that this sum enabled them to receive four additional scholars, whom they promised to cloath at the periods mentioned in the statutes of the institution.

Another, or perhaps the same person, released 30 persons from Whitechapel prison, in August, 1717, cloathed them, gave them a dinner, and 2*s.* 6*d.* each; six months afterwards, the same benevolent unknown, repeated his charities at Whitechapel, and released all confined for small debts, one of whom was imprisoned near six months for 5*s.* 6*d.* which had been swelled by charges and fees to 40*s.*

Jan. 1717-18, the King gave 1000*l.* for the discharge of insolvent debtors, in the gaols of London and the county of Middlesex.

The King gave 1000*l. per annum*, towards the relief of poor housekeepers in London and Westminster[25:A]; that sum was increased to 1900*l.* in 1718, by collections under his Majesty's letters patent for the same purpose.

The Prince appears to have given 250*l.* annually to the Charter-house.

A repetition of the liberality of the unknown occurred again in September 1719, at Whitechapel, when he released 35 prisoners, besides giving them money.

1720, the earl of Thanet gave 1000*l.* to the widows and children of clergymen.

The Society for the relief of the Widows and Children of Clergymen has been already noticed, in the first volume of "Londinium Redivivum;" it will therefore only be necessary to state their gifts in 1720, which amounted to 2645*l.* 10*s.* exclusive of a considerable sum expended in placing out apprentices.

Mrs. Mary Turner, in the same year, commenced that noble foundation, which has since flourished with so much success, for the reception of incurable lunatics at Bethlehem hospital, by a handsome legacy.

Shortly after an examination of the Marshalsea books took place, when it was found that upwards of eleven hundred persons confined for small debts had been discharged within three years, by the charitable contributions of Roman catholics.

Amongst the charities of 1720, was that of lady Holford, who left 10*l.* each to 27 clergymen, on condition they attended her funeral; and eleven exhibitions of about 10*l.* each to as many boys, educated at the Charter-house upon the foundation.

The collection for the Sons of the Clergy amounted to 239*l.* 10*s.* in 1720, which was distributed to 16 children, in sums from 10*l.* to 20*l.* each; the annual contributions generally average now at 1000*l.*[27:A]

The year closed with the unequalled donation of Thomas Guy, who then determined to found that hospital on the site of the antient St. Thomas's, in Southwark, which has immortalized his name.

Certain charitable persons established an Infirmary in 1719. Two years afterwards they published one year's statement of their proceedings, from which it appears 108 patients had been received, of whom 52 were cured, 6 incurable, 8 died, 19 discharged for non-attendance, 1 for irregularity, 11 out-patients, and 11 within the infirmary, who received, with food and medicines, the exhortations of such clergymen as the Society could procure.

The London Workhouse received from March 1720 to March 1721, 683 vagabonds, beggars, pilferers, and young vagrants, and lewd and disorderly persons, of whom 620 were discharged, 2 buried, and 61 remained. In the same period, 27 children were bound to tradesmen, 2 were buried, and 86 remained; the latter were religiously educated in the doctrines of the Established Church; and were employed in spinning wool, sewing, and knitting, and taught to read, write, and cast accompts.

A treaty was completed in 1721, between the British Government and the Emperor of Morocco, by means of which, 280 persons were restored to their country; who went in procession, clad in the Moorish habit, to St. Paul's, where a Sermon suited to the occasion was preached by Mr. Berriman, chaplain to the bishop of London. The curiosity of the citizens to see the emancipated slaves was such, that the benevolent intentions of many charitable persons were frustrated; the collectors however obtained about 100*l.* After the Sermon, they proceeded to St. James's, and were admitted to the garden, where the King did them the honour of viewing their grateful countenances, and afterwards ordered them 500*l.* The captives went thence to Leicester-house, and received 250*l.* from the Prince of Wales.

The newspapers of December 1721, mention the revival of an antient custom upon the eve of great festivals; which was the Lord Mayor's visiting the Markets in person, to solicit contributions of provisions for the poor. It is said that his lordship was very successful at this period.

The spring of 1725 was extremely wet, and serious apprehensions of a total failure of the crops very generally prevailed. Those fears fortunately proved fallacious; but the useful body of labourers who resort to the neighbourhood of London as haymakers suffered dreadfully, and several actually died for want of food and lodging. One sentiment of compassion seems to have prevailed for these wretched people, and 20 and 30*l.* at a time was collected at the Exchange and in several parishes: the duke of Chandos gave 150 of them 2*s.* 6*d.* and a sixpenny loaf each, at his gate at Canons. Mr. Carey, vicar of Islington, went to every house in the parish soliciting for them; and, having received a handsome sum, he afterwards distributed it in the church.

The following January was very propitious to the funds of Bethlehem hospital, several gentlemen having subscribed towards the erection of the wings for incurables. One of these gifts was 500*l.* a second 200*l.* and another 100*l.* with a promise of the same sum annually for four years; they unanimously concealed their names.

M. Mahomet, a Turk, and a valet-de-chambre to George I. died in 1726, of whom it was said, "He wore the habit of a Turk, but had many Christian virtues, being profusely liberal to the poor; and is said to have discharged near 300 debtors from prison for small sums, since his coming into England."

A Mrs. Palmer died in 1727, who bequeathed the following large sums in charities: 4000*l.* for propagating the Gospel abroad; 4000*l.* for promoting Christian knowledge in the Highlands of Scotland; 2000*l.* to queen Anne's bounty; 2000*l.* to Bethlehem hospital; 500*l.* to the charity school of St. Andrew's, Holborn; and 500*l.* to poor widows, who received no alms from the parish. She resided in the parish of St. Andrew; but was buried at St. Giles's, Cripplegate.

The King honoured the Corporation of London with his company to dinner, in October, 1727; when on his way, a person presented him a petition, beseeching relief for the various prisoners for debt in London; this he received in the most gracious manner, and immediately ordered 1000*l.* to be paid to the Sheriffs for that purpose.

A Committee of the House of Commons visited the various prisons of the Metropolis, by order of the House, in March, 1729, when they found 30 miserable wretches in the greatest extremity, through illness and want, at the Marshalsea; which operated so forcibly on their feelings, that they immediately contributed sufficient to procure them medical assistance, nurses, cloaths, and food.

Bloomsbury-market, built by the duke of Bedford, was opened in March, 1730, to the great satisfaction of the neighbourhood. On the following

Monday, the Duke bought all the unsold meat at the market-price, and had it distributed to the reduced housekeepers, and other necessitous persons, inhabitants of the parish of St. Giles's[31:A].

630 chaldrons of coals were purchased in June, 1730, for the use of the poor of the several wards within the city of London.

There were dreadfully destructive fires at Blandford and Tiverton in 1731; the sufferers from which received unusual commiseration from the whole kingdom, and large subscriptions. The King gave 100*l*. to each of those towns, and the several wards of London made considerable collections.

In the year 1733, four Charity Sermons were preached in the parish of St. Margaret, Westminster, and a collection made from door to door, which amounted to 125*l*. intended for certain inhabitants of Saltzburg, who were persecuted for their religious opinions, and desirous of emigrating to Georgia.

The Weekly Miscellany of May 19, 1733, contains the following account of the Charity Schools then established in London, with the rules by which they were governed; they cannot but be read with avidity.

"The most charitable and useful design of setting up Schools, for the instructing children of the meanest and poorest of the people, was begun in the year 1698. What has now diffused itself through the whole nation, sprung from a very small seed, which was first planted in this great city, and by the blessing of the Divine Providence has, in a wonderful manner, been increased; so that there is now, within the cities of London and Westminster and bills of mortality, 132 charity schools. This charitable design meeting with such encouragement from the very liberal benefactions of the inhabitants almost in every parish, trustees were chosen in each district to oversee the management of the masters and mistresses, and to prescribe rules and orders for the government of each school; and treasurers were appointed, to whom all contributions were to be paid, who annually make up accounts of all money received and disbursed. The trustees frequently meet, to examine into the behaviour of the masters and mistresses, and whether due care is taken to preserve a regular discipline, and that the boys and girls be instructed, not only to read, but to be examined in the repetition of the Catechism, with the explanation thereof; which is brought in many schools to such perfection, that the children, upon their examination before the trustees, repeat, with great exactness, the texts in the Holy Scripture, to prove all the articles of the Creed, and other parts of the Catechism. These children are all cloathed at the expence of the trustees and subscribers; and when they have been fully taught to read, write, and cast accompts, they are then either put out to services, or to some handicraft trade. The girls are bred up not only to read, but to work in linen, knitting, and washing, so as to be fit for menial services.

"These schools thus increasing, it was thought necessary, in the year 1706, that the trustees should be formed into a voluntary Society, and that a chairman should be elected to preside, and summon meetings of the trustees as often as occasion should render it necessary. These meetings have regularly been continued to this time, where orders from time to time have been, by the majority of votes, agreed upon; and in the year 1729, rules and orders for the better regulation of the said schools, were recommended to the several trustees of the schools in the country; which being laid before the archbishops and bishops of the several dioceses in the kingdom, the said rules and orders were by them, under their hands, approved and established; which orders are here inserted: by which it will appear that the utmost care has been taken, not only to instruct the Children in the knowledge of the Christian religion, but also to breed them up in such a manner, that, as they are descended from the laborious part of mankind, they may be bred up and enured to the meanest services. If these orders be candidly considered, there is no reason for the objections that are commonly made against the Charity schools; and it must be a great satisfaction to those that have engaged in this charitable and useful design, that out of so great a number of children as have been thus educated, there is but one instance that any of them have been convicted of any crime; and this person, being transported, was so far influenced by his first education, that he was so thoroughly reclaimed, that he became a very industrious and sober man, and is so sensible of the benefit of his education, that, being in good circumstances, he is an annual contributor to the school where he was educated. Let it be considered, that as this city has vastly increased, and by consequence the poor proportionably multiplied, what must have become of all their children, if this method had not been taken for putting them out in an honest way to get their livelihoods, either by services or trades, the happy effects whereof is very evident. For there are now in the city of London many substantial tradesmen, who are constant contributors to the schools in which they were educated. To this may be added, that by particular benefactions a school is established for teaching the art of Navigation, to qualify the boys, bred up in the Charity schools, to be skilful and able seamen; since which a considerable number have been actually sent to sea; and by all the accounts received from captains of the ships where they were placed, they have fully answered the intention of their benefactors.

"In some schools, both in London, and in the country, where the benefactions would allow it, the children are both fed and cloathed; and in these both boys and girls are enured to labour, and the profit of their work applied towards their maintenance and setting them up; and in most of the schools in the country, the children in the time of harvest, are to be absent from coming to school, that they may glean, or do other work; and when they are fully taught to read, they are put out to handicraft trades, or to be servants in husbandry.

"That great Prince the Czar took with him not only the models of English ships, but also the scheme that was then newly projected for establishing Charity schools, which upon return to his own country, he ordered to be erected in all parts of his vast Empire, which he inforced by an edict, that none should be married that could not read the Bible: so differently did this wonderful genius think from some politicians amongst *us*, who have laid it down for a maxim in government, that the *servile* part of mankind are to be kept as *ignorant* as possible; whereas *he* endeavoured to promote knowledge and religion, even in the lowest conditions of life, as a means of making his Nation a flourishing and powerful people, and himself a great and glorious Monarch.

"*Rules for the good Order and Government of Charity Schools; drawn up by the Trustees of those Schools within the Bills of Mortality.*

"I. That the directions given by the present Lord Bishop of London to the masters and mistresses of the Charity schools within the bills of mortality and diocese of London, in the year 1724 (a copy of which hath been formerly sent to the several Charity schools), be duly observed. Particularly,

"1. The cautions there given against teaching the children any thing that may set them above the condition of servants, or the more laborious employments.

"2. The directions laid down concerning the Psalms to be sung by the children on the days of collection, that they be taken out of the book of Psalms only, and sung in the most common and usual tunes.

"3. The method there prescribed to the masters and mistresses in several rules, for possessing the minds of the children with the just sense of the duty and affection they owe to the present Government, and the succession in the Protestant line, and with a just dread of the persecutions and cruelties to be expected from a Popish Government.

"II. That the trustees of every school, according to the custom of the place, or the appointment of the founder, do frequently meet, and examine into the management of the school, and report the state and condition of the same at every general meeting of the subscribers.

"III. That they be very careful in the choice of a treasurer, who is to keep a fair account of all receipts and disbursements, for the view of all subscribers and contributors, who may desire to know how the money is disposed of.

"IV. That the person who shall be chosen for master or mistress of any school, be a member of the Church of England, of known affection to His Majesty King George, and to the Protestant succession as by law established; of a religious life, and sober conversation, a constant communicant, understanding the grounds and principles of the Christian religion, and having a capacity for educating children, according to the rules herein recommended.

"V. That, in training up of children, particular regard be had to the business they are most like to be employed in, either as servants, or in husbandry, or else in the woollen, iron, or such other manufactures, as are most used in those places where charity-schools are maintained. And in order thereto, that the children whilst at school be (so far as is consistent with their necessary learning, and the different circumstances of particular places) inured to some kind of work or labour, and in some measure daily employed in it; so that they may be rendered most useful to the publick; and for this end it may be proper that their earnings be applied towards finding them in diet, lodgings, and other necessaries.

"VI. Whereas Thomas Neale, esq. deceased, did devise part of his estate to be applied for supporting of Charity schools, or for such other charitable uses as his executors thought fit; and Frederick Slare, doctor in physick, the surviving executor of the said Mr. Neale's will, hath, out of the surplus of the said estate, appointed a considerable sum of money for the payment of an annual salary for a master, to instruct poor children in such part of the mathematicks as may fit them for the sea service; and this appointment hath been established by a decree of the high court of Chancery; and a Charity-school for that purpose is erected in the City of London; and the Trustees of the said school have ordered that each boy that should be sent from any of the Charity schools, shall be taught the said science, upon the payment of twenty shillings a year for each boy: It is therefore in a particular manner recommended to the trustees of each school within the cities of London and Westminster, that such boys as may be thought fit for the sea-service, be sent to the said school, to be instructed in an art which will render them so very useful to the publick.

"VII. That the trustees do insist upon it with parents, as a necessary condition on which their children are to be taken into school, that they send them clean washed and combed, regularly and constantly, at the hours of schooling; that they comply with all orders relating to them, and freely submit them to be chastised for their faults, without quarrelling or coming to the school on such occasions; that children be not countenanced in their faults, or masters and mistresses discouraged in the performance of their duty. But if there be any just reason of complaint, that it be made to the trustees, in whose determination they are to acquiesce; or if persons neglect, or refuse to observe these orders, then their children to be dismissed the school; and if they are cloathed, to forfeit their school cloaths.

"VIII. That the trustees do likewise, as far as in them lies, oblige the parents of all such children as they take into their schools, to agree that their children be put out to such services, employments, or trades, as the trustees shall think most proper and advantageous to the publick, and the places where they live.

"IX. And lastly, that the trustees do what they can to engage parents to give their children good examples at home, of a sober and religious behaviour, frequently to call upon them to repeat the Church Catechism, to read the Holy Scriptures, especially on the Lord's day, and cause prayers to be read morning and evening in their families: so that both parents and children may be the better informed of their duty, and by a constant and sincere practice thereof, promote the pious and useful design of charity schools, and so procure the blessing of God upon them.

"*Rules proper to be observed by the Masters and Mistresses.*

"I. That the masters and mistresses do themselves attend the school at the times appointed by the founders and trustees, and keep the children diligently to their business, during the hours of schooling, suffering none to be absent at any time, but upon account of sickness, or some such reasonable excuse, unless in the time of harvest, and when the trustees think it proper that they should be employed in husbandry, spinning, carding, or some other manufactures; but, if children are kept away, the trustees to be acquainted with it, that others more conformable may be taken into their places.

"II. That they teach the children the true spelling of words, make them mind their stops, and bring them to pronounce and read distinctly without a tone: and because it is found by experience, that in several places in the country due care has not been taken in these respects (the masters and mistresses being paid for teaching the children either by a monthly or quarterly allowance), it is proposed to such founders and trustees as shall think it requisite, that their payments be hereafter made in the following manner: The *first* to begin so soon as each child can name and distinguish all the letters in the alphabet; the *second*, when the child can spell well; and the *third*, when it can read well and distinctly, and can repeat the Church Catechism.

"III. That they make it their principal care to teach the children to read the Bible, to instruct them in the principles of the Christian religion, according to the doctrine of the Church of England; and that they explain the Church

Catechism to them by some exposition, which, together with the Catechism, the children should publicly repeat in church, or elsewhere, so often as the minister and the trustees shall require; and be frequently examined in school, as to their improvements of every sort.

"IV. That they teach the children those doctrines and principles of religion which are in their nature most useful in the course of a private life, and especially such as concern faith and good manners.

"V. That they bring the children to church, so often as divine service is there performed, before it begins, and instruct them to behave themselves orderly, kneeling, or standing as the rubrick directs, and to join in the public service with, and regularly to repeat after, the minister, with an humble low voice, and in the most devout manner, in all places where the people are so directed, in such manner as not to disturb the rest of the congregation, and particularly in singing of Psalms: and that they likewise take care, that the children bring their Bibles and Common-prayer books always to church; and in order to prevent their spending the Lord's-day idly or profanely, it will be proper that every master and mistress give each child some task out of the most useful parts of Scripture, to be learnt on each Lord's-day, according to their capacities; and that they require a strict performance of it every Monday morning, and also oblige them to say the texts of the sermons preached the day before.

"VI. That they never fail to pray morning and evening in the school, and teach the children to do the same at home, devoutly upon their knees, when they rise and go to bed, as also to say grace before and after meat.

"VII. That they take particular care of the manners and behaviour of the children, and by all proper methods discourage idleness, and suppress the beginnings of vice; such as lying, cursing, swearing, profaning the Lord's-day, obscene discourse, stealing, &c. putting them often in mind, and obliging them to get by heart such parts of the Holy Scriptures, where those things are forbid, and where Christians are commanded to be faithful and obedient to their masters, to be diligent in their business, and quiet and peaceable to all men.

"VIII. That they call over in school the children's names every morning and afternoon; and, if any be missing, that they put them down in rolls kept for that purpose, as tardy or absent; as also for their being guilty of breaking any of the aforesaid rules and orders; and that they lay those rolls before the founders or trustees of every school, where required so to do, or before any other person empowered by the founder, trustees, or subscribers, who have a right to enquire into their behaviour, in order to their encouragement, correction, or expulsion.

"IX. That they take care that where the children are cloathed, they wear their caps, bands, and cloaths every day; whereby the trustees, benefactors, and others, may know and see what their behaviour is abroad.

"These rules were approved by the archbishops and bishops whose names are underwritten: and they were pleased to direct, that the same be observed by all the charity-schools in their respective dioceses.

- W. Cant.
- Lan. Ebor.
- Edm. London.
- W. Duresme.
- R. Winchester.
- J. Wigorn.
- J. Bath and Wells.
- Jo. Oxford.
- B. Sarum.
- E. Cov. and Lich.
- Sa. Roffen.
- Tho. Ely.
- R. Lincoln.
- Jos. Gloucester.
- W. Norwich.
- Jo. Carliol.
- H. Hereford.
- Ric. St. David's.
- E. Chichester.
- W. Bristol.
- Steph. Exon.
- Rob. Peterborough.
- Sam. Cestriens.

- Fr. Asaph.
- Tho. Bangor.

"The foregoing rules for the good order and government of Charity-schools, being laid before the *Society for Promoting Christian Knowledge*, they have approved the same, as being agreeable to the rules of Charity-schools formerly published by the said Society; and have therefore directed that the same be printed, and dispersed among all the Charity-schools in South Britain."

135 captive Britons, nine of whom were commanders of vessels, arrived in England from the States of Barbary in 1734, and were presented to the King and the Lords Commissioners of the Admiralty. The King gave them 100*l*. and several of the nobility and gentry five and ten guineas each, to which sir Charles Wager added 50*l*. They afterwards dined together at Ironmongers' hall.

The practice of placing infants in baskets, and those at the doors of opulent persons, was a common trait in the characters of imprudent females previous to 1734; of which the following advertisement will be a forcible illustration:

"Last Tuesday evening a female child of about three weeks old was left in a basket at the door of Buckingham-house. The servants would have carried it into the Park; but the case being some time after made known to the Duchess, who was told it was too late to send to the Overseers of the parish, and that the child must perish in the cold without speedy relief; her Grace was touched with compassion, and ordered it to be taken care of. The person who left the letter in the basket, is desired by a penny-post letter to inform whether the child has been baptized; because, if not, her Grace will take care to have it done; and likewise to procure a nurse for it. Her Grace doth not propose that this instance of her tenderness should encourage any further presents of this nature, because such future attempts will be found fruitless."

It gives me great pleasure to add, that *dropping* of children is but little known at present.

A charitable institution called the *Stepney feast*, produced a sufficient sum, in 1734, to apprentice 16 boys at 5*l*. each, and to cloath seven, and one poor man.

The duke of Bedford, the earl of Litchfield, and admiral Haddock, were three of the eight stewards for the year 1735; when the ensuing verses, set to music by Dr. Green, were sung at the anniversary dinner.

"From Zembla's ever icy plain,

From where eternal Summer burns,

> From all the terrors of the main,
>
> The wearied Mariner returns.
>
> Old Thames extends his parent arms,
>
> And all his rising towers shows,
>
> To welcome him from War's alarms
>
> To glorious ease and sweet repose.
>
> Tritons wind their coral shells,
>
> And every cliff in echo tells:
>
> Thus Britain is grateful, thus Britain bestows
>
> For a youth of brave toil, an age of repose[44:A]."

The Hospital at Hyde-park corner was instituted Oct. 19, 1733, and has been supported by voluntary contributions from that day to the present; this is one of the many instances which might be produced of the *hereditary* charity of the inhabitants of London; a species of benevolence silently handed from generation to generation; a bequest not inforced by forms of law, and parchment and seals.

In the year 1734, the Prince of Wales acted as president; the Queen and Princesses became subscribers; and the most eminent physicians, surgeons, and apothecaries attended the sick, &c. *gratis*. An additional wing was voted to the building, and the following statement[45:A] published:

"Cured from 1st Jan. to 26th Dec. 1734	379
Discharged for non-attendance, most of them supposed to be cured	196
Dead	77
Discharged incurable	26
For irregularities	15
Discharged as improper objects	4
Sent to Guy's hospital	2
Patients in the house	87
Out-patients	50
Under the care of the house in the whole	840

Receipts for the year 1734.	£.	s.	d.
Subscriptions from Oct. 19, 1733, to Dec. 26, 1734	2277	5	6
Benefactions, ditto ditto	1859	11	0
	4136	16	6
Disbursements 1734	2559	5	0-1/2
Remainder	1577	11	5-1/2

The necessity of Alms-houses, Hospitals, and, in short, every description of receptacles for the miserable poor, was apparent to every friend of humanity at this period; and it is to the honour of the then publick that the necessity was in a great measure removed. The parish-officers were universally negligent, and even the public papers asserted, "That the present laws (those of 1735) are defective; and that notwithstanding they impose heavy burthens on parishes, yet the poor, in most of them, are ill taken care of. That the laws relating to the settlement of the poor, and concerning vagrants, are very difficult to be executed, and chargeable in their execution, vexatious to the poor, and of little advantage to the publick, and ineffectual to promote the good ends for which they are intended."

They proposed these remedies, which will at least explain the deficiencies of the day:

"That a public workhouse or workhouses, hospital or hospitals, house or houses of correction, be established in proper places, and under proper regulations, in each county.

"That in such workhouses all poor persons able to labour be set to work, who shall either be sent thither, or come voluntarily for employment.

"That in such hospitals, foundlings, or other poor children not having parents able to provide for them, be taken care of; as also all poor persons impotent or infirm.

"That in such houses of correction, all idle and disorderly persons, vagrants, and such other criminals as shall be thought proper, be confined to hard labour.

"That toward the charge of such workhouses, hospitals, and houses of correction, each parish be assessed or rated; and that proper persons be empowered to receive the money so to be assessed or rated, when collected; also all voluntary contributions or collections, either given or made for such purposes," &c. &c.

The centre of Bancrofts Almshouses

Whether Bancroft was influenced by having viewed the state of the poor in the same light, or whether he acted from an innate impulse of charity, is of little importance at present; but it is certain that his alms-houses were most opportunely erected in 1735, to supply part of the wants of the community, on the ground at Mile-end, where a fair was previously held. This gentleman left 28,000*l.* to accomplish his intentions; which were, that 24 houses should be built for 24 aged men, a school-room for 100 poor boys, two houses for as many masters, and a chapel, under the direction of the company of Drapers[47:A].

A person who concealed his name gave, in May, 1736, the sum of 1000*l.* to each of the following charities: the Society for propagating the Gospel in foreign parts; for the Augmentation of poor livings; and the Corporation of the Sons of the Clergy; with 500*l.* for the promotion of Christian knowledge.

The Prince of Wales sent the Lord Mayor 500*l.* in January 1737, to be applied in discharging poor freemen from prison, by the payment of their debts and fees.

The governors and the publick at large had enabled the conductors of the Small-pox hospital (who at that time had two separate buildings for the purpose, the one at Islington, the other in Cold Bath Fields) to receive 500 patients in six months, so long since as 1757. Those who have seen the present elegant building at Battle-bridge, will be aware of the excellent accommodations it contains; and those who have not are referred to the view of it annexed.

In the year 1758, another pleasing act of benevolence distinguished the natives of London, under the title of "an Asylum, or house of refuge for orphans, and other deserted girls of the poor within the bills of mortality, situated near Westminster-bridge on the Surrey side." The following notice appeared in the newspapers of the above period:

"The guardians of this charity (the intention of which is to preserve poor friendless girls from ruin, and to render them useful members of the community) have engaged three matrons: the first to superintend the affairs of the house in general; the second a school-mistress to teach reading, knitting, sewing, making linen, &c.; the third to preside in the kitchen, and instruct the children in plain cookery, curing provisions, pickling, and other branches of housewifery.

"The house will soon be prepared and furnished for the reception of *poor deserted girls*, from the age of eight to twelve years.

"As in the beginning of these institutions considerable expences are necessarily incurred, the guardians hope the benevolence of the publick will be excited, to enable them effectually to carry this laudable design into present execution; and to extend their plan hereafter as they shall see occasion."

This forcible appeal was by no means made in vain; subscriptions followed immediately, and the Asylum *now flourishes* in full vigour.

The Small Pox Hospital.

The efforts of the humane at present, in attempting to cure the ruptured poor, deserve every commendation; but it should at the same time be remembered, that the community of 1759 were equally desirous of alleviating the sufferings of the miserable. Mr. Lee, of Arundel-street, surgeon, superintended the hospital at that period; and according to his statement to the committee of subscribers, 60 men, women, and children, and upwards of fifty soldiers, had been perfectly cured, without the loss of a single life, from the day of its institution.

Mr. Paterson, secretary to a charitable fund, gave the following account of it in a letter to the editor of the London Chronicle, April 21, 1759.

"SIR,

"The distressed circumstances in which many of our inferior Clergy necessarily leave their numerous families, induced the piety of our ancestors to establish a Corporation for their relief; in aid of which, the stewards of the feast of the Sons of the Clergy have promoted an annual collection for putting some of their helpless orphans apprentices to reputable trades. But there being still wanting a fund for the maintenance and education of these poor children in their more helpless infant state; some gentlemen in the year 1749, formed themselves into a Society for raising such a fund by a small annual subscription, and for seeing it faithfully applied to this very humane and necessary purpose.

"The Society's income, small as it has hitherto proved, yet not being burthened with salaries of any kind, has enabled them in the course of nine years, to take care of 28 boys, selected out of the most numerous and distressed families that applied.

"Of these, 13 have been placed out apprentices, and to the remaining number the Society have agreed to add two, besides filling up the vacancies that will happen, by the placing out of others who are now properly qualified.

"The Society's general account at their last audit in February, stood as follows:

"Total receipts 971*l.* 15*s.* 6*d.* Disbursements, for schooling and maintenance, 713*l.* 11*s.* 6*d.* Children's travelling charges 32*l.* 15*s.* 10*d.* Printing 62*l.* 12*s.* 6*d.* Balance in the Treasurer's hands 162*l.* 16*s.* 8*d.*

"The Society's circumstances have hitherto prevented them from extending their care to the poor girls, whose situation, no doubt, is full as deserving of compassion; but this they hope the benevolence of other well-wishers to the Church of England will soon enable them to do; and in the plan and management of this branch of the Charity, they shall be glad of the advice and assistance of the ladies.

"Several Bishops and other persons of rank of both sexes have been pleased to approve of the design and conduct of the Society, and to honour the subscription with their names.

JOHN PATERSON, *Sec.*

"Mr. Hayter (treasurer) desires I will, in his name, acknowledge the receipt of a bank-note for 20*l.* sent in a penny-post letter signed P. Q. R. and also of one guinea sent in the name of E. B. for the benefit of the above charity."

A fire attended with many distressing circumstances occurred in King-street, Covent-garden, at the close of 1759, in consequence of which the managers of the Theatre there granted the sufferers a benefit, when every person employed on the occasion gave their salaries for the night cheerfully. The produce of another at Drury-lane was 230*l.*

A subscription in imitation of that which took place in 1745 for rewarding the soldiers with money and clothing who assisted in suppressing the Rebellion, distinguished the winter of 1760; and a very considerable sum was obtained for those then in the field.

Another subscription, far more disinterested, amounting to 1782*l.* 17*s.* 3*d.* in January 1760, was intended for the relief of French prisoners. As the prologue spoken at the Drury-lane benefit alludes to each of the above traits of national benevolence, I think, the reader will pardon its insertion.

> "Cowards to cruelty are still inclin'd,
>
> But generous pity fills each Briton's mind.
>
> Bounteous as brave; and though their hearts are steel'd
>
> With native intrepidity, they yield
>
> To Charity's soft impulse: this their praise,
>
> The proud to humble, and th' oppress'd to raise:
>
> Nor partial limits can their bounty know;—
>
> It aids the helpless alien, though a foe.
>
> Hear this, ye French, who urge the insidious strife
>
> That arms the Indian with the murdering knife;
>
> Who, to your foes less cruel, leave your own
>
> Starving in sad captivity to groan.
>
> Think of th' inhuman policy—and then

Confess, ye fight not, nor ye feel, like men.

Britons, this night your kind compassion flows

For near-felt mis'ries and domestic woes;

The dire distress with horror we recall;—

'Twas death, 'twas dreadful devastation all.

The sleepers were alarm'd with wild dismay,

As lull'd in calm security they lay;

While each perhaps in dreams forgot his pains,

And fondly counted o'er his honest gains.

But oh! the poor mechanic, scarce with life

Himself escap'd, his children and his wife,

Cold, naked, hungry, whither can they roam,

No friend to succour, and without a home?

Their little *all* with sorrow they survive,

And hardly deem it mercy, that they live.

Your tender care their present wants supplies,

And gives to industry new means to rise;

Nor needed yet this bounteous act to prove

Your wide humanity, and social love;

All, all who want it, your protection find;

For Britons are the friends of all mankind."

The continued rains of May 1761 had almost ruined the haymakers assembled near the Metropolis, and compelled them to enter it as suitors for charity, which they received to the amount of 16*l.* 12*s.* from the Merchants on Change spontaneously. 129 persons shared the above sum.

In a work of this description the thoughts of respectable writers cannot but be acceptable; one of those observed, in July 1761, "that parish charges (were) every where justly complained of; but how insupportable would they be, were it not for the hospitals erected in the Metropolis, and of late in several county towns, which, so far as they extend, for they go no farther than to relieve such sick or lame poor as there is a probability of curing, are of infinite use, not only to London and the county towns, but to the country for many miles around them.

"In St. Bartholomew's hospital, in the year 1760, there were 3,539 in-patients cured. The number of in-patients in that hospital at that time is 405, and in Guy's and St. Thomas's about 400 in each. Supposing the numbers of in-patients cured in the two last to be the same, therefore, with that in St. Bartholomew's hospital, the total in the three will be 10,617: add to these, the number cured in the hospitals at Hyde-park corner and Westminster, the London Infirmary, the Middlesex, Small-pox, Bethlehem, and other hospitals in London, and they will amount to 15,000 at least. Add to this number the patients cured in the hospitals at Winchester, Bath, Bristol, Newcastle, Shrewsbury, Northampton, Liverpool, and the two hospitals at Exeter; I think there are fourteen of them out of London in different counties; and I believe I shall not exceed when I put the whole number, including those at London, at 20,000. All these are entirely maintained, and do nothing towards a subsistence; except that in some houses, those who are tolerably well assist in cleaning the house, making the beds, &c.

"And it is very observable, that these hospitals for the sustenance and relief of the sick and lame poor have all of them been founded (St. Bartholomew's, St. Thomas's, &c. excepted) within these forty years: Hyde-park hospital was founded in 1733.

"The London hospitals are so many and large, and under such prudent management, that scarce any persons are so destitute of friends, but they can procure admittance into one or other of them. In this, as in all other instances, Providence seems to have proportioned the quantity of pity and compassion to the real wants and distresses of the indigent."

There are numbers of well-disposed persons who would contribute to the support of charitable institutions, were they introduced to their notice in a manner congenial to the bent of their inclination. A man of a grave and sedentary turn of mind may be prevailed upon by a tale of distress to open his purse, but similar methods will not succeed with the *bon vivant*; full of life and spirit, he drives care from him by every artifice in his power; and yet the governors of our hospitals and benevolent foundations have contrived a trap for him, and he cheerfully catches at the bait.—*Ecce signum!*

Magdalen-house charity, Prescot-street,
Goodman's fields, Feb. 10, 1762.

"The *anniversary feast* of the Governors of this Charity will be held on Thursday, the 18th of March next, at Drapers-hall, in Throgmorton-street; after a Sermon to be preached at the parish church of St George's, Hanover-square, before the Right honourable the earl of Hertford, president, the vice-presidents, treasurer, and governors of this Charity, by the Rev. William Dodd, A. M. chaplain to the bishop of St. David's. Prayers will begin at 11 o'clock precisely.

"*And dinner will be on the table at three o'clock.*

"N. B. A *Te Deum* composed by Mr. Handel, for the late duke of Chandos's chapel, with *Jubilate* and other Anthems, will be performed by Mr. Beard, and a proper band of the best performers, both vocal and instrumental.

"Tickets for the feast may be had at the following places at *five shillings each*," &c. &c.

The readers of the newspapers of our day will thus perceive that Solomon was right in saying, 'there is nothing new under the Sun;' from the above hour, nay long before, conviviality and charity have coalesced. Dinners, and collections after dinners, when the mind generously dilates, have relieved thousands from the deepest misery; and I hope this mode of filling the chasms of more disinterested benevolence will prevail till such methods are unnecessary.

An occurrence happened in 1762, which places the humanity of his present Majesty in a very amiable point of view. A female infant had been left in one of the courts of the palace of St. James's; some of the officers in waiting sent it to the overseers of St. Martin's parish, who, with those of St. Margaret's afterwards applied to, refused to receive the child under the plea that the palace was an independent jurisdiction. When the King heard of the circumstance, he immediately ordered that a nurse should be provided, and the fortunate orphan was subsequently honoured with the name of Georgiana Charlotta Sophia.

The City of London Lying-in hospital, established many years past, has served as a pattern for several others in various parts of the Metropolis. From the date of its commencement to 1762, 3655 married women had been received, 45 of whom were delivered of twins, and one of three children; including which, 1896 male and 1806 female infants were indebted for life to this humane establishment[57:A].

Collections have been frequently made during severe weather, or on some particularly distressing occasion, from door to door in the various parishes within the bills of mortality, and considerable sums obtained. In the winter of 1763, the inhabitants of St. Anne's, Westminster, gave 169*l*. 15*s*. 3*d*. the Princess dowager of Wales 100*l*. and the duke of York 50*l*. to the poor not relieved by the regular assessments. Nor was this a solitary instance of generosity, as the duke of Newcastle gave above 400*l*. to different places at the same period; and the rich parish of St. James's relieved 1200 persons with gifts of money and coals.

Though so much had been done to prevent the calamities of poverty, wretchedness prevailed in places where benevolence could not imagine it existed. Garrets in retired alleys and lanes always afford inmates in the last stages of disease and starvation; and the instances that might be adduced would prove very distressing in the recital; but that *supposed empty houses* should contain wretches expiring with want, was beyond the imagination of the most exalted charity; and yet the following melancholy fact actually occurred in November 1763, the narrative of which may serve as a hint to overseers, whose duty it is, I should conceive, to prevent actual *death through want* in their respective districts.

A Mr. Stephens, of Fleet-market, was commissioned to shew some empty houses in Stonecutter-street intended for sale, and one day accompanied a gentleman to them, who had thoughts of purchasing the estate on which they were situated. On entering a room on the first floor, an object of horror attracted their attention, *a naked female corpse*! Stephens, alarmed beyond expression, fled from the scene; but the other more courageous ascended to the next floor, where he was soon after joined by his terrified attendant, and they discovered a second and a third woman dead, and nearly destitute of clothing; pursuing this dreadful research, they found in the upper story two women, and a girl about eighteen years of age, one of whom, and the latter, appeared emaciated beyond description, but their companion in misery was in better condition. Prudence and humanity dictated that an examination should take place as to the cause of so singular and dreadful an occurrence; in consequence, the survivors were taken into custody, and the ensuing particulars were related by them before the Coroner and his Jury.

"It appeared on the inquisition, from the evidence of Elizabeth Stanton, one of these women, that on the Wednesday preceding the inquiry she came from Westminster, and being in want of lodging, strolled to this house, and laid herself down on the ground-floor, where she saw nobody; that about eleven that evening the woman in good condition (Elizabeth Pattent) a stranger to her, came into the room where she (Stanton) had laid herself down, and by treading on her awakened her, at the same time crying out 'Who is there?' To which Stanton replied, 'No person that will hurt you, for that she was going away in the morning.' Pattent therefore advised her to go up to the garret with her, which she did, and stayed there all that night, and the following day and night, and until she was taken into custody in the garret upon the above discovery.

"Pattent, being out of place, attended the Fleet-market as a basket-woman; where she became acquainted with the deceased women, who were basket-women, and both known by no other names than Bet. Pattent, being destitute of lodging, was recommended to this ruinous house by the deceased women, who had lived, or rather starved, there for some time. Pattent, in the day-time, used to go to her late mistress's, who kept a Cook's-shop in King-street, Westminster, and worked for her victuals, and lodged in this house at night, where she continued till she was taken into custody. About the middle of the week preceding the inquisition, the deceased women were taken ill; and on Saturday the 12th instant, Pattent pawned her apron for sixpence, and bought some beef and plumb-pudding at a Cook's-shop in Shoe-lane, and both the deceased women on Saturday and Sunday ate heartily thereof, and on Sunday night she heard the deceased women groan. One had the itch, and the other a fever; and, being fearful of catching the one or the other, she did not go to them any more; nor did she know of their deaths till taken into custody.

"Elizabeth Surman, the girl, was the daughter of a deceased Jeweller, in Bell-alley, Coleman-street; her parents died when she was about six years of age, and she was taken care of by Mrs. Jones, a next door neighbour, with whom she lived about four years; Mrs. Jones then dying, Surman was left destitute; and on being informed she could get employment in Spital-fields, she went there, and assisted a woman in winding quills, but she retiring into the country, Surman was again left destitute; however, she found employment in Spital-fields market, with Mrs. Bennet, in winding silk, but, not pleasing her, was discharged in a week. She then went to Mrs. Roach's in that market, who took in washing and nursed children, where Surman continued six years, and until she was taken ill, on which account she was discharged her service. She then went to the churchwarden of the parish where her father had been housekeeper many years, to desire relief; *but he refused, without so much as expostulating with her about her legal settlement, or informing her that she had gained a settlement by servitude.* She being very ill and weak, *lay all night at the churchwarden's door, but it had no effect on him*; and this girl was obliged to lie about in the streets, until she was informed of this empty house, where she lay every night for near two months; the deceased women being there when she came, and both then lying on straw in the two pair of stairs room. For the first week of Surman's being there, she lay in the room with them on straw, all which week *she was ill with an ague, and had no sustenance* whatever; *that then Elizabeth Pattent relieved her*; and as Surman grew better, she went abroad and received alms, returning at night, and delivering her money to Pattent, who bought her victuals. Surman was afterwards received into St. Andrew's workhouse, where she continued a week; and, about a fortnight ago, she returned to this empty house, and lodged in the garret; and being very ill, *was assisted by Pattent*, and for the last fortnight was not out of the garret till last Friday, when she, with the two other women, were found in the garret, and taken into custody, and never saw or heard, all that time, any thing of the deceased women till she was apprehended.

"On Pattent's being interrogated with respect to the woman's being stripped naked and selling her cloaths, she strictly denied knowing any thing of it; alledging, that as they all entered the house at the cellar, and she being mostly out in the day-time, and attending the poor girl at night, other persons might strip the deceased unknown to her.

"There were no marks of violence about the deceased women, *but they appeared as if starved.*

"The Jury were well satisfied with the account they had received from their most deplorable evidence. The Coroner gave them some money; and the Jury ordered them a supper, and that care might be taken of them in the Casualty-house."

These pitiable objects, worthy of a far better fate, who starved rather than they would steal, and met death surrounded with tenfold terrors, supported by pure consciences, deserve statues to their memory; nay, Pattent would have done honour to Roman virtue, who worked the day through for a miserable subsistence, and passed the night in watching and relieving the sick—and yet I should be afraid to know the sequel of her eventful story. Is it not shocking to think on this catastrophe, when we reflect how many would have contributed to the relief of this family of misery, had they known their wants, when advertisements for relief daily appeared from the distressed and were successful. Even at the moment they were dying a thousand lingering deaths through every possible privation, Catharine Shaw, a widow, with seven children and a mother, acknowledged the bounty of the publick in the receipt of 191*l.* 13*s.* 9*d.* and presentations to Christ's hospital for two of her boys.

The Marine Society, mentioned in "Londinium Redivivum," relieved 295 youths *a second time* in 1763. These lads, rescued originally from ruin, and sent by the Society into the King's service, were discharged on the conclusion of peace; when they apprenticed 15 to fishermen, 71 to trades, 17 to manufacturers, 6 to public-houses, 29 to the merchant's service, 80 to naval officers for three years, one to agriculture, and nine to water and lightermen; assisted 17 to procure masters, sent 29 to their friends, and 21 provided for themselves.

The unfavourable weather which occurred in July 1764, did infinite damage to the grain near London; and a hail-storm that fell on the 23d injured the inferior farmers' property to the amount of 4864*l.* in Middlesex only: the benevolent inhabitants of the Metropolis, touched with their misfortunes, opened a subscription, and restored their losses[64:A].

A second scene of wretchedness and distress attracted commiseration in the above year, for certain Germans; who, deceived by splendid offers of prosperity provided they emigrated to America, were left by their inhuman deceivers to perish in the neighbourhood of London, because they found some deficiencies in their own calculations of profit. Such was the miserable situation of those poor Palatines, that they actually lay in the fields near Bow, where, it is asserted, they had not eaten for two days previous to the following generous act recorded of a baker, who should have been a Prince. This worthy man (whose name has unfortunately not been mentioned) passing along the road near the Germans with his basket on his shoulder, containing 28 two-penny loaves, perceiving their forlorn situation, threw it down, and observed, that his customers must fast a little longer that day, and immediately distributed the bread, for no other return than signs of gratitude and tears of joy.

This affecting circumstance is the first intimation the publick received of their situation; but Mr. Wachsel, Minister of the German Lutheran church, in Little Ayliffe-street, Goodman's-fields, thus addressed the publick immediately afterwards, through the medium of the newspapers:

"I hope you will permit me, by means of your paper, to inform those who have the power to redress it, of the very deplorable situation of the poor unhappy Palatines, lately arrived here from Germany. They are in number, men, women, and children, about *six hundred*, consisting of Wurtzburghers and Palatines, all Protestants; and were brought hither from their native country by a German officer, with a promise of being sent to settle, at his own expence, in the Island of St. John and Le Croix, in America; but *by inability he has been obliged to decline the undertaking*; so that, instead of their being shipped off for those places, some of them have lain during the late heavy rains, and are now lying, in the open fields adjacent to this Metropolis, without covering, without money, and, in short, without the common necessaries of life; others lie languishing under the complicated evils of sickness and extreme want, at the Statute-hall in Goodman's-fields; and more than 200 remain on board the ship which brought them over, on account of their passage not being paid for, where they are perishing for food, and rotting in filth and nastiness. Collections have been made at the German churches and chapels here, several times, to afford them some relief; but as the number of these poor creatures is so considerable, it is impossible, by such means, to furnish them with a regular and continued supply, adequate to their wants; so that, unless some provision is very speedily made for them, they must inevitably perish. These unfortunate people would think themselves inexpressibly happy, if the English Government would be graciously pleased to take them under its protection; to allow them, for the present, some ground to lie on; tents to cover them; and any manner of subsistence, till it shall be thought proper to ship them off, and settle them in any of the English colonies in America; where, I doubt not, they will give their protectors and benefactors constant proofs of their affection and gratitude for such kindness, by behaving as becometh honest, industrious, and dutiful subjects to the British government. I take the liberty of thus expressing the hopes and wishes of these wretched beings, as they have no friend to intercede for them who has interest sufficient for such an undertaking, or even a knowledge of the proper method of application.

"That their distresses are unutterably great, I myself have been too often a mournful witness of, in my attendance on them to administer the duties of my function; with one instance of which I shall conclude this melancholy detail. One of the poor women was seized with the pangs of labour in the open fields, and was delivered by the ignorant people about her in the best manner they were able; but, from the injury the tender infant received in the operation, it died soon after I had baptized it; and the wretched mother, after receiving the Sacrament at my hands, expired from the want of proper care and necessaries suitable to her afflicting and truly lamentable condition.

"That the Almighty may, of his infinite mercy, incline the hearts of the great and good of this Kingdom, distinguished for its charity and hospitality, to take under their protection these their unhappy fellow Christians, who did not intrude themselves into this country, but were invited hither, and send them whithersoever they in their wisdom and goodness shall think proper, is the most ardent prayer of

G. A. WACHSEL."

A subscription was opened at Batson's Coffee-house, where eight hundred pounds was instantly subscribed; and Government, fully impressed with the urgency of the case, immediately sent 100 tents and other necessaries from the Tower. On the following Sunday 120*l.* was collected at Whitechapel-church, and several other parishes followed this most urgent example; but one unknown good Samaritan sent Mr. Wachsel an 100*l.* bank note, who soon after addressed the Editors of the Newspapers with the following welcome information:

"As I have twice solicited the attention of the publick through your paper in regard to the German Emigrants, give me leave now to inform those beloved servants of the Lord, of every rank, who so cheerfully fulfilled the will of their Divine Master, in kindly receiving, feeding, clothing, and visiting these poor strangers, that the remainder of them on the 6th instant (November 1764), left this Christian hospitable shore, to settle in America, on the spot assigned them by the bounty of the gracious Ruler of this happy realm. For all which extraordinary and unparalleled instances of beneficence, and likewise for the attention paid to them by the most worthy gentlemen of the Committee, who not only generously contributed to their relief, but have also been indefatigably employed in conducting this charity with the utmost wisdom and integrity, my warmest and most respectful thanks, as well as those of my poor brethren, are too mean a tribute. But, though they earnestly entreated me to convey their humble and sincere acknowledgments to their very humane and generous benefactors, it is out of the power of language justly to describe their grateful feelings on this occasion: I am, however, confident, that the remembrance of the benefits so seasonably and liberally bestowed on them will remain on their minds to the latest period of their existence; and that they will seize every opportunity of testifying their gratitude to this nation.

"I have been applied to by anonymous letters, complaining of the delay of the promised account of receipts and disbursements; to which I take this opportunity of replying, that when the gentlemen subscribers, after the publication of my first letter, had formed themselves into a Committee for the management of this Charity, I gave into their hands an account of what I had received and expended before their establishment; and to them I have paid all the monies since received by me, &c. &c.

G. A. WACHSEL."

The King sent 300*l.* to the Committee alluded to by the indefatigable Wachsel, who exerted themselves with the utmost perseverance, in providing food and other necessaries, while the Minister read prayers and preached daily before the Palatines, in addition to his other unwearied exertions in their favour. After the more immediate attentions had been paid to their wants, the Committee determined to petition the King, that he would be pleased to grant the Germans lands in some of the American provinces; which they had no sooner done, than they were informed land in South Carolina should be appropriated for that purpose, and that they would be allowed 150 stand of arms to be used by them on their settlements for defence from the Indians and for hunting. Upon this favourable result, the Committee agreed with certain ship-owners to convey the objects of their care to the place of their destination, on the following liberal terms:

"Two ships of not less than 200 tons each, and to carry no more than 200 persons in each ship, to be ready to sail in ten days: the necessaries to be provided were, one pound of bread of sixteen ounces for each person, men, women, and children, every day; one man, one woman, and three children to a mess: Sunday, for each mess, a piece of beef of four pounds, flour three pounds, fruit or suet half a pound, and a quart of pease. Monday, stock-fish three pounds, butter one pound, cheese one pound, potatoes three pounds. Tuesday, two pieces of pork six pounds, rice two pounds. Wednesday, grits five pounds, butter two pounds, cheese two pounds. Thursday, the same as Sunday, only potatoes instead of pease. Friday, grey pease two quarts, butter two pounds, cheese two pounds. Saturday, flour three pounds, fruit half a pound, potatoes two pounds, butter two pounds, and cheese two pounds. Sufficient of vinegar, pepper, and salt every day; a ton of water for every three persons; six quarts of good ship beer each mess, for the first three weeks; and for the remainder of the voyage, a pint of British spirits each day; medicines, and a doctor to each ship, provided by the Committee.

"Half the freight to be paid before sailing from Gravesend, the other moiety at their delivery at South Carolina, deducting one half of the second payment for every person that dies on their passage: all that exceed fourteen years on the first of September, to be deemed whole passengers; all under two to be deemed as one passenger. Security is required for the exact performance of the above contract."

On Saturday, October 6, the Germans left their tents, to embark on board of lighters which were to convey them to Blackwall, attended by the Treasurer and several gentlemen of the Committee.

The parting between those poor people and their guardian Wachsel was exceedingly affecting; nor were their expressions of gratitude to the inhabitants of London less fervent, who accompanied them in crowds in boats, admiring the devotion with which they sung various hymns on their way.

One detestable act disgraced this dignified scene of disinterested Charity, which seems almost beyond credibility, and yet it is certainly a fact; the Committee had filled four tents with clothing, which were guarded by children during the time their parents were attending Divine Service; at that critical moment, several wretches decoyed the guards away by a distribution of half-pence to buy cakes, and immediately stole every article worth conveyance.

The above splendid æra in the annals of Charity was equally distinguished by the exertions of other individuals, who obtained large sums by contributions from the publick, with which they relieved 4931 persons who had been compelled to pawn their clothes, and other necessary articles, to supply the deficiencies in their earnings, through the decline of the Silk manufactory in Spitalfields. I am, however, sorry to add that the conduct of those artizans did not in the least resemble that of the Germans; clamorous assemblies of men, women, and children, under turbulent leaders, with a black flag carried before them, approached the Royal residence of St. James's; where, disappointed of meeting the King, many of the most violent presumed to follow his Majesty to Richmond with a petition, which certainly ought to have been presented to the House of Commons through the medium of a Member; others met in Old Palace-yard, where they obstructed the passage of the Peers, and were only prevented from committing acts of violence by a party of guards. Thus disappointed of their aim, they spread in various directions, and almost filled Bloomsbury-square in defiance of parties of horse and foot soldiers sent to keep the peace. After suffering several severe injuries, self-committed by pressure, they returned towards home; but in their way broke all Messrs. Carr and Co.'s windows on Ludgate-hill, and would have done other damage, had not a patrole of grenadier guards interfered and dispersed them; but, as this article should be wholly devoted to the peaceful operations of benevolence, I must refer the reader to "Popular Tumults," for the remainder of the event.

The King gave 1000*l*. to the sufferers by a fire in Bishopsgate-street, London, in November 1765; and the Society of Quakers 500*l*.

During the severity of the winter of 1767-8, a great deal was done for the relief of the poor, particularly in the following instances: Earl Percy gave 400*l*.; 200*l*. was collected at Almack's; Daniel Giles, esq. distributed 20 chaldrons of coals; the Archbishop of Canterbury gave 5*s*. 3*d*. each, to upwards of 200 watermen of Lambeth; the Lord Mayor had 50 pounds of beef boiled every day, and distributed it and the broth from it; an unknown person released 26 prisoners from the Poultry, and others from Wood-street, confined for debts between forty shillings and six pounds, and each received thirty shillings, the surplus of the cash sent; besides these generous acts, large sums were collected in various parishes, and the Queen gave 500*l*. under a feigned name, through the hands of Dr. Hill[74:A].

Sir John Fielding, long celebrated for his activity as the supreme director of the Police Westward of Temple-bar, thus addressed the publick in March 1770:

"The worthy and ingenious Mr. Nelson, in a book, intituled, 'An Address to Persons of Quality and Estate,' relative to the different methods of doing good, seems from the benevolence of his mind, and from that rich fountain of humanity in his heart, to have furnished hints for almost all the charities which have been established since his time; and, indeed, from the present number of them, one should imagine, that scarce a distress could arise to the poor, but there is an hospital, infirmary, or asylum to relieve; yet, alas, how short-sighted is the eye of man! for, behold a new Charity makes its appearance, of a most striking nature indeed; namely, a Dispensary for the benefit of the infants of the industrious poor; and how objects so essential to the community should have been so long overlooked by the ingenious and benevolent, is very surprising. The fate of those children that have fallen to the lot of workhouses in their tender state, has been proved, beyond contradiction, to have been dreadful to the last degree; few, indeed, of such lives having been preserved. For this evil some remedies have been provided by law, which, I hope to God, may prove effectual. The next class of distressed objects of this kind are, the infants of the industrious poor, who, being careful and temperate, have frequently large families, which they may indeed subsist, but numbers of these sort of children are precipitately snatched from the fond mother's embrace by sudden diseases, which the poverty and the ignorance of the parent render them incapable of contending with. The lives of children hang on a slender thread, and their diseases, though few, require immediate and able assistance: behold then Armstrong's Dispensary opening its bosom for the relief of these tender patients! It seems a work of supererogation to recommend such a charity as this; it speaks for itself, and needs but to be considered to be encouraged; and to the mother's breast it speaks a feeling language indeed; for the experience that may be acquired in the knowledge and cure of diseases incident to children, by this institution, may be the happy means of preserving heirs to many valuable families, and of preventing much of that sorrow which swells the mother's heart when the little object of her affection is snatched from her tender arms.

"J. FIELDING.

"The remarkable success hitherto experienced in treating the little patients, as appears from the account published after the meetings of the Committee, must doubtless be no small recommendation of this charity."

This Dispensary, calculated for infants only, was accompanied by a plan (separately recommended by Mr. Daniel Sutton) for the *eradication* of the Small-pox by inoculation, at receiving-houses in various parts of the Metropolis. The latter, however, appears to have been the most successful application to the feelings of the publick, as I believe amongst the numerous Dispensaries, which at present do honour to London, there is not one appropriated exclusively to children; nor is it necessary when relief is afforded at all to every description of disease in either infants or adults.

The excellent Institution for the relief of persons confined for Small Debts, which originated from the active mind of the late unfortunate Dr. Dodd, and which has been continued to the present moment, principally through the exertions of Mr. Neild, gave the following flattering account of their success, even in the infancy of the undertaking, Jan. 1773: "535 persons discharged, together with 245 wives and 1496 children, amounting in all to 2276 souls relieved by means of the public humanity."

An Act was passed in 1773, for the better regulation of Lying-in hospitals and other places of reception for pregnant women, and to provide for the safety of illegitimate children born within them; a clause of which enacts, "That from and after the first day of November, 1773, no hospital or place shall be established, used, or appropriated, or continue to be used or appropriated, for the public reception of pregnant women, under public or private support, regulation, and management, in any parish in England, unless a licence shall be first had and obtained, in manner therein-mentioned, from the Justices of the Peace at some one of their General Quarter Sessions to be held for the County, Riding, Division, City, or Corporation, wherein such hospital or place shall be situated."

One of the most singular methods of obtaining charity perhaps ever adopted, occurred in January 1774. The severity of the weather had rendered navigable canals useless; and with others, those of Oxford and Coventry; consequently the persons employed on them were distressed for want of employment. Eighteen of the sufferers obtained a waggon, which a gentleman of Willoughby generously filled with the best coals; and thus furnished, they harnessed themselves to the vehicle, and set off from Bedworth in Warwickshire to draw it to St. James's, there to present the coals to the King. The oddity of their contrivance proved highly beneficial to them on their road; and when they arrived at the Palace, the Board of Green-cloth ordered them twenty guineas, but refused the coals, which were disposed of, and the produce greatly augmented by gifts from numbers of persons who witnessed the exertions of these human *drafts-men*[78:A].

Several instances have been already given of individuals endeavouring to alleviate the calamities arising from the resentment of inexorable creditors, by the discharge of the debts which excited it. Every possible praise is certainly due those philanthropists; nor is the Society just mentioned less deserving of the thanks of the community; but their's is an Herculean labour, and a sum equal to the revenues of a state would be little more than sufficient to accomplish the release of all entitled to commiseration. Impressed with similar sentiments, John Howard, esq. determined to explore the various prisons in England, and indeed throughout Europe, not so much with a view to discharge captives, as to render them the most essential service while such, by exposing their unwarranted sufferings, inflicted in defiance of the dictates of humanity, and even contrary to law. His labours in this pursuit, his disregard of opposition, his manly reprobation of oppression to the oppressor, disdain of personal danger from vindictive revenge and disease, his death, and the honours decreed him by public bodies and public gratitude, are all fresh in the memories of my readers: I shall therefore merely quote his own words in explanation of his intentions, when they were perhaps not fully developed to himself.

"To the Publisher of the London Chronicle.

Cardington, March 6, 1774.

"Mr. WILKIE,

"The account I gave before the House of the state of Gaols being somewhat misrepresented in the papers, I must beg the favour in your next to set it right.

"I am, Sir, &c.

JOHN HOWARD.

"I informed the House that I had travelled and seen 38 out of the 42 gaols in the Lent circuit, besides others, as Bristol, Ely, Litchfield, &c.: that those I had not seen in the circuit, in a few days I should set out to visit them: that I released a person out of Norwich City gaol, who had been confined five weeks for the gaoler's fee of 13*s.* 4*d.*: that at Launceston the keeper, deputy keeper, and ten out of eleven prisoners, lay ill of the gaol distemper; at Monmouth, last Wednesday se'night, the keeper lay dangerously ill, and three of the prisoners were ill; at Oxford, eleven died last year of the small-pox.

"That as to fees, those in the Western counties were highest, as at Dorchester, 1*l.* 3*s.* 9*d.* Winchester, 1*l.* 7*s.* 4*d.* Salisbury, 1*l.* 6*s.* 4*d.*: but in the county of York only 9*s.*

"That the gaols were generally close and confined, the felons wards nasty, dirty, confined, and unhealthy. That even York-castle, which to a superficial viewer might be thought a very fine gaol, I thought quite otherwise; with regard to felons their wards were dark, dirty, and small, no way proportioned to the number of unhappy persons confined there. Many others are the same; as Gloucester, Warwick, Hereford, Sussex, &c. The latter had not for felons, or even for debtors, at their county gaol at Horsham, the least outlet; but the poor unhappy creatures were ever confined within doors without the least breath of fresh air.

 "I was asked my reasons for visiting the gaols? I answered, I had seen and heard the distress of gaols, and had an earnest desire to relieve it in my own district as well as others. It was then asked me, if it was done at my own expence? I answered, undoubtedly. Some conversation passed relative to gaolers taking off their prisoners irons; but that was private, and not at the bar of the House.

"The above account, including that of garnish, which was from 3 and 4*s.* to 8*s.* which I said was a cruel custom, and connived at and permitted by gaolers, was the whole of what passed at the House as to myself, except the great honour they did me in their thanks *nem. con.*"

This true Patriot addressed the printer a second time, March 7, in the same year.

"SIR,

"I shall set off for the gaols in Westmoreland, Cumberland, and Northumberland, next Monday, and also visit again some which I have already seen, likewise Lancaster, Chester, and Shrewsbury, *if I am not taken off with the gaol distemper*, as Dr. Fothergill says, 'I carry my life in my hand, and it is a wonder I have not been taken off.'

"The misery in gaols is great beyond description; Sheriffs for many years not having set foot into the prisons of most of the counties in England. There are many of them (the felons wards I mean) dirty, infectious, miserable places; so that, instead of sending healthy useful hands to our Colonies as transports out of our gaols, they become infectious, sickly, miserable objects: half of whom die on their passage; and many of those that arrive at the places of their destination infect the families they enter into. I saw lately in your paper, what I knew our Colonies complained of from Philadelphia: 'An Act passed to prevent infectious diseases being brought into that Province.'

"Another great evil in gaols is, that the poor debtors on the common side in most counties have not even the felons' county allowance of bread; and I have not found twelve people that have sued out their groats in all the county gaols; that benevolent Act of 32 George II. being frustrated, as no attornies will, without pay, take a poor debtor's case in hand. These I have found some of the most pitiable objects in our gaols.

"I am, &c.

JOHN HOWARD."

The result of the visits thus announced has long been before the publick, and that infinite improvement followed must be admitted; yet much still remains to be done, merely to obtain that order and cleanliness which the Legislature has at various periods declared should be maintained in each prison throughout the Kingdom. Mr. Neild, the worthy magistrate, has undertaken the task left incomplete by his exalted predecessor; and there cannot be a doubt that he has done incredible service to the criminal, and the debtor, most unaccountably immured within the *inclosures intended for the purpose of justice only*.

The same distresses which accompany every severe winter recurred in 1776, and the utmost exertions were made to alleviate them; when the Corporation of London gave 1500*l.* and several rich Citizens from 100*l.* to 20*l.* each, to be distributed to poor housekeepers. This fund was augmented by the exertions of the Sheriffs, Aldermen, and Deputies, who went from house to house soliciting contributions.

The Humane Society, instituted for the recovery of persons supposed to be dead from the effect of disease, suffocation, and drowning, had arrived to that degree of importance in 1776, as to be enabled to distribute several gold and silver medals, from a die executed by Lewis Pingo, from a design by Dr. Watkinson. The four gentlemen first honoured with this mark of distinction were Dr. Hawes, who had frequently advertised, before the Society was formed, offering a reward to those who would call for his assistance in cases where the functions of life were suspended; and Dr. Cogan, his colleague, in establishing the first principles of the Institution; Alderman Bull, president; and Dr. Watkinson.

Since the above period, the enterprising spirit and activity of Dr. Hawes has been constantly exerted in promoting the continuation of the Humane Society, which, though under Royal Patronage, derives very small pecuniary aid from the publick, compared with some Institutions of less importance; nor has the Legislature granted it a farthing; though, as the Doctor once observed to me, there are benefactions recorded in the Journals of the House of Commons for a Veterinary College, to recover horses from diseases[84:A].

Sermons, and an annual dinner, with a procession of those recovered from death by the Society, are substituted to obtain contributions; and I am happy to add, that they have always amounted, with other voluntary gifts, to a sum which has enabled the Governors to render thousands of persons supremely blest by the restoration of their relatives from the relentless grave.

Similar Institutions now existing throughout Europe and America, are strong proofs of the honours due to the founders, Hawes and Cogan—honours to be paid by posterity.

A most melancholy circumstance occurred in 1777, which deprived the inhabitants of London of one of the best orators in the cause of benevolence they had ever possessed. The reader must be aware that I allude to the ignominious death of Dr. Dodd, whose conduct cannot but be allowed to have been inconsistent beyond parallel; a teacher of the most exalted benevolence, and one who practised it to the degree he taught; and yet a luxurious spendthrift, and a violator of the penal laws of his country, to support unjustifiable extravagance and splendour of living. When we reflect on the thousands of pounds his exertions *have* collected, and *will yet* collect, for the relief of penitent Prostitutes, in the establishment (in conjunction with Mr. Dingley) of the Magdalen hospital, and the Society for the relief of prisoners confined for Small Debts; besides those, the fruits of his preaching on numerous occasions; we cannot but lament that mercy was withheld which *a Nation* solicited. His was a singular case—but enough—Justice required his life; and Death, the portion of forgery, closed the scene.

We have now arrived at a period within the recollection of most of my readers; it will not therefore be necessary to notice every Institution existing at present, the result of recent exertion; they are numerous beyond all former example. From the temporary relief afforded during severe winters, and the charities even to passing mendicancy, with that to individuals advertising for assistance, up to the incorporated Societies for constant duration; all are successful, and none more so than the Patriotic Fund, established for relieving and rewarding military and naval sufferings and merit.

Exclusive of the various means, described in the preceding pages, for effecting the great work of alleviating the wants of mankind, there are others of established and permanent operation. I mean, the constant charitable bequests, continued even from the establishment of masses for the repose of the souls of the testators. In those the poor were always remembered; but the Protestant, more disinterested, has long given the whole of his money to the wretched, and *required* no prayers in return. Were I to collect the items of bequests from the days of Henry VIII. to the present moment, this work would not contain them, and the reader would barely credit the enormous amount: and yet this is independent of the Alms-houses and Hospitals which we meet with in every direction, where many thousands are absolutely supported by the benevolence of those who have very long since paid the debt of nature.

Such are the effects of the general charity of the Natives of London; such their attempts to smooth the path of life, and to render the person those services which are necessary to maintain its dignity and proportion. I am now compelled to turn from this grateful scene, and to exhibit what has been done by depravity and laxity of manners, to shorten life, and destroy the fine proportions of the Citizen.

FOOTNOTES:

[13:A] Gent. Mag.

[13:B] Jour. of House of Commons.

[15:A] See the plate of the North side of the Foundling.

[15:B] Gent. Mag. The origin of the Welsh Society, and the subsequent charity school, may perhaps be dated from the celebration of the birth-day of the Princess of Wales, Feb. 1715, when several distinguished sons of St. David heard a Sermon preached in their native language, by Dr. Lewis, at St. Paul's, Covent-garden; whence they adjourned to Haberdashers hall, where, invigorated by repletion, the Antient British Society was planned for the double celebration of the Prince's birth-day, and the commemoration of their Patron Saint.

[23:A] Original proposal.

[24:A] Statement of the trustees.

[24:B] Newspapers.

[25:A] This Royal donation is still annually repeated; and a collection under the King's letters patent is also made in all the parishes within the Bills of Mortality.

[27:A] All these statements are from the Daily papers.

[31:A] Statements in Newspapers.

[44:A] Newspapers.

[45:A] Treasurer's statement.

[47:A] See the view of this superb structure—Seymour's London.

[57:A] London Chronicle.

[64:A] London Chronicle.

[74:A] London Chronicle.

[78:A] London Chronicle.

[84:A] The worthy Doctor died in December 1808. See a Tribute to his Memory in Gent. Mag. vol. LXXVIII. p. 1121.

CHAPTER. II.
ANECDOTES OF DEPRAVITY, FROM 1700 TO 1800.

Mankind may be universally divided into two classes, the honest and dishonest; for I admit of no medium. That those distinctions have existed from the very remotest periods, I believe no one will deny; therefore it is perfectly natural to suppose, that depraved and idle wretches, who would rather steal the effects of another than labour to acquire property for themselves, have infested London, from the hour in which an hundred persons inhabited it in huts or caverns. How those depredators on Society were treated by the Cits of very very very antient times is not worth enquiry; but that death was often inflicted cannot be doubted; and that might be effected by twenty different methods. Strangulation was certainly used before the time of Henry I. in London: punishment for crimes of inferior magnitude are always species of torture; to repeat the probable modes would be far from pleasant.

Whatever may have been the other inventions of the idle to obtain bread, that of begging in all its ramifications was the most antient; the fraternity of mendicants have resisted every attempt to dissolve their body, nor will they vanish till the last day shall remove every living creature from the surface of the earth. After the establishment of Christianity, flocks of Christians determined to devote themselves to the service of the Lord *in their way*, and work no more; such were some orders of Monks and Friars mendicants! The monasteries afterwards, acting upon a mistaken idea of charity, gave alms, and fed the poor and idle indiscriminately at their gates: thus a wretch might invigorate his body with the viands of the Abbots and Monks in the day, and pass the night in attacks upon the defenceless traveller, perhaps often relieved in presence of the depredator by the blind religious.

In vain have the Monarch, the Law, and the Judge, from the days of the Aborigines down to the present moment, exerted their authority and terrors; and I am compelled, for brevity's sake, to confine myself to the disgraceful acts of a single century. To mention the numbers who were condemned at the Old Bailey in 14 years from 1700, will be sufficient, without particularizing their crimes.

Years.	Condemned.		Executed.
1701	118	4 died after conviction	66
1702	49		13
1703	38		18

1704	35		17
1705	44		16
1706	33		5
1707	23		18
1708	34		18
1709	39		10
1710	36		8
1711	36		13
1712	43		15
1713	60		25
1714	108		59
	———		———
	696	Reprieved 391	301

In the mayoralty of Sir Francis Child, 1732, 502 persons were indicted at the Old Bailey; 70 of whom received sentence of death; 208 of transportation; eight fined, imprisoned, or pilloried; four burnt in the hand; four whipped; and 288 acquitted.

In 1722, ten pounds reward was offered by the Clerk of the New River Company, for the apprehension of persons who had wantonly tapped the pipes, and others that had cut the banks to let water on their own possessions.

Lotteries.—These pernicious contrivances to raise money were in full vigour at the commencement of the century. There was the "Greenwich Hospital adventure," sanctioned by an Act of Parliament, which the managers describe as "liable to none of the objections made against other Lotteries, *as to the fairness* of the drawing, it being not possible there should be any deceit in it, *as it has been suspected in others.*" Mr. Sydenham's Land Lottery, who declared it was "found very difficult and troublesome for the adventurers for to search and find out what prizes they have come up in their number tickets, *from the badness of the print*, the *many errors in them*, and the *great quantity of the number of the prizes.*" the Twelve-penny or Nonsuch: and "the Fortunatus."

Esquire Sydenham's lady's gentlewoman obtained an estate worth 600*l.* per annum, in her master's Lottery; but the unfortunate holders of blanks, suspecting foul play, advertized an intended meeting on the 11th January 1700, for the purpose of entering into an investigation of their real or fancied wrongs. This produced a denial on the part of his Trustees, but did not prevent the meeting from taking place, when it was unanimously resolved to appoint an eminent goldsmith in Lombard-street cashier, for the receipt of subscriptions to carry their purposes into effect; which being accomplished, they exhibited a Bill in Chancery against the unfortunate Squire[90;A].

Guinea-dropping was practised in 1700; and it was customary for thieves to carry cocks into retired or vacant places to throw at them, in order to collect spectators, and empty their pockets. The following extract from the Protestant Mercury of February 14, 1700, point out three of those places of iniquity: "Last Tuesday, a Brewer's servant in Southwark took his walks round *Tower-hill, Moor-fields,* and *Lincoln's-Inn-fields,* and knocked down so many cocks, that, by selling them again, he returned home twenty-eight shillings odd pence a richer man than he came out."

In collecting materials for this portion of my review of London, order and regularity are unnecessary; cheats, impostors, knaves, and thieves, members of one great family, will be indiscriminately introduced, with their schemes and crimes to mark *them,* and the cullibility of the good Citizens of London, a large portion of whom are ever ready to catch at the most silly and absurd baits, provided they happen to agree with their pursuits. Money-lenders, those excellent members of Society, the friends of youth, the alleviators of distress, who hold forth their thousands to the publick, merely with a view to accommodate the wants of their countrymen, and without the least wish of private advantage to themselves, were known to the inhabitants of this Metropolis at the period from which I date my present researches. The reader will find a wonderful similarity in the ensuing advertisement to some of very recent date. "From our house, New Tuttle-street, near the Royal-oak, Westminster, or Young Man's Coffee-house, at Charing-cross, in the morning. All gentlemen and others that have business in Treasury, Admiralty, or Navy offices, or any of the Courts of Law or Equity, may have it faithfully solicited. We buy and sell estates, *help persons to money* on good security. We help persons to employments, &c. and have now several to be disposed of, of 400*l.* 100*l.* 80*l.* 60*l.* 40*l. per annum*[92;A]; any that shall give in timely notice of places to be disposed of shall be rewarded for the same. *And because many have been defrauded of considerable sums of money* by one that lately printed from Salisbury-court, Fleet-street; that none may be served so that apply themselves to us, *nor the reputation of this undertaking ruined, because ill men have had the management of it,* we shall not take our gratuity, *till we have done their business;* which must be allowed to be a candid acknowledgment of *our intention.*"

In so populous a City as London, no place is sacred from the contrivances of Sharpers. Even plate used at the Coronation feast of Queen Anne, in

Westminster-hall, April 1702, was stolen, with table-linen and a great deal of pewter[22:B].

To second the operations of the Royal Proclamation for the Suppression of Vice, certain well-disposed Citizens entered into the following agreement, to promote the Reformation of Manners.

"We whose names are hereunto subscribed, out of a sense of the duty we owe to Almighty God, in pursuance of His Majesty's Proclamation for the discouragement and prosecution of debauchery and prophaneness, and for the suppressing of them, do agree as followeth:

"That we meet weekly at ——, under the penalty of —— each default without a just cause; to consult how we may be most serviceable in promoting the execution of the Laws against prophaneness and debauchery. That we use all proper means to prevail with men of all ranks to concur with us in this design, especially such as are under the obligation of oaths to do so; and in order to their acting vigorously therein, that we endeavour to persuade them to form themselves into Societies, at least to have frequent meetings for this purpose.

"That we encourage and assist officers in the discharge of their duty, of discovering disorderly houses, of taking up of offenders, and carrying them before the magistrates, and, moreover, endeavour to assist both magistrates and officers, by giving information ourselves as we have opportunity.

"That, for order sake, every Member in his turn be Chairman (unless any desire to be excused) for four successive days of meeting; that as soon as four members are met, the Chairman, or, in his absence, the next in order upon the list (that shall be made for that purpose) shall take his place: and that from that time to the breaking up of the meeting, we forbear all discourse of public news or our private affairs, as also all unnecessary disputes upon speculative and controversial points of Religion.

"That when any thing is proposed and seconded, the Chairman shall put it to the question, which shall be determined by the majority; and such determination shall remain till altered by a majority upon another meeting.

"That, if upon any matter in debate the voices are equal, the question shall be again proposed by the Chairman at the same meeting, if more of the members come in, or otherwise at the next or some other meeting.

"That it be part of the office of the Chairman to take notice of the breach of any of our orders, to enquire of every member how he hath discharged the business that was allotted him at the last meeting, and what difficulties he hath met with, in order to find out proper remedies. To read over the agreement of this Society once a month. To read over the minutes of what hath been resolved upon at the end of every meeting, and the list of the members; and to go or send to such as have been absent twice successively, without a just excuse known to some member of the Society; and, the next time any such persons shall be present, the Chairman for the time being shall put them in mind of the great importance of the business they are engaged in, and of the obligations they have laid themselves under by their subscriptions to attend the meetings of this Society.

"That we endeavour to find out proper persons to be brought into this Society; and that no member shall be proposed for a member but when four or more of the Society are present; and that none shall be admitted into this Society till he hath been proposed by three several meetings, and are thought to be men of piety and temper; and that after any person hath been proposed a second time for a member, two persons shall be appointed by the major part of the Society to make enquiry concerning his life and conversation.

"That in cases of difficulty that shall occur, we consult the learned in the Law, or other proper persons, that we by no means go further than the Law will warrant us.

"That we keep an exact account of our proceedings in a book kept for that purpose.

"That the debates and resolutions of the Society be kept secret; and, therefore, no person shall be admitted to be present at any debate, in any meeting, that is not a member, unless upon special occasion, and by agreement of the majority present.

"That we look upon ourselves as under a peculiar obligation to pray for the Reformation of the Nation in general, and to implore the Divine direction and blessing upon this our undertaking in particular[96:A]."

Every man may be considered as included within this class, who hazards a falsehood to forward his views, whether they are in the course of trade, or deviate into cheating. Mr. Sheridan, in the Critick, forcibly exposes the various kinds of puffs used by Tradesmen and Authors; and he classes them very justly into the puff direct, indirect, &c. The first instance which occurs of a case in point, after 1700, is the following from a Hair-dresser, which fraternity is notorious for extreme modesty and truth in their addresses to the publick: "Whereas a pretended Hair-cutter, between the Maypole in the Strand and St. Clement's church, hath, without any provocation, maliciously abused Jenkin Cuthbeartson behind his back, at several persons' houses, and at his own shop, which hath been very much to his disadvantage, by saying that he was a pitiful fellow and a blockhead, and that he did not understand how to cut hair or shave: I therefore, the said Jenkin Cuthbeartson, think myself obliged to justify myself, and *to let the world know* that I do understand my trade so far, that I challenge the aforesaid pretended hair-cutter, or any that belongs to him, either to shave or cut hair, or any thing that belongs to the trade, for five or ten pounds, to be judged by two sufficient men of our trade, as witness my hand this 9th day of November, 1702, Jenkin Cuthbeartson, King-street, Westminster[97:A]."

Fellows who pretended to calculate Nativities were to be met with in several parts of London at the same period: they sold ridiculous inventions which they termed *Sigils*; and the possessor of those had but to fancy they would protect themselves and property, and the object of the Conjurer was accomplished. Almanack John obtained great celebrity in this art. It appears that he was a Shoe-maker, and resided in the Strand. This fellow, and others of his fraternity, preyed upon fools or very silly people only; their losses were therefore of little moment, and the turpitude of Almanack John was not quite so great as that of the villains who affected illness and deformity, thus to rob the charitable, whose gifts would otherwise have been directed to the relief of the *real* sufferer.

The reader will presently perceive that, in one instance, the depravity of the community of Beggars is but too stationary since 1702. "That people may not be imposed upon by Beggars who pretend to be lame, dumb, &c. which really are not so; this is to give notice, that the President and Governors for the poor of London, pitying the case of one Richard Alegil, a boy of 11 years of age, who pretended himself lame of both his legs, so that he used to go shoving himself along on his breech; they ordered him to be taken into their workhouse, intending to make him a taylor, upon which he confessed that his brother, a boy of 17 years of age, about four years ago, by the advice of other beggars, contracted his legs, and turned them backwards, so that he never used them from that time to this, but followed the trade of begging; that he usually got 5*s*. a day, sometimes 10*s*.; that he hath been all over the counties, especially the West of England, where his brother carried him on a horse, and pretended he was born so, and cut out of his mother's womb. He hath also given an account that he knows of other beggars that pretend to be dumb and lame, and of some that tie their arms in their breeches, and wear a wooden stump in their sleeve. The said President and Governors have caused the legs of the said Alegil to be set straight; he now has the use of them, and walks upright; they have ordered him to be put to spinning, and his brother to be kept to hard labour. Several other able beggars are by their order taken up and set to work, and when brought into the Workhouse have from 10*s*. to 5*l*. in their pockets."

A person during the fair of 1703 had the audacity to advertise, that the spoils taken at Vigo were to be seen for sixpence at his booth; and he imposed upon the public curiosity by exhibiting fictitious representations of an Altar-piece of silver, with six Angels in full proportion, four Apostles supporting the four pillars, and four Angels attending them, with each a lamp for incense in their hands; also a Crown set with valuable stones, a Holy-water pot garnished with filligree-work, &c. &c. "*all brought from Vigo*, having been first lodged in the Tower, *and never exposed before but in the Tower.*"

John Bonner, of Short's Gardens, had the barefaced effrontery, in 1703, to offer his assistance, by necromancy, to those who had lost any thing at Sturbridge Fair, at Churches or other assemblies, "he being paid for his labour and expences."

The Corporation of London aimed a severe blow, in the same year, at impostors and sturdy beggars, by offering a reward of one shilling each for such as were apprehended, and sent to the Workhouse in Bishopsgate-street.

The Post-boy of July 21, 1711, contains the following paragraph: "It is thought proper to give notice of a common notorious cheat frequently practised by men who pretend to be soldiers, and others, in a game by them called Cups and Balls, particularly at the wall next the Mewsgate, within the Verge of the Court."

At a petty Sessions for Westminster held in April 1714, an account was returned from the proper officers of the receipt of 42*l*. in the preceding six months, as penalties for profanations of the Sabbath, swearing, and drunkenness.

There was a place of resort for the vicious, called the Cave, at Highgate, which was indicted, and the indictment opposed by the proprietors, in a trial before Lord Chief Justice Parker, December 1714; but the defendants lost the cause, and the Cave was suppressed, to the satisfaction, as a paragraph expresses it in the Flying Post, of those "who are enemies to such a nursery of profaneness and debauchery."

A shocking instance of depravity occurred in March 1718. A Quaker potter, of the name of Oades, who resided in Gravel-lane, Southwark, had four sons, whom he admitted into partnership with him, and at the same time suffered them to carry on business on their own account. This method of proceeding naturally led to jealousies and envy on both sides, which increased to a degree of rancour, that the father and sons appear to have acted towards each other as if no connection subsisted between them. The immediate cause of the horrid event that renders the tale odious, was the arrest of Oades by his sons, for the violation of the peace, which they had bound him in a penalty to observe, and the consequent expulsion of their mother from her dwelling. This act attracted the notice of the populace, who seldom fail to adopt the right side of a question of justice, and as usual they began to execute summary vengeance on the house. The sons, an attorney, and another person, secured themselves within it, whence they read the Riot Act, and fired immediately after; a bullet entered the head of a woman, who fell dead; the assault then became more furious, and persons were sent for Mr. Lade, a Justice; that gentleman bailed the father, and commanded the sons to submit in vain: he therefore found it necessary to send for a guard of Soldiers, who arrived and commenced a regular siege, but the fortress was not stormed till two o'clock in the morning, when a courageous fellow scaled a palisade on the back part of the house, and admitted his party, who rushed in, and secured the garrison. The son of Oades, who shot the woman, was tried for the murder, found guilty, but pardoned on his father's intercession, provided he banished himself.

The villain who occasioned the ensuing advertisement mixed cruelty with his fraud. "Whereas a person who went by the name of Dr. Cock, did about two months since come to Mrs. Robinson, in Putney, being indisposed; he pretended to come from an acquaintance of hers from London to give her advice; accordingly he applied a plaster to her stomach, by which she has received a great deal of injury. He had for his fee ten shillings, and demanded six shillings for his plaster; it is supposed he took a handkerchief with him and a shirt. It appearing that nobody sent him, whoever can give notice of him, &c."

The next Sharper upon *public* record worthy notice was Jones, a footman, who had contrived to attract the favours of the lady of Esquire Dormer, of Rousam, Oxfordshire, a gentleman worth 3500*l. per annum*; which being discovered by the injured husband, an action was commenced for Crim. Con. against the party-coloured enamorato, and pursued to conviction; but, just as sir Thomas Cross, the foreman of the Jury, was about to pronounce the tremendous sound of 5000*l.* damages, or, in other words, imprisonment for life, master Jones rushed through the Hall, flew to a boat, was rowed across the Thames, and took sanctuary in the Mint, before the Lord Chief Justice's Tip-staff could prevent him.

An escape accomplished by a still greater villain in 1716, was far more extraordinary: a highwayman, named Goodman, had been apprehended with great exertion and difficulty, and brought to trial at the Old Bailey, where the Jury pronounced him guilty; but, at the instant their verdict was given, he sprang over the enclosure, and eluded every endeavour to arrest his progress.

Such was the daring folly of this man, that he frequently appeared in public, and presuming on his supposed security, actually went to Mackerel's Quaker Coffee-house in Bartlett's-buildings, for the purpose of procuring the arrest of a Carrier, to whom he had intrusted 16*l.* to be conveyed to his wife in the country, and who, supposing Goodman would be hanged, had converted it to his own use: there he met an Attorney by appointment, and stationed four desperadoes at the door armed with pistols, in order to repel any attempt at seizing him. The Attorney, aware of his precaution, listened to the case of the Carrier, and studiously avoided betraying him; but the instant Goodman departed, he declared who his client was, upon which several persons watched the wretch to his place of concealment, where they attacked him, and he them, with the utmost resolution; after a severe conflict, in which the assailants were compelled to bruise him dreadfully, he was secured; but, throwing himself down in the streets, they were at last compelled to bind and carry him in a cart to prison: he was hanged not long after[104:A].

The Mistress of Child's Coffee-house was defrauded of a considerable sum, in September 1716, by an artful stratagem. She received a note by the Penny-post, which appeared to come from Dr. Mead, who frequented her house; saying, that a parcel would be sent there for him from Bristol, containing choice drugs, and begging her to pay the sum of 6*l.* 11*s.* to the bearer of it. The reader will probably anticipate the *denouement*; the bundle was brought, the money paid; the Doctor declared his ignorance of the transaction, the parcel was opened, and the contents found to be —— rags[104:A].

It is not often that thefts can be narrated which are calculated to excite a smile; and yet I am much mistaken if the reader doth not relax his risible faculties, when he is informed of a singular method of stealing wigs, practised in 1717. This I present him *verbatim* from the Weekly Journal of March 30. "The Thieves have got such a villainous way now of robbing gentlemen, that they cut holes through the backs of Hackney coaches, and take away their wigs, or fine head-dresses of gentlewomen; so a gentleman was served last Sunday in Tooley-street, and another but last Tuesday in Fenchurch-street; wherefore, this may serve for a caution to gentlemen or gentlewomen that ride single in the night-time, to sit on the fore-seat, which will prevent that way of robbing."

The first notice of Mr. Law, the chief Director of the Royal Bank at Paris, that I have met with, was in August 1717; when it was said he had betted that the French State-bills would not fall 10 *per cent.* within a year, and given 10 Louis to receive 100 if he won; he offered the earl of Stair 100 for 1000 in the same way, which was refused; and the event proved, that the bills fell 50 *per cent.*

Gaming was dreadfully prevalent in 1718. This will be demonstrated by the effect of one night's search by the Leet Jury of Westminster, who presented no less than 35 houses to the Justices for prosecution.

The Society for the Reformation of Manners published the ensuing effects of their labours for one year, ending in December 1718.

Prosecuted for lewd and disorderly practices, 1253.

Keeping of bawdy and disorderly houses, 31.

Exercising their trades or callings on the Lord's-day, 492.

Profane swearing and cursing, 202.

Drunkenness, 17.

Keeping common gaming-houses, 8.

We have now arrived at a grand æra of villainy, the golden harvest of scheming, in which Mr. Law acted the first part in France. A person under the signature of Publicus, in the Thursday's Journal of December 17, 1719, very justly observes: "If any of the days of us or our forefathers might be called the *projecting* age, I think this is the time. If ever there was a nation that had been 23 years ruining itself and recovered in a moment, this is the time. If ever a government paid its debts without money, and exchanged all the cash in the kingdom for bits of paper, which had neither anybody to pay them for, or any intrinsic fund to pay themselves, this is the time. If ever a credit was raised without a foundation, and built up to a height that not only was likely to fall, but indeed was impossible to stand, this is the time."

Speaking of Mr. Law, he says, "First, he has entirely restored credit in France; or, as it may be said, he has planted credit in a soil where credit never could thrive, and never did thrive before; I mean in a tyrannic absolute government, a thing inconsistent with credit, and the very name of it; for when was ever credit established to any degree, where the Sovereign was able to seize upon the foundation on which it stood, by his absolute power, and at his pleasure.

"2dly, He has established such a bank, and so fortified it with an established settlement, and on such a stock, as nothing can come up to it in the world, except only the Banks of London and Amsterdam.

"3dly, He has erected a Company immense and inimitable on a trifling fund, and the trifle made up of the most precarious things that could be then imagined, being State bills, Town-house rents, and public funds, which in their own esteem were not at that time to be rated at above 35 or 40 *per cent.* nor would they have fetched more to have been sold then in open market; and these has he brought up to be worth 2000*l. per cent.* in the same market where they were under 40 *per cent.* before. The man that has done all this was here but a contemptible person, a Silversmith's son at Edinburgh, then a rake, then a soldier, then a kind of bully, then a murderer; he was tried at the Old Bailey for killing Mr. Wilson, commonly called *Beau* Wilson, in a duel; he was condemned to be hanged, but found means to break out of Newgate; some say he got out by a silver key, and from thence made his escape into France: there he lived without character and without employment, till entering into the schemes which he has since laid open, and talking freely of them, it came to the ears of the Regent, who employing some men to talk with him, and they finding his head turned for great projects, he was heard by more considerable persons, and finally by the Regent himself, with whom he established these just maxims as fundamentals; namely: That a fund of credit was equal to a fund of money. That credit might be raised upon personal funds, not upon the publick, because the power was absolute. Upon these foundations he first erected the Royal bank; which, having been done by a subscription, and having a sufficient fund in specie to answer all the bills on demand, began to take, and having stood several severe shocks from the attempts of merchants and others to ruin its reputation, established itself upon the punctual discharge of its first credit, till by time it increased to such a magnitude as we now see it, being able to pay bills as was tried by its enemy for a million and a quarter, sterling, in one day. This Bank, being thus past the first hazards, stands too fast for the power of art to shake it; and immense sums being lodged with them, their payments are much safer than the money in any man's pocket.

"This raised Mr. Law's fame to the pitch it is now at, and set him above the power of all his enemies. From thence he grounded his Mississippi project, got it filled up, joined it to the East-India Company; undertook the whole coinage, embraced several other projects, as a Royal fishery, the Tobacco farm, and at last the trade to Norway for naval stores, deals, timber, &c.

"It is true that a stock advanced to 2000 *per cent.* may undertake any thing; but depend upon it, a stock advanced to 2000 *per cent.* upon no foundation, must at last come to nothing, and the only use is to raise estates upon the first advance of it; and perhaps it may appear at last, that the imaginary value of the stock declining in the humours of the times, it will by no means be able to support itself, which, whenever it happens, blows it up all at once."

Such were the prophetic reasonings of our observer, which the event fully justified by the ruin of thousands in England. To authenticate this assertion, I shall present the reader a succession of paragraphs from the Newspapers, pointing out the ramifications from the parent *stock*, and the facility with which the publick were imposed upon.

"Here has been the oddest bite put upon the Town that ever was heard of. We having of late had several new subscriptions set on foot, for raising great sums of money for erecting Offices of Insurance, &c.; at length, some gentlemen, to convince the world how easy it was for projectors to impose upon mankind, set up a pretended office in Exchange-alley, for the receiving subscriptions for raising a million of money to establish an *effectual* Company of Insurers as they called it. Upon which, the day being come to subscribe, the people flocked in, and paid down 5*s.* for every 1000*l.* they subscribed, pursuant to the Company's proposals; but, after some hundreds had so subscribed (that the thing might be fully known), the gentlemen were at the expence to advertise, that the people might have their money again without any deductions; and to let them know that the persons who paid in their money, contented themselves with a fictitious name, set by an unknown hand to the receipts delivered out for the money so paid in; and that the said name was composed only of the first letters of six persons names concerned in the said publication." Weekly Packet, January 2, 1719-20.

The original Weekly Journal immediately after observes: "It was the observation of a very witty knight many years ago, that the English people were something like a flight of birds at a barn door; shoot among them and kill ever so many, the rest shall return to the same place in a very little time, without any remembrance of the evil that had befallen their fellows. Thus the English, though they have had examples enough in these latter times of people ruined by engaging in Projects, yet they still fall in with the next that appears. Thus, after Neal's Lottery, how many were trumped up in a year or two's time, till the Legislature itself was fain to suppress them. Sometime after this, there was a new project set on foot for the prodigious improvement of small sums of money, in which they who put in, for example, 5*l.* must by the proposal make above 100*l.* of it in a year's time. People never examined how they could perform this proposal; but, blind with the hopes of gain, threw their money into the Denmark-court Office in so extravagant a manner, that, if the humour could have gone on, they must have had passed through their hands in a few months half the cash of the nation. The success of this Office begot many more in all parts of the Town, all which ended in the ruin of many families.

"Our cunning men are now carrying on a cause very much like these that are past, but infinitely more extravagant than all of them; though I believe it will prove less detrimental than any of them, because they are already multiplied to that degree, that the sharpers, *alias* projectors, are infinitely too numerous for the bubbles; since the Stocks they have proposed to raise amounts to 28,000,000*l.*; above twice as much as the current coin of the Nation, nay more than the third-part of all the payments the circulation of that current coin performs in the whole kingdom; but, because the placing these projects all in one view must certainly be useful to your readers, I here send you an abstract of them.

"For a general insurance on houses and merchandize, at the three Tuns, Swithin's-alley, 2,000,000*l.*

For building and buying ships to let or freight, at Garraway's, Exchange-alley, 1,200,000*l.*

To be lent by way of Loan on Stock at Garraway's, 1,200,000*l.*

For granting annuities by way of survivorship, and providing for widows, orphans, &c. at the Rainbow, Cornhill, 1,200,000*l.*

For the raising the growth of raw silk, 1,000,000*l*.

For lending upon the deposit of goods, stock, annuities, tallies, &c. at Robin's, Exchange-alley, 1,200,000*l*.

For settling and carrying on a trade to Germany, 1,200,000*l*. at the Rainbow.

For insuring of houses and goods from fire, at Sadlers-hall, 2,000,000*l*.

For carrying on a trade to Germany, 1,200,000*l*. at the Virginia Coffee-house.

For securing goods and houses from fire, at the Swan and Rummer, 2,000,000*l*.

For buying and selling of estates, public stocks, government securities, and to lend money, 3,000,000*l*.

For insuring ships and merchandize, 2,000,000*l*. at the Marine Coffee-house, Birchin-lane.

For purchasing government securities, and lending money to merchants to pay their duties with, 1,500,000*l*.

For carrying on the *undertaking* business, for *furnishing funerals*, 1,200,000*l*. at the Fleece-tavern, Cornhill.

For carrying on trade between Great-Britain and Ireland, and the Kingdoms of Portugal and Spain, 1,000,000*l*.

For carrying on the coal-trade from Newcastle to London, 2,000,000*l*. Cooper's Coffee-house.

For preventing and suppressing of thieves and robbers, and for insuring all persons goods from the same, 2,000,000*l*. at Cooper's."

Here ceases the enumeration of the Journalist, but his hiatus shall be supplied faithfully from other original advertisements.

A grand Dispensary, 3,000,000*l*. at the Buffaloe's-head.

Subscription for a sail-cloth manufactory in Ireland, at the Swan and Hoop, Cornhill.

4,000,000*l*. for a trade to Norway and Sweden, to procure pitch, tar, deals, and oak, at Waghorn's.

For buying lead mines and working them, Ship-tavern.

A subscription for manufacturing Ditties or Manchester stuffs of thread and cotton, Mulford's.

4,000,000*l*. for purchasing and improving commons and waste lands, Hanover Coffee-house.

A Royal fishery, Skinners-hall.

A subscription for effectually settling the Islands of Blanco and Saltortugas.

For supplying the London-market with cattle, Garraway's.

For smelting lead-ore in Derbyshire, Swan and Rummer.

For manufacturing of muslins and calico, Portugal Coffee-house.

2,000,000*l.* for the purchase of pitch, tar, and turpentine, Castle-tavern.

2,000,000*l.* for importing walnut-tree from Virginia, Garraway's.

2,000,000*l.* for making crystal mirrors, coach glasses, and for sash windows, Cole's.

For purchasing tin and lead mines in Cornwall and Derbyshire, Half-moon Tavern.

For preventing the running of wool, and encouraging the wool manufactory, King's Arms.

For a manufactory of rape-seed oil, Fleece-tavern.

2,000,000*l.* for an engine to supply Deal with fresh water, &c. Black Swan.

2,000,000*l.* at the Sun Tavern, for importing beaver fur.

For making of Joppa and Castile soap, Castle Tavern.

4,000,000*l.* for exporting woollen stuffs, and importing copper, brass, and iron, and carrying on a general foundery, Virginia Coffee-house.

For making pasteboard, packing-paper, &c. Montague Coffee-house.

A *Hair* copartnership, permits 5*s.* 6*d.* each, at the Ship Tavern, Paternoster-row; "*by reason all places near the Exchange are so much crowded at this juncture.*"

For importing masts, spars, oak, &c. for the Navy, Ship Tavern.

"This day, the 8th instant, at Sam's Coffee-house, behind the Royal Exchange, at three in the afternoon, a book will be opened for entering into a joint-copartnership for carrying *on a thing* that will turn to the advantage of the concerned."

For importing oils and materials for the woollen manufactory, permits 10*s.* each, Rainbow.

For a settlement in the Island of St. Croix, Cross Keys.

Improving the manufacture of silk, Sun Tavern.

For purchasing a Manor and Royalty in Essex, Garraway's.

5,000,000*l.* for buying and selling lands, and lending on landed security, Garraway's.

For raising and manufacturing madder in Great Britain, Pennsylvania Coffee-house.

2000 shares for discounting pensions, &c. Globe Tavern.

4,000,000*l.* for improving all kinds of malt-liquors, Ship Tavern.

2,500,000*l.* for importing linens from Holland, and Flanders lace.

A Society for landing and entering goods at the Custom-house on commissions, Robin's.

For making of glass and bottles, Salutation Tavern.

The grand American fishery, Ship and Castle.

2,000,000*l.* for a friendly Society, for purchasing merchandize, and lending money, King's-arms.

2,000,000*l.* for purchasing and improving Fens in Lincolnshire, Sam's.

Improving soap-making, Mulford's Coffee-house.

For making English pitch and tar, Castle Tavern.

4,000,000*l.* for improving lands in Great-Britain, Pope's-head.

A woollen manufactory in the North of England, Swan and Rummer.

A paper manufactory, Hamlin's Coffee-house.

For improving gardens, and raising fruit-trees, Garraway's.

For insuring Seamen's wages, Sam's Coffee-house.

The North-America Society, Swan and Rummer.

The gold and silver Society.

2,000,000*l.* for manufacturing baize and flannel, Virginia Coffee-house.

For extracting silver from lead, Vine Tavern.

1,000,000*l.* for manufacturing China and Delft wares, Rainbow.

4,000,000*l.* for importing tobacco from Virginia, Salutation Tavern.

For trading to Barbary and Africa, Lloyd's.

For the clothing and pantile trade, Swan and Hoop.

Making iron with pit-coal.

A copartnership for buying and selling *live hair*, Castle Tavern.

Insurance office for horses, dying natural deaths, stolen, or disabled, Crown Tavern, Smithfield.

A rival to the above for 2,000,000*l.* at Robin's.

Insurance office for servants' thefts, &c. 3000 shares of 1000*l.* each, Devil Tavern.

For tillage and breeding cattle, Cross-keys.

For furnishing London with hay and straw, Great James's Tavern.

For bleaching coarse sugars to a fine colour without fire or loss of substance, Fleece.

1,000,000*l.* for a perpetual motion, by means of a wheel moving by force of its own weight, Ship Tavern.

A copartnership for insuring and increasing children's fortunes, Fountain Tavern.

4,000,000*l.* for manufacturing iron and steel, Black Swan Tavern.

2,000,000*l.* for dealing in lace, &c. &c. &c. Sam's.

10,000,000*l.* for a Royal fishery of Great-Britain, Black Swan.

2,000,000*l.* to be lent upon pledges, Blue-coat Coffee-house.

Turnpikes and wharfs, Sword-blade Coffee-house.

For the British alum works, Salutation.

2,000,000*l.* for erecting salt-pans in Holy Island, John's Coffee-house.

2,000,000*l.* for a snuff manufactory, Garraway's.

3,000,000*l.* for building and rebuilding houses, Globe Tavern.

The reader will find that I have given him the titles of *ninety* of these symptoms of public phrenzy, exclusive of the South-Sea scheme[118:A]. Such of the projects as have not mentioned millions, appear to have been forlorn wights, who were contented perforce to receive the few loose pounds left in the pockets of the subscribers, by those whose aggregate sums amount to *one hundred and ten millions.*

The sufferers in this monstrous scene of wickedness and folly could not plead ignorance or deception; the baits were so clumsily affixed to the hooks, that the Journalists were continually employed in warning the publick, sometimes seriously, and frequently piercing them with the keenest shafts of ridicule: Sir Richard Steele endeavoured to warn the maniacs of the South-Sea Stock, fruitlessly.

"Notwithstanding what has been published, that the annuitants would not subscribe their annuities in the South-Sea Stock, we find that they now run in crowds to subscribe them, though they know not how much Stock they are to have. Some people say as much as will make 30 years' purchase; but this is uncertain. It was, indeed, expected that before the Company would take those subscriptions, they would have given notice of it in the Gazette, and have put up advertisements at their house and at the Royal Exchange, at least eight days before; but it seems the Annuitants have such a good opinion of the Directors of the South-Sea, that without this they come and surrender their ALL as it were, leaving it to the pleasure, discretion, and honour of the Directors, to give them as much Stock as they shall think fit. The like, we suppose, never was heard of before. It is said there has already been above 300,000*l. per annum* subscribed. The reason of people running to it in such haste is, that it has been whispered the first subscribers would receive a greater advantage than those that shall stay longer. A million has also been subscribed, at the rate of 400*l. per cent.* the money to be paid in three years' time, but they are to have the benefit of the next half year's dividend; by this last subscription the Company will get 3,000,000*l.* of money; and it is said they will shortly take another subscription at 500*l.* to pay in seven years, and to have the next half year's dividend; by which means they will get, together with those before, above 11 millions of money. In all appearance, the Company will carry every thing before them; for we see that, notwithstanding what has been said against their Stock by Sir Richard Steele and others, that people are as eager for it as if nothing had been said against it. Those fine writers might as well have attempted to stop the tide under London-bridge, as to stop the people from buying or subscribing in that Stock: as to the first of these, they know something of what they do, but the Annuitants run blindfold into the hands of the Directors, as if they should say: 'Gentlemen, We have so many 1000*l.* or 100*l. per annum* in the annuities for 99 years; we know you to be both just and honourable, give us as much of your South-Sea Stock as you please, we oblige ourselves to be content with whatever you shall give us;' and this is, in short, the sum and substance of the case." London Journal, May 7, 1720.

The Weekly Packet of the same date adds: "The subscriptions that were lately carried on for raising more millions of money than all Europe can afford, are not as yet quite dead, but are very much withered by the breath of the Senate, or a nipping blast from Westminster. It is observed, that many of those projects are so ridiculous and chimerical, that it is hard to tell which is most to be wondered at, the impudence of those that make the proposals, or the stupid folly of those that subscribe to them; yet many a gudgeon hath been caught in the net, though one would think that, with half an eye, they might discern the cheat. When these bites can no longer go on with their bubbles, happy will be the consequence to many honest but unthinking men that stand in danger to be drawn in by them; but unhappy to themselves that they have been used to such dishonest ways of living, and hardly will take up with any course of life that is not so; insomuch that it is feared, as one says, that many of them will go out a marauding; then stand clear the Bristol Mail."

On the 4th of June, the Newspapers intimated the intentions of Parliament, directed to the prevention of any farther mischief from Schemes and Stock-jobbing; and yet, so willing were people to be ruined, that the London Journal of the 11th declares: "The hurry of our Stock-jobbing bubblers, especially, has been so great this week, that it has even exceeded all that ever was known before. The subscriptions are innumerable; and so eager all sorts of people have been to engage in them, how improbable or ridiculous soever they have appeared, that there has been nothing but running about from one Coffee-house to another, and from one Tavern to another, to subscribe, and without examining what the proposals were. The general cry has been, 'For G—'s sake let us but subscribe to something, we do not care what it is!' So that, in short, many have taken them at their words, and entered them adventurers in some of the grossest cheats and improbable undertakings that ever the world heard of: and yet, by all these, the projectors have got money, and have had their subscriptions full as soon as desired."

The auspicious 24th of June at length arrived, which gave the force of law to the following words: "And it is further enacted, by the authority aforesaid, that if any Merchant or Trader, after the 24th day of June 1720, shall suffer any particular damage in his, her, or their trade, commerce, or their lawful occasions, by occasion or means of any undertaking, or attempt, matter, or thing, by this Act declared to be unlawful as aforesaid, and will sue to be relieved therein: then, and in every such case, such Merchant or Trader shall and may have his remedy for the same, by an action or actions, to be grounded upon this Statute, against the persons, societies, or partnerships, or any of them, who, contrary to this Act, shall be engaged or interested in any such unlawful undertaking or attempt; and any such action and actions shall be heard and determined in any of His Majesty's Courts of Record, wherein no Essoign shall be allowed."

This necessary Act was faintly opposed in an attempt to evade its penalties, by the projectors terming themselves and their Subscribers co-partners; but the interposition of the Legislature stamped all their schemes with discredit, and the elopement of several principals utterly destroyed the contrivances of those who dared popular vengeance by keeping their posts.

"The destruction of the bubbles has been a very heavy blow to many families here, and some are entirely ruined by them. There appeared the utmost consternation in Exchange-alley, the day the Act for suppressing them took place, which, because of the confusion and terror it struck among those brethren in iniquity, they called the day of judgment. It might be well indeed with many of them, if no future inquisition would be made into their conduct in this matter, though, if so, they would not wholly escape; for many of those who have been the most assiduous in drawing other poor wretches in to their ruin have, besides their wealth, acquired an infamy they can never wipe off; and as the rage of those who have drunk deep of the delusion is at this time pretty great, the others do not seem fond of appearing too much in public for the present; they being followed with the reproaches, threats, and bitterest curses, of the poor people they have deluded to their destruction. So that if all of them escape the resentment of the populace, it must be more owing to the care of the Magistracy, than the want of will or desperation in the injured." London Journal, July 2.

A waggish Scale-maker ventured, at the same time, into Exchange-alley, at the very height of business, with his right hand extended, holding a pair of scales, exclaiming, "Make room for Justice: I sell Justice, who buys Justice *here*?" And the butchers' boys, actuated by the same, though less civilized principle, made a tumultuous sham funeral for the entertainment of the vicinity.

Although this great point was accomplished, the grand fortress yet remained to be subdued.

Applebee's Journal of August 5, says, "Our South-sea equipages increase every day; the City ladies buy South-Sea jewels; hire South-Sea maids; and take new country South-Sea houses; the gentlemen set up South-Sea coaches, and buy South-Sea estates, that they neither examine the situation, the nature or quality of the soil, or price of the purchase, only the annual rent and the title: for the rest, they take all by the lump, and give 40 to 50 years' purchase. This has brought so many estates to market, that the number of land-jobbers begin to increase to a great degree, almost equal to the Stock-jobbers we had before."

On the 10th of August, the Lords Justices gave positive orders to the Attorney-General, to bring Writs of *scire facias* against the York-buildings Company, the Lustring, the English Copper, and Welsh Copper and Lead Companies, or any others that persisted in their endeavours to evade the Law; and the Royal proclamation issued in aid of it.

Government received numberless adventitious aids in their exertions. Pamphlets, paragraphs, and calculations, proving the losses that must follow from the monstrous price of 1000 *per cent.* for South-Sea Stock; issued in shoals from the press; and, as usual, much malignity and some wit composed the ingredients. One scrap of doggrel may be worth inserting:

In London stands a famous pile,
And near that pile an alley,
Where merry crowds for riches toil,
And Wisdom stoops to Folly.
Here sad and joyful, high and low,
Court Fortune for her graces,
And as she smiles or frowns, they show
Their gestures and grimaces.

Here stars and garters too appear
Among our lords the rabble;
To buy and sell, to see and hear,
The Jews and Gentiles squabble.
Here crafty Courtiers are too wise
For those who trust to Fortune:
They see the cheat with clearer eyes,
Who peep behind the curtain.

Our greatest ladies hither come,
And ply in chariots daily,
Oft pawn their jewels for a sum,
To venture it in the Alley,
Young harlots, too, from Drury-lane,
Approach the 'Change in coaches,
To fool away the gold they gain
By their obscene debauches.

Long heads may thrive by sober rules,
Because they think, and drink not;
But headlongs are our thriving fools,
Who only drink, and think not.

The lucky rogues, like spaniel dogs,
Leap into South-Sea water,
And there they fish for golden frogs,
Not caring what comes after.

'Tis said that Alchemists of old
Could turn a brazen kettle,
Or leaden cistern, into gold,
That noble tempting metal;
But if it here may be allow'd
To bring in great with small things,
Our cunning South-Sea, like a god,
Turns nothing into all things.

What need have we of Indian wealth,
Or commerce with our neighbours,
Our constitution is in health,
And riches crown our labours:
Our South-Sea ships have golden shrouds,
They bring us wealth, 'tis granted;
But lodge their treasure in the clouds,
To hide it till it's wanted.

O Britain, bless thy present state,
Thou only happy Nation,
So oddly rich, so madly great,
Since bubbles came in fashion.
Successful rakes exert their pride,
And count their airy millions;
Whilst homely drabs in coaches ride,
Brought up to town on pillions.

Few men who follow Reason's rules

Grow fat with South-Sea diet;

Young rattles and unthinking fools,

Are those that flourish by it.

Old musty jades and pushing blades,

Who've least consideration,

Grow rich apace, whilst wiser heads

Are struck with admiration.

A race of men who t'other day

Lay crush'd beneath disasters,

Are now by stock brought into play,

And made our lords and masters.

But should our South-Sea Babel fall,

What numbers would be frowning;

The losers then must ease their gall,

By hanging or by drowning.

Five hundred millions notes and bonds,

Our stocks are worth in value;

But neither lie in goods or lands,

Or money, let me tell you;

Yet, though our foreign trade is lost,

Of mighty wealth we vapour;

When all the riches that we boast,

Consist in scraps of paper.

October 1, South-Sea Stock had fallen to 370; on the 6th to 180. The consternation occasioned by this event to those who had purchased at 980, may readily be conceived. The Saturday's Post of the 1st remarks: "It is impossible to express the vast alterations made by the sudden and unaccountable fall of the South-Sea Stock, as well as other Stocks; some few of the dealers in them, indeed, had happily secured themselves before the storm arose; but the far greater number who are involved in this public calamity, appear with such dejected looks, that a man of little skill in the art of physiognomy may easily distinguish them.

"Exchange-alley sounds no longer of thousands got in an instant; but, on the contrary, all corners of the town are filled with the groans of the afflicted; and they who lately rode in great state to that famous mart of money, now condescend to walk the streets on foot, and, instead of adding to their equipages, have at once lost their estates. And even those of the trading rank who talked loudly of retiring into the country, purchasing estates, there building fine houses, and in every thing imitating their betters, are now become bankrupts, and have, by necessity, shut up their shops, because they could not keep them open any longer; however, for the comfort of such whose condition will admit of a remedy, it is said, a gentleman has formed a scheme for the relief of those concerned."

Mist's Journal contains a paragraph, said to have been copied from a work, intituled, "The Lord knows what, by the Lord knows who;" which seems to place the South-Sea Stock in a true light: "I shall make a familiar simile, which every reader may carry in his mind without the help of figures, and which, I think, has a very near resemblance to the South-Sea scheme, as it has been executed: *viz*. A, having 100*l.* Stock in Trade, though pretty much in debt, gives it out to be worth 300*l.* on account of many privileges and advantages to which he is entitled. B, relying on his great wisdom and integrity, sues to be admitted a partner on those terms, and accordingly brings 300*l.* into the partnership. The trade being afterwards given out or discovered to be very improving, C comes in at 500*l.*; and afterwards D, at 1100*l.*; and the capital is then completed to 2000*l.* If the partnership had gone on no farther than A and B, then A had got and B had lost 100*l.*; if it had stopt at C, A had got and C had lost 200*l.*; and B had been as he was before. But D also coming in, A gains 400*l.* and B 200*l.* and C neither gains nor loses, but D loses 600*l.* Indeed, if A could show that the said capital was intrinsically worth 4,400*l.*, there would be no harm done to D, and B and C would have been much obliged to him. But if the capital at first was worth but 100*l.* and increased only by the subsequent partnerships, it must then be acknowledged that B and C have been imposed on in their turns; and that unfortunate, thoughtless D pays the piper."

I shall conclude my notices of the money-making schemes of 1720, with a beautiful invocation written by Mr. Philips: "O Eunomius (Earl Cowper), oraculous in thy speech! happy had it been for thy country if thy wisdom and integrity could have prevailed over the rashness of some, and the avarice of others! Hereafter may'st thou never speak in vain; and may thy counsels help to remedy those evils they might have prevented! may the King hasten his return to his deluded, abused subjects, and the Council of the Nation be speedily summoned for the redress of the land! In the mean time let us mutually bear with, and assist one another in our present necessities: and since we are as free, though not so rich, a people as we have been; and still claim, as our birthright, the liberty to debate, to speak, to write manfully for the public good; let us not be dejected like our neighbours, after whose inventions we have gone astray, not sorrow, even as others who have no hope.

"Have we been delivered from the curse of arbitrary power; have we been preserved from the destruction of the sword, the rage of fire, the scourge of pestilence, and the ghastly terrors of famine, to suffer by the mean artifices of money-changers? O my fellow citizens, you have joined with the spoilers; yet have you not added to your stores. Let me print the remembrance of your past inadvertency upon your hearts, that it may abide as a memorial to you and to your children; that deceivers may not hereafter inherit your possessions. And whereunto shall I liken our past inadvertency, that it may abide as a memorial to us and to our children? O my fellow-citizens, we have waged a civil war throughout the land; who hath not committed hostilities against his neighbour, and what hath it profited? The wealth, the inheritance of the Island, are transferred to the meanest of the people; those chiefly have gained who had nothing to lose: the nobility, the gentry, the merchants, have been a prey to the idle, the licentious, the spendthrifts; men whose habitations were not known. All the calamities have we felt of a civil war, bloodshed only excepted: they who abounded suffer want. The industry, the trade of the Nation, has been suspended, and even arts and sciences have languished in the general confusion: the very women have been exposed to plunder, whose condition is the more deplorable, because they are not acquainted with the methods of gain to repair their broken fortunes. Some are driven from their country, others forced into confinement, some are weary of life; and others there are who can neither be comforted nor recovered to the use of reason. Had his Majesty been present to see the wild proceedings of the people, his goodness would have saved us from these extremities; for though a King can, in his absence, delegate his power and authority, yet can he not delegate his wisdom and his justice."

Immediately after the disclosure of the shocking villainy practised by Stock-jobbers and the South-Sea Directors, another impostor was exposed to public view, and the Charity that had voluntarily flown into his pockets turned to more worthy channels. It is true, the fellow was a little villain, but his arts may serve as a beacon to the unwary. This wretch pretended to be subject to epileptic fits, and would fall purposely into some dirty pool, whence he never failed to be conveyed to a dry place, or to receive handsome donations; sometimes he terrified the spectators with frightful gestures and convulsive motions, as if he would beat his head and limbs to pieces, and, gradually recovering, receive the rewards of his performance; but the frequency of the exploit at length attracted the notice of the Police, by whom he was conveyed in a dreadful fit to the Lord Mayor, in whose presence the symptoms continued with the utmost violence; that respectable Magistrate, undertaking the office of physician, prescribed the Compter, and finally the Workhouse, where he had no sooner arrived, than, finding it useless to counterfeit, he began to amend, and beat his hemp with double earnestness.

A brother in iniquity went to as many as twenty taverns in one afternoon, the landlords of which were ordered by him to prepare a supper for three officers of the guards, and to pay him a shilling for his trouble, and charge it to the officers.

The following Report of a Committee was made to his Majesty's Justices of the Peace for the County of Middlesex, in their General Quarter Sessions, assembled 1725.

"In pursuance of an order made in the last Quarter Sessions held for this County; whereby it was referred to us, among others, to enquire into the number of houses and places within such parts of this town and county as are therein mentioned, where Geneva and other strong waters are sold by retail, and the mischiefs occasioned thereby: We, whose names are subscribed, do hereby certify, that by the returns of the high and petty constables, made upon their oaths, it appears there are within the weekly Bills of Mortality, and such other parts of this County as are now by the contiguity of buildings become part of this Town, exclusive of London and Southwark, 6187 houses and shops, wherein Geneva or other strong waters are sold by retail. And, although this number is exceeding great, and far beyond all proportion to the real wants of the inhabitants (being in some parishes every tenth house, in others every seventh, and in one of the largest every fifth house), we have great reason to believe it is very short of the true number, there being none returned but such who sell publicly in shops or houses, though it is known there are many others who sell by retail, even in the streets and highways, some on bulks and stalls set up for that purpose, and others in wheelbarrows, who are not returned; and many more who sell privately in garrets, cellars, back-rooms, and other places not publicly exposed to view, and which thereby escaped the notice of our officers; and yet there have been a considerable number lately suppressed, or obliged to leave off, by the Justices within their parishes, though it has proved of no effect, having only served to drive those who before were used to these liquors into greater shops, which are now to be seen full of poor people from morning to night.

"But in this number of 6187 are included such victuallers who sell Geneva or other strong waters, as well as Ale and Beer: though it is highly probable, from the great and sudden decay of the brewing-trade, without any diminution in the number of victuallers, that the quantities of strong waters now drank in Alehouses is vastly increased of late beyond what was usual; and it appears by the constables' returns, where they are distinguished, that the number of Geneva and other strong water shops are fully equal to the number of Alehouses, and rather exceed than otherwise.

"It is with the deepest concern your Committee observe the strong inclination of the inferior sort of people to these destructive liquors; and yet, as if that were not sufficient, all arts are used to tempt and invite them. All Chandlers, many Tobacconists, and several who sell fruit or herbs in stalls or wheelbarrows, sell Geneva; and many inferior tradesmen begin now to keep it in their shops for their customers; whereby it is scarce possible for soldiers, seamen, servants, or others of their rank, to go any where without being drawn in, either by those who sell it, or by their acquaintance they meet with in the streets, who generally begin with inviting them to a dram, which is every where near at hand; especially where, of all other places, it ought to be kept at the greatest distance; near churches, work-houses, stables, yards, and markets.

"Your Committee, after having informed themselves as well as they were able of the numbers of those houses, proceeded to enquire according to your directions into the mischiefs arising from them, and from the immoderate use of these liquors, and more especially Geneva; and those appear to be endless and innumerable, affecting not only particular persons and families, but also the trade of the Nation and the public welfare.

"With respect to particular persons; it deprives them of their money, time, health, and understanding, weakens and enfeebles them to the last degree; and yet, while under its immediate influence, raises the most violent and outrageous passions, renders them incapable of hard labour, as well as indisposes them to it, ruins their health, and destroys their lives; besides the fatal effects it has on their morals and religion. And among the women (who seem to be almost equally infected) it has this farther effect, by inflaming their blood, and stupifying their senses, to expose them an easy prey to the attacks of vicious men; and yet many of them are so blind to these dismal consequences, that they are often seen to give it to their youngest children, even to such whom they carry in their arms.

"With regard to their families, this pernicious liquor is still more fatal: whilst the husband, and perhaps his wife also, are drinking and spending their money in Geneva-shops, their children are starved and naked at home, without bread to eat, or clothes to put on, and either become a burden to their parishes, or, being suffered to ramble about the streets, are forced to beg while they are children, and learn as they grow up to pilfer and steal; which your Committee conceive to be one of the chief causes of the vast increase of thieves and pilferers of all kinds, notwithstanding the great numbers who have been transported by virtue of the excellent law made for that purpose. Under this head may also be added, the common practice of pawning their own and children's clothes (which exposes them to all the extortions of pawnbrokers), and their running in debt, and cheating by all the ways and means they can devise, to get money to spend in this destructive liquor, which generally ends in the husband's being thrown into a gaol, and his whole family on the parish. And this your Committee conceive to be one of the principal causes of the great increase of beggars and parish poor, notwithstanding the high wages now given to all sorts of workmen and servants.

"And lastly, with regard to trade, and the public welfare, the consequences are yet more ruinous and destructive. It has been already observed, that the constant use of strong-waters, and particularly of Geneva, never fails to produce an invincible aversion to work and labour; this, by necessary consequence, deprives us of great numbers of useful hands, which would otherwise be employed to the advantage of the publick. And as to those who yet do work sometimes, or follow any employment, the loss of their time in frequent tippling, the getting often drunk in the morning, and the spending of their money this way, must very much cramp and straiten them, and so far diminish their trade, and the profit which would accrue from thence to the publick, as well as to themselves. But it is farther to be observed, that although the retail trade of wine and ale is generally confined to Vintners and Victuallers, this of Geneva is now sold, not only by Distillers and Geneva-shops, but by most other inferior traders, particularly by all chandlers, many weavers, and several tobacconists, dyers, carpenters, gardeners, barbers, shoemakers, labourers, and others, there being in the hamlet of Bethnal-green only above 40 weavers who sell this liquor; and these and other trades which make our manufactures, generally employing many journeymen and artificers under them, who having always this liquor ready at hand, are easily tempted to drink freely of it, especially as they may drink the whole week upon score, and perhaps without minding how fast the score rises upon them, whereby at the week's end they find themselves without any surplusage to carry home to their families, which of course must starve, or be thrown on the parish. And as this evil (wherein the masters may perhaps find their own account, by drawing back the greatest part of their workmen's wages) will naturally go on increasing, and extend to most other trades where numbers of workmen are employed, your Committee apprehend, it may (if not timely prevented) affect our manufactures in the most sensible manner, and be of the last consequence to our trade and welfare.

"Under this head it may be proper also to take some notice of the pernicious influence, the permitting of chandlers, and other inferior trades, to deal in this destructive liquor, or any other strong-waters, has in this town, on the servants of the nobility and gentry; it being too common a practice among chandlers and others, where servants are continually going on one occasion or other, to tempt and press them to drink, and even to give them drams of this liquor, which we may reasonably suppose must be paid for by the masters, either in the price, weight, or measure of the goods they are sent for, and which, besides the immediate damage, encourages them to wrong their masters in greater matters, and, as we conceive, may be one cause of the great complaints that are made against servants.

"And if we may judge what will happen in other workhouses now erecting, by what has already happened by that of St. Giles's in the Fields, we have reason to fear, that the violent fondness and desire of this liquor, which unaccountably possesses all our poor, may prevent in great measure the good effects proposed by them, and which in all other respects seem very hopeful and promising; it appearing by the return from Holborn division, wherein that workhouse is situate, that notwithstanding all the care that has been taken, Geneva is clandestinely brought in among the poor there, and that they will suffer any punishment or inconveniences rather than live without it, though they cannot avoid seeing its fatal effects by the death of those amongst them who had drank most freely of it; and it is found by experience there, that those who use this liquor are not only the most lazy and unfit for work, but also the most turbulent and ungovernable, and on that account several of them have been turned out, and left to struggle with the greatest wants abroad, which they submit to, rather than they will discover who brought in the Geneva to them, though they have been offered to be forgiven on that condition.

"Your Committee, having thus laid before you the numbers of the houses and places wherein Geneva and other strong-waters are sold, as also some of the many mischievous effects derived from them, submit to the consideration and judgment of the Sessions, how far it is in their power, and by what means, to suppress this great nuisance; or whether any, and what application to superiors may be proper in order to a more effectual remedy.

"*Jan. 13, 1725.*

- "JOHN MILNER,
- ISAAC TILLARD,
- R. THORNHILL,
- THOMAS PINDER,
- JOHN MERCER,

- WM. COTESWORTH,

- JOHN ELLIS."

The Society for the Reformation of Manners published a Statement of their proceedings almost immediately after, by which it appears, they had prosecuted from December 1, 1724, to December 1, 1725, 2506 persons for keeping lewd and disorderly houses, swearing, drunkenness, gaming, and proceeding in their usual occupations on Sundays. The total amount of their prosecutions for 34 years amounted to the amazing number of 91,899[14];[A].

A grand masqued ball, given at the Opera-house in February 1726, commenced at 12 o'clock on Monday night the 13th; deep play at Hazard succeeded, when one of the company threw for 50*l.* and lost; and still holding the box without paying, threw a second time for 150*l.* with no better success; the winners then insisted upon a deposit of the money, which was complied with in four supposed roleaus, of 50 guineas each; but, some suspicions arising, they were opened and found to be rolls or parcels of halfpence; the sharper was immediately seized and committed to the custody of an officer of the guard, whom he soon terrified into a release, by declaring he was a lawyer thoroughly acquainted with the acts concerning unlawful games at Hazard, and, at the same time, advising him not to incur the penalties usually inflicted on those who committed trespasses on the liberty of the subject by false imprisonment. When carried to a Magistrate, he obliged that respectable guardian of the public peace to acknowledge that he could do nothing with him, and he was discharged accordingly.

The King directed the following note

"To the Right Honourable the Lord De la Warr, Chairman of the Session for the City and Liberty of Westminster; or, in his Lordship's absence, to the Deputy Chairman.

Windsor Castle, Oct. 8, 1728.

"MY LORD,

"His Majesty, being very much concerned at the frequent robberies of late committed in the streets of London, Westminster, and parts adjacent; and being informed, that they are greatly to be imputed to the unlawful return of felons convict who have been transported to his Majesty's Plantations, has been graciously pleased, for the better discovering and apprehending of such felons, to give orders to the Lords Commissioners of his Majesty's Treasury, to cause to be paid to any person or persons, who, before the first day of March next, shall discover any of them, so as they may be apprehended and brought to justice, a reward of 40*l.* for each felon convict returned, or that shall return from transportation before the expiration of the term for which he or she was transported; who shall, by the means of such discovery, be brought to condign punishment.

"And it having been farther represented to his Majesty, that such felons and other robbers, and their accomplices, are greatly encouraged and harboured by persons who make it their business to keep night-houses, which are resorted to by great numbers of loose and disorderly people; and that the gaming-houses, as also the shops where Geneva and other spirits and strong liquors are drank to excess, much contribute to the corruption of the morals of those of an inferior rank, and to the leading them into these wicked courses: His Majesty has commanded me to recommend it, in his name, in the strongest manner, to his Majesty's Justices of the Peace for the City and Liberty of Westminster, to employ their utmost care and vigilance, in the preventing and suppressing of these disorders; and that they do, in their several parishes or other divisions, hold frequent petty Sessions for this purpose, and call before them the High Constable, Petty Constables, and other proper officers under their direction, and give them the strictest orders and warrants, from time to time, as there shall be occasion, to search for and apprehend rogues, vagabonds, idle and disorderly persons, in order to their being examined and dealt with according to the statutes and laws in that behalf; and the said Justices are also to proceed according to law, as well against all persons harbouring such offenders in their houses, as against those that sell Geneva or other spirits and strong liquors, who shall suffer tippling in their houses or shops, contrary to law; and against such as keep common gaming-houses, or practise or encourage unlawful gaming. And his Majesty, having very much at heart the performance of this service, wherein the honour of his government, the preserving of the peace, and the safety of his Majesty's subjects are so much concerned, does further require the said Justices, in their respective Sessions, to draw up in writing, from time to time, an account of their proceedings herein, inserting the names of the Justices of the Peace attending such meetings, and of the Peace-officers whom they shall employ, taking particular notice of the zeal and diligence of each of them in the performance of his duty; which accounts are to be transmitted from the said several Sessions to one of his Majesty's principal Secretaries of State, to be laid before his Majesty; who, being himself informed of their behaviour, may bestow marks of his Royal bounty upon such of the said officers as shall remarkably distinguish themselves by the faithful and diligent execution of their office; his Majesty not doubting but the said Justices, on their part, will take care to punish with rigour, as by law they may, those who shall appear to have been guilty of corruption or negligence therein.

"Your Lordship will be pleased to acquaint the Justices of the Peace for the said City and Liberty, and all others whom it may concern, with this his Majesty's pleasure; that the same may be duly and punctually complied with.

"I am, &c.

TOWNSHEND."

When Government issues such notices as the preceding, it authenticates the paragraphs of Newspapers, which might otherwise be doubted; indeed, they abound at this period with the most horrid tales of murders, beatings, and robberies, in every direction.

The Post-man of October 19, observes: "The persons authorized by Government to employ men to drive Hackney-coaches have made great complaints for the want of trade, occasioned by the increase of street-robbers; so that people, especially in an evening, choose rather to walk than ride in a coach, on account that they are in a readier posture to defend themselves, or call out for help if attacked. Mean-time it is apparent, that whereas a figure for driving of an Hackney-coach used lately to be sold for about 60*l.* besides paying the usual duties to the Commissioners for licensing, they are at this time, for the reasons aforesaid, sold for 3*l. per figure* good-will."

The year 1730 introduced a new and dreadful trait in the customs of thieves and other villains, which seems to have originated in the lazy constitutions of some predatory wretches in Bristol; where they sent a letter to a Ship's Carpenter, threatening destruction to himself and property, if he did not deposit a certain sum in a place pointed out by them. As that unfortunate person neglected to do so, his house was burnt in defiance of every precaution; and the practice was immediately adopted throughout the Kingdom, to the constant terror of the opulent. London had a threefold share of incendiaries; indeed, the letters inserted in the newspapers, received by various persons, are disgraceful even to the most abandoned character. The King was at length induced to issue his Proclamation, forbidding any person to comply with demands for money, and offering 300*l.* reward for the apprehension of such as had, for four months previous to the date of the Proclamation, sent incendiary letters, or maimed or injured his subjects for non-compliance.

A female of tolerable appearance, and between 30 and 40 years of age, was the cause of much alarm in 1731, by pretending to *hang herself* in different parts of the town. Her method was thus: she found a convenient situation for the experiment, and suspended herself; an accomplice, always at hand for the purpose, immediately released her from the rope, and after rousing the neighbourhood absconded. Humanity induced the spectators sometimes to take her into houses, and always to relieve her, who were told, *when sufficiently recovered to articulate*, that she had possessed 1500*l.*; but that, marrying an Irish Captain, he robbed her of every penny, and fled, which produced despair, and a determination to commit suicide.

According to the Report of Thomas Railton, Esq. eldest Justice of the Peace, in April 1731, it appeared that a Committee appointed for the suppression of night-houses, night-cellars, and other disorderly houses, had bound over to the Quarter Sessions 58 persons charged with keeping houses of the above description, and committed 16 to prison for the same offence; besides 24 who were indicted, and their neighbours bound to prosecute them; 26 houses were utterly suppressed, and their landlords absconded. In addition to this laudable reformation, the Committee sent 127 vagabonds to the House of Correction, and convicted 11 persons for profane swearing.

I have too frequently had occasion to notice the general depravity of the publick, which must have had its origin from the same indifference towards religion, observable in the Cathedral of St. Paul, where unthinking people walked and talked as much at their ease as if they trod the Mall in St. James's-park. One wretched family, neglecting those precepts which are aimed against despondency and suicide, *reasoned* themselves into a contempt of death. Pernicious and detestable as the doctrine is, and contrary to every visible operation of nature placed in our view by the Divinity; too many, I am afraid, *still cherish* an idea that the soul perishes with the body. As an antidote for such persons, let them read the horrid murders committed by Richard Smith and his wife in April 1732. This wretched pair were found in their lodgings, within the Liberties of the King's-bench, hanged, and their infant child shot to death in its cradle. The following letters will explain the opinions entertained by them, which, if adopted, would soon render the world a desert. It is the essence of cowardice to fly from misfortunes.

"To Mr. BRIGHTRED.

"SIR,

"The necessity of my affairs has obliged me to give you this trouble; I hope I have left more than is sufficient for the money I owe you. I beg of you that you will be pleased to send these inclosed papers, as directed, immediately by some porter, and that without shewing them to any one, &c.

RICHARD SMITH."

"I have a suit of black clothes at the Cock, in Mint-street, which lies for 17*s.* 6*d.* If you can find any chap for my dog and antient cat, it would be kind. I have here sent a shilling for the porter."

"Cousin Brindley,

"It is now about the time I promised payment to Mr. Brooks, which I have performed in the best manner I was able. I wish it had been done more to your satisfaction; but the thing was impossible. I here return you my hearty thanks for the favours which I have received; it being all the tribute I am able to pay. There is a certain anonymous person whom you have some knowledge of, who, I am informed, has taken some pains to make the world believe he has done me services: I wish that said person had never troubled his head about my affairs; I am sure he had no business with them; for it is entirely owing to his meddling that I came pennyless into this place; whereas, had I brought 20*l.* in with me, which I could easily have done, I could not then have missed getting my bread here, and in time have been able to come to terms with my plaintiff; whose lunacy, I believe, could not have lasted always. I must not here conclude, for my meddling friend's man Sancho Panca would perhaps take it ill, did I not make mention of him; therefore, if it lies in your way, let Sancho know that his impudence and insolence was not so much forgotten as despised. I shall now make an end of this epistle, desiring you to publish the inclosed; as to the manner how, I leave it entirely to your judgment.

"That all happiness may attend you and yours, is the prayer of, your affectionate kinsman even to death,

Richard Smith.

"If it lies in your way, let that good-natured man Mr. Duncome know that I remembered him with my latest breath."

"These actions, considered in all their circumstances, being somewhat uncommon, it may not be improper to give some account of the cause, and that it was an inveterate hatred we conceived against poverty and rags; evils that, through a train of unlucky accidents, were become inevitable; for we appeal to all that ever knew us, whether we were either idle or extravagant, whether or no we have not taken as much pains to our living as our neighbours, although not attended with the same success. We apprehend that the taking our child's life away, to be a circumstance for which we shall be generally condemned; but for our own parts, we are perfectly easy upon that head. We are satisfied it is less cruel to take the child with us, even supposing a state of annihilation (as some dream of) than to leave her friendless in the world, exposed to ignorance and misery. Now in order to obviate some censures, which may proceed either from ignorance or malice, we think it proper to inform the world, that we firmly believe the existence of Almighty God; that this belief of ours is not an implicit faith, but deduced from the nature and reason of things. We believe the existence of an Almighty Being, from the consideration of his wonderful works; from a consideration of those innumerable celestial and glorious bodies, and from their wonderful order and harmony. We have also spent some time in viewing those wonders which are to be seen in the minute part of the world, and that with great pleasure and satisfaction; from all which particulars, we are satisfied that such amazing things could not possibly be without a first mover, without the existence of an Almighty Being; and as we know the wonderful God to be Almighty, so we cannot help believing but that he is also good, not implacable; not like such wretches as men are, not taking delight in the miseries of his creature; for which reason we resign up our breaths unto him without any terrible apprehensions, submitting ourselves to those ways, which in his goodness he shall please to appoint after death. We also believe the existence of unbodied creatures, and think we have reason for that belief; although we do not pretend to know their way of subsisting. We are not ignorant of those laws made *in terrorem*, but leave the disposal of our bodies to the wisdom of the Coroner and his Jury; the thing being indifferent to us where our bodies are laid; from whence it will appear how little anxious we are about a *Hic jacet*; we for our parts neither expect nor desire such honours, but shall content ourselves with a borrowed epitaph, which we shall insert in this paper:

> Without a name, for ever silent, dumb;
>
> Dust, ashes, nought else is within this tomb;
>
> Where we were born or bred it matters not,
>
> Who were our parents, or hath us begot;
>
> We were, but now are not; think no more of us,
>
> For as we are, so you'll be turn'd to dust.

"It is the opinion of naturalists, that our bodies are, at certain stages of life, composed of new matter; so that a great many poor men have new bodies oftener than new clothes; now, as Divines are not able to inform us which of those several bodies shall rise at the resurrection; it is very probable that the deceased body may be for ever silent as well as any other.

"RICHARD SMITH,
BRIDGET SMITH."

Smith was pronounced by the Coroner's Jury, *felo de se*, and guilty of murder with respect to the child: his wife they declared a lunatic.

At a Sermon preached at Bow-church in 1734, before eight Bishops, many Magistrates, and a numerous auditory, by the Rev. Mr. Bedford, on the Anniversary of the Society for the Reformation of Manners; it was stated, that the Society had prosecuted, between December 1732 and December 1733, 89 persons for disorderly and lewd practices; 13 for keeping disorderly houses, and for exercising their trades on Sundays 395.

Three different sets of sharpers infested the Metropolis in the following winter, who went from house to house with counterfeited letters of request from the Magistrates and Rectors of Tid St. Mary's, Lincolnshire, and Outwell and Terrington, Norfolk; representing, that dreadful fires had almost desolated those places; when, in truth, no such events had happened.

The Weekly Register of December 8, 1733, declares: "Those honest City Tradesmen and others, who so lovingly carry their wives and mistresses to the neighbouring villages in chaises to regale them on a Sunday, are seldom sensible of the great inconveniencies and dangers they are exposed to; for besides the common accidents of the road, there are a set of regular rogues kept constantly in pay to incommode them in their passage, and these are the drivers of what are called waiting jobs, and other Hackney travelling coaches, with sets of horses, who are commissioned by their masters to annoy, sink, and destroy all the single and double horse chaises they can conveniently meet with, or overtake in their way, without regard to the lives or limbs of the persons who travel in them. What havock these industrious sons of blood and wounds have made within twenty miles of London, in the compass of a Summer's season, is best known by the articles of accidents in the newspapers; the miserable shrieks of women and children not being sufficient to deter the villains from doing what they call their duty to their masters; for, besides their daily or weekly wages, they have an extraordinary stated allowance for every chaise they can reverse, ditch, or *bring by the road*, as the term or phrase is.

"I heard a fellow, who drove a hired coach and four horses, give a long detail of a hard chace he gave last Summer to a two-horse chaise which was going with a gentleman and three ladies to Windsor. He said he first came in view of the chaise at Knightsbridge, and there put on hard after it to Kensington; but that being drawn by a pair of good cattle, and the gentleman in the seat pretty expert at driving, they made the town before him; and there stopping at a tavern-door to take a glass of wine, he halted also; but the chaise not yet coming on, he affected another delay, by pretending that one of his horses had taken up a stone, and so dismounting, as if to search, lay by till the enemy had passed him; that then they kept a trot on together to Turnham-green, when the people suspecting his design, again put on; that he then whipped after them for *dear blood*, thinking to have done their business between that place and Brentford. But here he was again disappointed, for the two horses still kept their courage, till they came between Longford and Colnbrook, where he plainly perceived them begin to droop or *knock-up*, and found he had then a sure game of it. He went on leisurely after them, till both parties came into a narrow road, where there was no possibility of an escape, when he gave his horses a sudden jerk, and came with such violence upon the people, that he pulled their machine quite over. He said, the cries of the women were so loud, that the B—s might be heard to his Majesty's garden, Piccadilly; that, there being nobody near to assist the people, he got clear off with two or three blind old women his passengers some miles beyond Maidenhead, safe both from pursuit and evidence.

"I have been credibly informed, that many of the coachmen and postillions belonging to the gentry, are seduced by the masters of the travelling-coaches to involve themselves in the guilt of this monstrous iniquity, and have certain fees for dismounting persons on single horses, and overturning chaises, when it shall suit with their convenience to do it with safety (that is, within the verge of the law); and in case of an action or indictment, if the master or mistress will not stand by their servant, and believe the mischief was merely accidental, the offender is then defended by a general contribution from all the Stage-coach masters within the Bills of Mortality.

"Those Hackney gentlemen who drive about the City and suburbs of London, have by their overgrown insolence obliged the Government to take notice of them, and make laws for their regulation; and as there are Commissioners for receiving the Tax they pay to the publick, so those Commissioners have power to hear and determine between the drivers and their passengers upon any abuse that happens: and yet these ordinary coachmen abate very little of their abusive conduct; but not only impose in price upon those that hire them, but refuse to go this or that way as they are called; whereas the Law obliges them to go wherever they are legally required, and at reasonable hours. This treatment, and the particular saucy impudent behaviour of the coachman, in demanding the other *twelver* or *tester* above their fare, has been the occasion of innumerable quarrels, fighting, and abuses; affronting gentlemen, frighting and insulting women; and such rudenesses, that no Civil Government will, or, indeed, ought to suffer; and above all, has been the occasion of killing several coachmen, by gentlemen that have been provoked by the villainous tongues of those fellows beyond the extent of their patience. Their intolerable behaviour has rendered them so contemptible and odious in the eyes of all degrees of people whatever, that there is more joy seen for one Hackney-coachman's going to the gallows, than for a dozen highwaymen and street-robbers.

"The driver of a Hackney-coach, having the misfortune to break a leg and an arm by a fall from his box, was rendered incapable of following that business any longer; and therefore posted himself at the corner of one of the principal avenues leading to Covent-garden, with his limbs bound up in the most advantageous manner to move the passengers to commiseration. He told his deplorable case to all, but all passed without pity; and the man must have inevitably perished, had it not come into his head to shift the scene and his situation. The transition was easy; he whipped on a leather apron, and from a Coachman became a poor Joiner, with a wife and four children, that had broke his limbs by a fall from the top of a house. Showers of pence poured daily into his hat, and in a few years he became able to purchase many figures as well as horses; and he is now master of one of the most considerable Livery-stables in London.

"The next are the Watermen; and indeed the insolence of these, though they are under some limitations too, is yet such at this time, that it stands in greater need than any other of severe Laws, and those Laws being put in speedy execution. A few months ago, one of these very people being steersman of a passage boat between Queenhithe and Windsor, drowned fifteen people at one time; and when many of them begged of him to put them on shore, or take down his sails, he impudently mocked them, asked some of the poor frighted women if they were afraid of going to the Devil, and bid them say their prayers; then used a vulgar water-phrase, which such fellows have in their mouths, '*Blow, Devil, the more wind the better boat.*' A man of a very considerable substance perishing with the rest of the unfortunate passengers, this villain, who had saved himself by swimming, had the surprising impudence to go the next morning to his widow, who lived at Kingston-upon-Thames. The poor woman, surrounded by a number of sorrowful friends, was astonished to think what could be the occasion of the fellow's coming to her; but thinking he was come to give some account of her husband's body being found, at last she condescended to see him. After a scurvy scrape or two, the monster very modestly 'hoped his good mistress would give him half a-crown to drink her health, by way of satisfaction for a pair of oars and a sail he had lost the night before, when her husband was drowned.'

"I have many times passed between London and Gravesend with these fellows; when I have seen them, in spite of the shrieks and cries of the women, and the persuasions of the men-passengers, and indeed, as if they were the more bold by how much the passengers were the more afraid; I have seen them run needless hazards, and go as it were within an inch of death, when they have been under no necessity of it; and if not in contempt of the passengers, it has been in mere laziness, to avoid their rowing. And I have been sometimes obliged, especially when there have been more men in the boat of the same mind, so that we have been strong enough for them, to threaten to cut their throats, to make them hand their sails, and keep under shore, not to fright, as well as hazard the lives of the passengers, when there was no need of it. But I am satisfied, that the less frighted and timorous their passengers are, the more cautious and careful the Watermen are, and the least apt to run into danger. Whereas, if their passengers appear frighted, then the Watermen grow saucy and audacious, show themselves venturous, and contemn the dangers they are really exposed to.

"*Set one knave to catch another*, is a proverbial saying of great antiquity and repute in this kingdom. Thus the vigilant Vintner, notwithstanding all his little arts of base brewings, abridging his bottles, and connecting his guests together, does not always reap the fruits of his own care and industry. Few people being aware of the underhand understandings, and petty partnerships these sons of Benecarlo and Cyder have topped upon them; and the many other private inconveniences that they, in the course of their business, are subjected to. Now, to let my readers into this great *arcanum* or secret, I must acquaint them, that nothing is more certain and frequent, than for some of the principal customers to a tavern to have a secret allowance, by way of drawback, of 6*d*. or 7*d*.; nay, sometimes I have heard of 8*d*. on every bottle of port-wine that themselves shall drink, or cause to be drank in the house, and for which they have seemingly paid the price of 2*s*.; and so are a sort of Vintners in vizards and setters of society. Those are mostly sharping Shopkeepers, who, by being considerable dealers, hold numbers of other inferior tradesmen in a state of dependency upon them; officers of parishes, old seasoned soakers, who, by having served an age to tippling, have contracted a boundless acquaintance; house-stewards, clerks of kitchens, song-singers, horse-racers, valets-de-chambre, merry story-tellers, attorneys and solicitors, with legions of wrangling clients always at their elbows. Wherefore, as they have got the lead upon a great part of mankind, they are for ever establishing clubs and friendly-societies at Taverns, and drawing to them every soul they have any dealings or acquaintance with.

"The young fellows are mostly sure to be their followers and admirers, as esteeming it a great favour to be admitted amongst their seniors and betters, thinking to learn to know the world and themselves. One constant topic of conversation is, the civility of the people, the diligent attendance, together with the goodness of the wines and cheapness of the eatables, with a side-wind reflection on another house. And, if at any time the wine is complained of, it is answered with 'People's palates are not at all times alike; my landlord generally hath as good, or better, than any one in the town.' And often the poor innocent bottle, or else the cork, falls under a false and heavy accusation.

"In a morning there is no passing through any part of the town without being *hemmed* and *yelped* after by these locusts from the windows of Taverns, where they post themselves at the most convenient views, to observe such passengers as they have but the least knowledge of; and if a person be in the greatest haste, going upon extraordinary occasions, or not caring to vitiate his palate before dinner, and so attempts an escape, then, like a pack of hounds, they join in full cry after him, and the landlord is detached upon his dropsical pedestals, or else a more nimble-footed drawer is at your heels, bawling out 'Sir, Sir, it is your old friend Mr. Swallow, who wants you upon particular business.'

"The sums which are expended daily by this method are really surprising. I knew a clerk to a vestry, a half-pay officer, a chancery solicitor, and a broken apothecary, that made a tolerable good livelihood, by calling into a tavern all their friends that passed by the window in this manner. Their custom was, to sit with a quart of white port before them in a morning; every person they decoyed into their company for a minute or two never threw down less than his sixpence, and few drank more than one gill; and, if two or three glasses, he seldom came off with less than one shilling. The master of the house constantly provided them with a plain dinner, *gratis*. All dinner-time they kept their room, still in full view of the street, and so sat catching gudgeons (as they used to call it) from morning till night; when, besides amply filling their own carcases, and discharging the whole reckoning, they seldom divided less than seven or eight shillings per man, *per diem*.

"Some people, unacquainted with this fellow-feeling at Taverns, often wonder how such-a-one does to hold it; that he spends a confounded deal of money, is seldom out of a Tavern, and never in his business: when, in reality, he is thus never out of his business, and so helps to run away with the chief profits of the house.

"Nor are these all the hardships many of the Vintners lie under; for, besides, their purses must too often stand a private examination behind the bar, when any of these sort of customers necessities shall require it.

"It is such dealings drives the poor Devils to all the little tricks and shifts imaginable. I went one day into a Tavern near Charing-cross, to enquire after a person whom I knew had once used the house. The Mistress being in the bar, cried out, 'What an unfortunate thing it was, Mr. ———being that instant gone out of the house, and was surprised I did not meet him at the door, but that he had left word he expected a gentleman to come to him, and would return immediately.' I staid the sipping of two or three half pints, and began to shew some uneasiness that he did not come according to her expectation, when she again wondered at it, saying, 'it was one of his times of coming; for that he was a worthy good gentleman, and constantly whetted four or five times in a morning.' At length being out of all patience, I paid, and went to my friend's house, about twenty doors farther; where his wife informed me, he had been gone about three months before to Jamaica.

"The bankruptcies so frequently happening among the sons of Bacchus, are doubtless to be attributed chiefly to such leeches as I have been describing, lying so closely upon them; and then an innocent industrious man is to be called forsworn rogue, villain, and what not: and to be told that he affected a failure, to sink a dozen or fourteen shillings in the pound upon his creditors, when, in reality, he hath not a single shilling left in the world, and shall oftentimes be obliged to become a common waiter to a more fortunate fellow, and one perhaps too that he once had thoughts of circumventing in his business and trade, by no other means than a more humble and tractable behaviour.

"A Vintner, who has been looked upon by all mankind to have been a 20,000*l.* man at least, hath died not worth eighteen-pence; and then the poor wretch has been worried to his grave, with the character of a private gamester."

Colonel De Veil, as celebrated for his address and the number of his commitments as Sir John Fielding afterwards was, had two legal culprits brought before him for examination, in 1737, who were a Counsellor and an Attorney, and as rare bucks and swindlers as ever disgraced the annals of turpitude. These gentlemen were charged with defrauding Mrs. Eddowes, keeper of a Bagnio in St. James's-street, and two other persons, of 12*l.*, by proceeding to the Bagnio in the characters of country gentlemen just arrived; the Attorney styling himself Sir John Peering, and the Counsellor plain *Tom*. After remaining a short time with Mrs. E. they sent a porter for *ladies*, and one kind soul even left her bed to visit them; they then proposed to hire a coach and four, in order to make an excursion for pleasure, and promised the woman a velvet cap and riding habit if she would make one of the party; this she consented to do, provided they would permit her to go home to dress; but Sir John and Tom, entertaining doubts whether she would return, demanded, and received, *and kept* two guineas as a pledge. The coach was hired and used, and two days and two nights were passed at the Bagnio; but when the *charges* were to be *discharged*, the Knight and Tom had nothing to produce but a valuable box carefully corded, containing the writings of Sir John's vast estates and several bank notes. This they offered to leave as *security* till *their return*; but Mrs. E. suspecting a fraud, had them immediately conveyed to the Magistrate, in whose presence the following *writings* were taken from the box: a parcel of rags and some hay, an empty bottle, an earthen pipkin, an earthen candlestick, and a japanned tin box. They were bound over for trial.

While the unthinking part of the community fled from place to place, rather in search of amusement than the means of preserving their health, the Police of the City appointed Beadles and Watchmen as follows, under the then recent Act, for better regulating the night watch of London:

	£.	s.
In Aldersgate ward, one beadle at 30*l. per annum*, 25 watchmen at 13*l. per annum*. To be raised, for defraying the charges	415	0
In Aldgate ward, one beadle at 40*l.* 31 watchmen 13*l.* each, charge	501	0
In Bassishaw ward, one beadle at 40*l.* 6 watchmen at 13*l.*	131	0
In Billingsgate ward, two beadles at 70*l.* 20 watchmen at 13*l.*	381	0
In Bishopsgate ward, two beadles at 100*l.* 49 watchmen at 13*l.*	794	0
In Bread-street ward, one beadle at 50*l.* 12 watchmen at 13*l.*	220	0
In Bridge ward, one beadle at 30*l.* 22 watchmen at 13*l.*	360	0
In Broad-street ward, one beadle at 50*l.* 38 watchmen at 13*l.*	634	0
In Candlewick ward, one beadle at 25*l.* 16 watchmen at 13*l.*	293	8
Castle-Baynard ward, one beadle at 50*l.* 24 watchmen at 13*l.*	442	0
Cheap ward, one beadle at 50*l.* 26 watchmen at 13*l.*	430	0
Coleman-street ward, one beadle at 40*l.* 24 watchmen at 13*l.*	407	0
Cordwainer's ward, one beadle at 45*l.* 16 watchmen at 13*l.*	318	14
Cornhill ward, one beadle at 50*l.* 18 watchmen at 13*l.*	305	0
Cripplegate Within, one beadle at 50*l.* 26 watchmen at 13*l.*	430	0
——— Without, one beadle at 32*l.* 28 watchmen at 13*l.*	550	0
Dowgate ward, one beadle at 50*l.* 16 watchmen at 13*l.*	300	0
Farringdon Within, two beadles at 85*l.* 49 watchmen at 13*l.*	764	10
——— Without, four beadles at 100*l.* 89 watchmen at 13*l.*	1550	0
Langbourn ward, one beadle at 40*l.* 23 watchmen at 13*l.*	450	0

Lime-street ward, one beadle at 50*l.* 10 watchmen at 13*l.*	200	0
Portsoken ward, one beadle at 50*l.* 28 watchmen at 13*l.*	474	5
Queenhithe ward, one beadle at 30*l.* 10 watchmen at 13*l.*	202	0
Tower ward, one beadle at 40*l.* 32 watchmen at 13*l.*	571	0
Vintry ward, one beadle at 40*l.* 16 watchmen at 13*l.*	312	0
Wallbrook ward, one beadle at 50*l.* 18 watchmen at 13*l.*	349	0

By this arrangement, the guardianship of the City was intrusted to 32 beadles and 913 watchmen.

The wretches, kept in some degree of awe by the above members of the Police, when nothing occurred to set their passions afloat, or to assemble them from all parts of the town to one point, committed horrid excesses at Tyburn this year, by the brutal practice of throwing stones and dirt; besides which they had one ludicrous contrivance that will force a smile, though disgust and abhorrence must succeed, when it is recollected it was performed at the hour of execution. The mob dug two large holes in the fields, and filled them with soil: those they carefully covered with turf; the populace of course walked into the filth, from which they were ushered amidst loud huzza's and laughter, while every effort was made to entice or force others into them.

The extreme misery of the lowest description of Londoners received some amelioration, about 1750, through the commendable inquiries and remedies made and applied by the Legislature, relating to their monstrous excesses in drinking ardent spirits. The evidence given before a Committee is too interesting to be omitted; yet it is a disgusting and melancholy picture of London, as it was at that date.

An eminent Physician to one of our Hospitals gave the following information: "That the increase of patients in all the hospitals from 1704 to 1718, being 14 years, the total increase was from 5612 to 8189, which was somewhat above one-fourth; that from 1718 to 1734, being 16 years, the total increase was from 8189 to 12,710, or perhaps 13,000, which was above one-third; but that from 1734 to 1749, being 15 years, the total increase was from 12,710 to 38,147, which was near three times the number." Being asked his opinion, whence he apprehended so great an increase could arise, he answered from the melancholy consequences of Gin-drinking principally; which opinion he enforced with such strong reasons (in which he was supported by another eminent Physician to one of the Hospitals) as gave full conviction to the house.

It appeared by the evidence of John Wyburn, of Whitechapel, and John Rogers, of Trinity-lane, both of whom had followed the trade of bakers for

30 years: "that the consumption of bread amongst the poor was greatly diminished since the excessive drinking of Gin, which would proportionably increase again as that vice abated; that the poor laid out their earnings in gin, which ought to purchase them bread for themselves and families; and that, in many of the out-parts, the bakers were obliged to cut their loaves into halfpenny-worths, a practice unknown to the trade till gin was so universally drank by the poor."

It appeared "that one house in seven, from the Hermitage to Bell-wharf, was a gin-shop: it appeared there were about 16,000 houses in the City of London, and that there were about 1050 licences granted yearly to victuallers, which was about one house to fifteen."

"It appeared by the evidence of the High Constable of Westminster, that there were in that City about 17,000 houses, of which 1300 licenced, and 900 unlicenced that sold liquors, which was about one house in eight.

"It appeared by the evidence of the High Constable of Holborn, that there were in his division 7066 houses, of which 1350 licenced and unlicenced, being about one house in five and a quarter. That in St. Giles's there were about 2000 houses and 506 gin-shops, being above one house in four; besides about 82 twopenny-houses of the greatest infamy, where gin was the principal liquor drank."

Hateful as the subject is, its ramifications spread, though rather softened, into higher scenes of life. Cordials, *alias* drams, were not *quite* unknown to the ladies; it was almost noon—

> ——ere Celia rose,
> But up she rear'd, and rang her bell,
> When in came dainty Mistress Nell;
> "Oh dear, my lady, e'ent you well?"
> "Well! yes—why what's o'clock?—Oh Heaven"—
> "A little bit a-past eleven."
> "No more! why then I'll lay me down—
> No, I'll get up—Child, bring my gown;
> My eyes so ache I scarce can see;
> Nelly, *a little Ratifia*[170:A]."

A vile impostor was detected in January 1757, and committed to Bridewell by John Fielding, Esq. This wretch had a practice of lying upon his back in some court or narrow passage, and feigning insensibility; at other times he would appear in the habit of a countryman just arrived in London, where he knew no person, and would declare that, being destitute of money, he had not eaten for four days: another trick represented him as an old worn-out and pennyless Soldier, just arrived from Jamaica; but the repetition of the first performance proved fatal to his *finesse*. A physician found him in the fainting scene, conveyed him to a comfortable bed, and gave him money; but meeting Master Anthony Needham a second time, to all appearance breathing his last, he adopted a new prescription, which procured the healthful exercises of Bridewell. Cash and provisions were found in his pockets when he arrived at the Police-office, though he had just declared he had fasted four days.

When an author is to be found who disinterestedly examines into any particular abuse, another writing on the same subject cannot surely do amiss in quoting such facts from his publication as may suit his purpose. A person who assumed the signature of Philanthropos exposed the villainy of Register-offices, as they were in 1757, in the following forcible manner: "I come now to the article of places under the Government, &c. to be sold, which we see frequently advertised from Register-offices in these or such like terms, and which you generally find in their hand-bills: 'A place to be disposed of for 100 guineas, which brings in 100*l. per annum*. A public office to be sold, where nothing less than gold is taken for any business transacted, &c.'

"I have the happiness to assure the publick, that most of the advertisements that have appeared within these twelve months past have been carefully perused, and an impartial enquiry made after several of the places to be disposed of (which are not confined to private life, but comprehend Church and State), by a public-spirited gentleman, who has been at the expence of applying to the offices from whence they were advertised, and was so kind as to furnish me with the remarks I offer to the publick, on the exposing to sale public offices and employments. The result of an enquiry after the place which brought in 100*l. per annum*, and might be purchased for 100 guineas, was, that the proprietor of the office took one shilling for answering to the question, 'What is the place?' notwithstanding it was so publicly advertised; and then told the gentleman, that it was a place in the Custom-house, and that he must apply for particulars to Mr. ———, at a certain Coffee-house. This the gentleman patiently submitted to; but when he came there, on enquiring for the person he was directed to, he was told at the bar, that he was just gone, and the place sold; and, notwithstanding the most diligent enquiry, the gentleman could never find out either who bought, or who sold the place. On his return to the Register-office, he naturally demanded his shilling again; but was told it was only the customary fee of the Office, that it was a pity he had not applied earlier (it was then only three o'clock on the very day the advertisement appeared in the paper); and if the place had not been gone, perhaps it would not have suited the gentleman's talents, as accompts were requisite; and if that had been the case, it was no fault of the Office; thus intimating, let what would be the success attending the enquiry, the Office-keeper was intitled to one shilling. It is highly probable that eight or ten more might have paid for the same enquiry."

Sir John Fielding received an *involuntary* present, in November 1757, from a number of Publicans, consisting of Billiard-tables, Mississippi-tables, Shuffle-boards, and Skittles, which the worthy Magistrate caused to be piled in a pyramidal form, near thirty-feet high, at the end of Bow-street near the Police-office, where they were consumed. A good hint for the Magistrates at present, as the word Billiards is really very conspicuous in various parts of the Metropolis every night, and, indeed, may be found not an hundred doors from the facetious Knight's old office.

One of the most wicked impositions practised by knaves in London, is the adulteration of Bread. The wretch who improves his circumstances by this detestable method of increasing his profits, is an assassin, full as wicked as the celebrated Italian Tophana: that human fiend poisoned her victims by degrees, suited to the malice of her employers; the Baker who throws slow poisons into his trough does worse, for he undermines the constitutions of his supporters, his customers. He that eats bread without butter or meat, throughout London, at the present moment, and afterwards visits a friend in the country who makes his own, cannot fail of perceiving the delicious sweetness which the mercy of our Creator hath diffused through the invaluable grain that produces it; the inducement held out to us, to preserve life by the most innocent means, is thus in a great measure lost to the inhabitants of London. I once broke a piece of alum with my teeth, which lay in the depth of a slice of bread, when at breakfast, as large as a pea; and was only deterred from prosecuting the baker by the dread of that obloquy which attends the least interested informers. At another time I lodged a week at a baker's house in a country-town, and during a lazy fit, strolled into the bake-house where bread was mixing; in an instant my landlord's countenance changed, and I was rudely desired to leave the place, as he would allow no one to pry into his business. This conduct from a man who had before behaved with the utmost civility, convinced me all was not right, and that other materials were within view than simple flour, yeast, and a little inoffensive salt. Let me not, however, be understood to apply this censure indiscriminately; it is aimed only at the guilty; the honest baker will adopt my sentiments, which are merely an echo of a little work published in 1757, intituled, "Poison detected: or, Frightful Truths, and alarming to the British Metropolis," &c. The Author asserts that, "Good bread ought to be composed of flour well kneaded with the slightest water, seasoned with a little salt, fermented with fine yeast or leaven, and sufficiently baked with a proper fire; but, to increase its weight, and deceive the buyer by its fraudulent fineness, lime, chalk, alum, &c. are constituent parts of that most common food in London. Alum is a very powerful astringent and styptic, occasioning heat and costiveness; the frequent use of it closes up the mouths of the small alimentary ducts, and by its corrosive concretions, seals up the lacteals, indurates every mass it is mixed with upon the stomach, makes it hard of digestion, and consolidates the fæces in the intestines. Experience convinces me (the Author was a physician) that any animal will live longer in health and vigour upon two ounces of good and wholesome bread, than upon one pound of this adulterated compound; a consideration which may be useful, if attended to in the times of scarcity."

After explaining many deleterious effects produced by alum, the Author proceeds, "But it is not alum alone that suffices the lucrative iniquity of bakers: there is also added a considerable portion of lime and chalk; so that if alum be prejudicial alone, what must be the consequences of eating our bread mingled with alum, chalk, and lime? Obstructions, the causes of most diseases, are naturally formed by bread thus abused. I have seen a quantity of lime and chalk, in the proportion of one to six, extracted from this kind of bread; possibly the baker was not so expert at his craft as to conceal it, the larger granules were visible enough: perhaps a more minute analysis would have produced a much greater portion of these pernicious materials."

An *Author* cannot be suspected of wishing to restrain the inoffensive liberty of the press; but he may, without fear or resentment, venture to reprobate the turpitude which it too often promotes. There have been, and still are, persons who will take a few facts, and compound them with many falsehoods, and, thus prepared, present them to some hungry printer or editor, to answer their own base purposes; the unsuspecting read them with avidity, and public bodies and individuals suffer without remedy; an instance of this description produced the following address to the community from John Fielding, Esq. in November 1759.

"About twelve months ago a very salutary law took place, to the great benefit of a large and useful body of men, commonly called Coal-heavers. By this law they were not only relieved from the impositions they then complained of, and the profits of their severe labour secured to themselves; but a provision was made for the infirm, sick, and disabled coal-heavers, and their dead buried, by their paying two shillings in the pound out of their earnings into an office established by the said law, and under the inspection of so worthy and so able a magistrate in the City, that it is impossible for any coal-heaver to be deprived of any advantage, privilege, or support, that the nature of this institution entitles them to. On Sunday the 28th of last month, one Patrick Crevey, a coal-heaver, chairman, and an Irishman, was buried according to the usual custom of burying coal-heavers, and was carried from Gravel-lane to St. Pancras church-yard; his corpse being preceded, as is customary, by the beadle of the coal-heavers' office, with a long staff in his hand, the common ensign of his office; the pall was supported by six chairmen, and eight others followed the corpse as mourners in black cloaks; for whenever a chairman is buried, he is constantly attended by as many of his brethren as can be got together: these mourners were followed by a considerable number of coal-heavers, who walked two and two. This procession gave rise to that extraordinary paragraph in the London Chronicle, on the 30th day of October last, wherein it is confidently asserted, that a Roman-catholic was carried through the streets of London to be buried at St. Pancras, and that the Host was carried, and Priests walked publicly before the corpse; and that the numerous attendants that followed, insulted and knocked down all who did not pay due obedience to their foreign foppery, and beat many persons whom common curiosity excited to ask any questions relative to the said procession. Should any part of this alarming account be true, the offenders cannot be punished with too much severity; but should it be a misrepresentation of facts, the publick would be equally pleased to be undeceived, and he who indiscreetly or wickedly propagated the report without foundation will be the only offender.

"In order therefore to get at the real truth of this matter, a few days ago, the informations on oath of the beadle of the said coal-heavers office, of the pall-bearers, mourners, undertaker, his servant, the landlord of the house from whence the corpse was carried, and some other inhabitants who followed the corpse (several of whom were Protestants), were taken before John Fielding, Esq.; and they all positively declared that at, or from the house, whence the man was carried to the grave in Pancras church-yard, no Host, representation of Host, crucifix, or other visible and external mark of the deceased Patrick Crevey being a Roman-catholick, was carried either before or after the said corpse; and that no Catholic Priest of any sort, to their knowledge, attended the said burial; but that the said Crevey (though a Roman-catholic) was buried by a Clergyman of the Church of England, and strictly conformable to the ceremonies of the said Church. And the aforesaid beadle, pall-bearers, mourners, and undertaker, further declare, that they themselves during their passage from the house to the grave, neither met with, nor were witnesses to any obstruction whatever; but that they afterwards heard that some of the coal-heavers who were at farther distance from the corpse behind had some dispute, which occasioned blows, with some persons who imitated the Irish howl, and called out *Paddy*, by way of derision to the deceased and his attendants, &c. &c.

"JOHN FIELDING."

THE COCK-LANE GHOST.

There is something so absurd and ridiculous in the terrors spread by *Miss Parsons*, that I think it hardly fair to class her operations with really serious offences against the laws of morality; but, recollecting that her *knockings indicated* a charge of poisoning, my scruples are removed, and I proceed to sketch the principal outlines of an incident that agitated the public mind till 1762, when all who had "three ideas in continuity" were convinced that the *spirit* possessed no *supernatural* powers.

For two years previous to the above date, knockings and scratchings had frequently been heard during the night in the first floor of a person named Parsons, who held the office of Clerk to St. Sepulchre's-church, and resided in Cock-lane, near West Smithfield. This man, *alarmed* at the circumstance, made several experiments to discover the cause, and at last had the amazing good fortune to trace the sounds to a bedstead, on which two of his children reposed after the fatigues of the day; the eldest of whom, *though a most surprising girl of her age*, had numbered but twelve winters. Justly supposing the children might suffer some dreadful injury from the knocker, this affectionate parent removed them a story higher; but, horror upon horror, the tremendous noise followed the *innocents*, and even disturbed their rest for whole nights. But this was not all: a publican, resident in the neighbourhood, was frightened into serious illness by the form of a fleeting female ghost, which saluted his vision one fatal evening when in Parsons's house; nay, that worthy Clerk saw it himself about an hour afterwards.

Facts of this description cannot be concealed: reports of the noises and of the appearance of the phantom spread from the lane into a vast circle of space; numbers visited the unfortunate house, and others sat the night through with the tortured infant, appalled by sounds terrific; at length a Clergyman determined to adjure the Spirit, and thus obtain direct replies to the following questions: "Whether any person in that house had been injured?" The answer, expressed by the *number* of knocks (as the ghost was denied the power of speech, and of shewing herself *within reach*), was in the affirmative. "Was she a woman?"—"Yes; the Spirit then explained, that she had been kept by Mr. ———, who poisoned her when ill of the Small-pox, and that her body was deposited in the vault of St. John's-church, Clerkenwell." During this examination, the girl exhibited a considerable deal of art, but betrayed herself decidedly in several instances. The result was, that the Spirit ardently desired the murderer might be punished for her alledged death. A wise-acre, who narrated the above particulars in a newspaper of the time, observes, with wonderful sagacity, "What *is* remarkable *is*, that the Spirit *is* never heard *till the children are in bed*. This knocking was heard by the *supposed woman* when alive, who declared it foretold her death." Another account of the affair asserts that the person accused had married two sisters, and that

Fanny, the daughter of Parsons, had slept with the lady that *appeared* by *knocking* and *scratching* during her husband's absence at a wedding; but the knocking the deceased heard, was declared by the girl to be caused by the Spirit of the previously deceased sister; if so, the girl's infernal acts may have caused the death of the woman, as it is well known the agitation of a mind under the terrors of supposed supernatural visitation must have a fatal tendency in such a disorder as the small-pox.

As an astonishing proof of the folly of certain persons on this occasion, I shall quote the following paragraphs from the London Chronicle, vol. XI. p. 74, which conclude a string of questions and answers, put to, and received from the horrid girl, who, young as she was, richly deserved hanging, with her prompters. "What must occasion credulity is, the afflicting an *innocent child*, whom this Spirit acknowledges to be so, and that it is not the part of a good Spirit so to do, while, *she knocks that she is*, and permitted by God, not by Satan, to appear. *What is more astonishing*, that she will not cease troubling the child after satisfaction had. There is such a mixture *of truth* and *contradictions*, that a person *cannot help doubting* of the veracity of this knocker. It is, we humbly presume, fit to be enquired into, for the satisfaction of the publick, and to bring to exemplary punishment the impostor or impostors, *if any*, to relieve a distressed family, to preserve the reputation of the innocent, or to vindicate the cause of the injured. The publick are desired to rest satisfied, as the fraud, *if any*, will be discovered soon; of which they may rest assured.

"The gentleman intended to be accused in this affair, of perpetrating upon two wives the most atrocious of all crimes, was married about six months since, to a very agreeable young lady, with a fortune of 3000*l.* The unhappy situation in which they must both be, from so horrid an aspersion upon the former, may be more easily conceived than expressed."

This shameful affair terminated in the manner described in the ensuing words, extracted from one of the newspapers published in February 1762. "February 1. On this night many gentlemen, eminent for their rank and character, were, by the invitation of the Rev. Mr. Aldrich, of Clerkenwell, assembled at his house, for the examination of the noises supposed to be made by a departed Spirit, for the detection of some enormous crime. About ten at night, the gentlemen met in the chamber, in which the girl supposed to be disturbed by a Spirit had, with proper caution, been put to bed by several ladies. They sat rather more than an hour, and hearing nothing went down stairs; when they interrogated the father of the girl, who denied, in the strongest terms, any *knowledge or belief* of fraud. The supposed Spirit had before publicly promised, by an affirmative knock, *that it would attend* one of the gentlemen *into the vault*, under the Church of St. John's Clerkenwell, where the body is deposited, and give a token of *her presence there*, by a knock upon her coffin. It was therefore determined to make this trial of the existence or veracity of the supposed Spirit.

"While they were enquiring and deliberating, they were summoned into the girl's chamber by some ladies, who were near her bed, and who had heard knocks and scratches. When the gentlemen entered, the girl declared that she felt the Spirit like a mouse upon her back, and was required to hold her hands out of bed. From that time, though the Spirit was very solemnly required to manifest its existence, by appearance, by impression on the hand or body of any present, by scratches, knocks, or any other agency, *no evidence of any preternatural power was exhibited.*

"*The Spirit was then very seriously advertised*, that the person to whom the promise was made, of striking the coffin, was then about to visit the vault, and that the performance of the promise was then claimed. The company, at one, went into the Church; and the gentleman to whom the promise was made went with one more into the vault. *The Spirit was solemnly required* to perform its promise; *but nothing more than silence ensued.* The person supposed to be accused by the Spirit then went down with several others, *but no effect was perceived.* Upon their return, they examined the girl, but *could draw no confession from her.* Between two and three she desired, and was permitted to go home with her father.

"It is therefore the opinion of the whole assembly, that the child has some art of making or counterfeiting particular noises[185:A], *and that there is no agency of any higher cause.*"

Completely exasperated at the base methods adopted by his enemies to ruin his character, if not to affect his life, the injured party at length had recourse to the justice of his Country; and exactly one year after the exposure of this ridiculous as well as wicked imposture, the principals made him pecuniary satisfaction, to avoid worse consequences; but Parsons received sentence of imprisonment for two years, and to be pilloried three times; his wife imprisonment one year, and their servant six months. Thus ended the serio-comedy of *Fanny the phantom*, which afforded fine sport for the wits of the day; nay, Parsons shared in the joke, for the populace pitied his *unmerited* sufferings, and, instead of pelting, cherished him when on the pillory, and even gathered money for him.

The Mayoralty of William Beckford, Esq. was distinguished by the trial of a greater number of felons than had occurred for many preceding years: 508 were placed at the bar of the Old Bailey; 58 received sentence of death; 187 were ordered to be transported; 15 to be branded in the hand, and five to be whipped.

Amongst the mal-practices of the Century may be included the Private Mad-houses. At first view such receptacles appear useful, and in many respects preferable to Public; but the avarice of the keepers, who were under no other controul than their own consciences, led them to assist in the most nefarious plans for confining sane persons, whose relations or guardians, impelled by the same motive, or private vengeance, sometimes forgot all the restraints of nature, and immured them in the horrors of a prison, under a charge of insanity.

Turlington kept a private Mad-house at Chelsea: to this place Mrs. Hawley was conveyed by her mother and husband, September 5, 1762, under pretence of their going on a party of pleasure to Turnham-green. She was rescued from the coercion of this man by a writ of *Habeas corpus*, obtained by Mr. La Fortune, to whom the lady was denied by Turlington and Dr. Riddle; but the latter having been fortunate enough to see her at a window, her release was accomplished. It was fully proved upon examination, that no medicines were offered to Mrs. Hawley, and that she was perfectly sane. This fact might be supported by the cases of Mrs. Smith, Mrs. Durant, &c.

"Mr. Turlington having, in defence of the proceedings of this house, referred himself to Mr. King as the person entrusted and employed by him, the Committee of the House of Commons thought it necessary to summons him. Mr. King said he had been in the Wool-trade, but for six years past he had been employed by Mr. Turlington to keep his Mad-house: that he had received no written directions from Mr. Turlington; that he found several patients in the house on his being employed, and all lunatic; that since his being employed *he had admitted several for drunkenness*, and for other reasons of the same sort alledged by their *friends* or relations bringing them, which he had always thought a sufficient authority. As to the treatment of the persons confined, he said, that they had the liberty of walking in the garden, and passing from one room to another; and as to their diet and apartments, he said, it was according to the allowance they paid, which was from 60*l.* to 20*l.* a year. He admitted that he knew Mrs. Hawley; that she was confined at the representation of a woman who called herself her mother; and that the reason alledged by her for the confinement of her daughter was drunkenness. He said, that he did not remember that she was refused pen, ink, and paper; but at the same time acknowledged it was the established order of the house, that no letter should be sent by any of the persons confined to their friends and relations."

Dr. Battie celebrated for his knowledge in cases of insanity, related the case "of a person whom he visited in confinement for Lunacy, in Macdonald's Mad-house, and who had been, as the Doctor believes, for some years in this confinement. Upon being desired by Macdonald to attend him by the order, as Macdonald pretended, of the relations of the patient, he found him chained to his bed, and without ever having had the assistance of any physician before; but some time after, upon being sent for by one of the relations to a house in the City, and then told, Macdonald had received no orders for desiring the Doctor's attendance, the Doctor understood this to be a dismission, and he never heard any thing more of the unhappy patient, till Macdonald told him some time after that he died of a fever, without having had any farther medical assistance; and a sum of money devolved upon his death to the person who had the care of him."

Upon those and other instances of wickedness and inhumanity, leave was given to bring in a Bill "for the regulation of Private Mad-houses in this Kingdom."

THE POLICE.

The report of a Committee of the House of Commons, appointed in 1770, will illustrate this subject from undoubted facts. "Sir John Fielding, being asked what number of houses have been broken open in and about the cities of London and Westminster, and whether it is a growing evil, said, that all robberies, with the circumstances attending them, and particulars of goods stolen, are registered at his office; and from that register informations are grounded, and offenders are detected several years after the offences are committed; and he delivered in lists of houses broken into, with computation of the goods stolen.

From Michaelmas 1766 to 14 March 1770, in half-yearly periods, by which it appeared that from Michaelmas 1766 to Lady-day 1767, 13 houses had been broken open, and goods stolen to the value of 289*l*.

From Lady-day 1767 to Michaelmas 1767, 36 houses, value 627*l*.

From Michaelmas 1767 to Lady-day 1768, 52 houses, value 569*l*.

From Lady-day 1768 to Michaelmas 1768, 48 houses, value 1332*l*.

From Michaelmas 1768 to Lady-day 1769, 35 houses, value 1448*l*. 15*s*.

From Lady-day 1769 to Michaelmas 1769, 63 houses, value 1616*l*.

From Michaelmas 1769 to 14 March 1770, 104 houses, value 4241*l*.

He farther informed the Committee, that it is supposed the last 104 houses were broken open by a number of house-breakers not exceeding 20, and few of them more than 20 years of age, 16 or 17 of whom are in custody with little probability of their being convicted: that the evil increases amazingly, and never was at so great a height as since last Michaelmas. Being asked, what is the cause of this increase of housebreaking; he said, that felons formerly carried their goods to pawnbrokers; but by the present method of quick notice to pawnbrokers, silversmiths, and others, that plan is defeated, and the housebreakers now go to Jews, who melt the plate immediately, and destroy other things that might be evidence, which in burglary can be nothing but the goods, though in other cases the person may be sworn to; that they disguise jewels by knocking them out of the sockets, so that they cannot be sworn to; that the present gang of house-breakers are sons of unfortunate people, and of no trade; that they began when boys as pick-pockets, but turned house-breakers when they grew up, in order to procure a greater income to supply their increased expences. And he informed the Committee, that for 20 years a footpad has not escaped; that highwaymen cannot escape, upon account of the early information given to the aforesaid office, and the great number of prosecutors who always appear against them, which he thinks must in time put an end to that evil[191:A]. He then said, he had detected several persons in Duke's-place with plate, and has offered a reward of five guineas for apprehending one person in the same place. Being asked what he thought of the present method of watching the town; he said, the watch is insufficient, their duty too hard, and their pay too small; that he has known serjeants in the guards employed as watchmen; that the watchmen are paid eightpence halfpenny in St. Margaret's parish, and a gratuity of two guineas a year, out of which they find their own candle; that as they are paid monthly, they borrow their money of an usurer once a week; that in other parishes the watch are paid from tenpence to one-shilling per night; that the watch in Westminster is in every parish under the direction of a separate commission, composed of persons who have served the offices of Churchwarden and Overseer; that Commissioners of the respective parishes appoint the beats of their watchmen without conferring together, which leaves the frontiers of each parish in a confused state; for that, where one side of a street lies in one parish, and the other side in another parish, the watchmen of one side cannot lend any assistance to persons on the other side, other than as a private person, except in cases of felony.

James Sayer, Esq. Deputy High-steward of Westminster, confirmed the above evidence; and added, that St. Margaret's parish has a select vestry, the majority of which is composed of tradesmen; that they will pay no more than eightpence halfpenny a night to their watchmen, and have no way of punishing them for neglect of duty than by dismissing them, which in fact is not a punishment, for they find it difficult to get men to serve in that office; and he further said, that their number is not sufficient. Being asked the reason for changing the constables from being parochial to be constables for the whole City and Liberty, he said, that before 29 George II. constables were parochial; that he apprehended the reason for the change was, that a constable could not execute any official act out of his parish without being specially authorised so to do. He mentioned an instance of a constable's being killed when he was serving a warrant out of his parish; that the person who killed him was tried and found guilty of manslaughter only, though he would have been guilty of murder, if it had happened in the parish to which the constable belonged.

Sir John Fielding being asked what remedies he could suggest to prevent the above evils; he produced two papers relating to constables, watchmen, and other officers, which were read to and confirmed by him, and are as follows:

"Watchmen too old—should be from 25 to 50; their beats too extensive—should not exceed 20 houses on each side of the way. Watchmen too few, the sum raised for the watch too little, being only fourpence in the pound—should be sixpence.

"Ward-officers to be chosen out of those inhabitants that have served the office of constable, and to have a good salary. One half of the constables to be discharged within the year, so that one half remaining two years will be able to instruct the new officers, and the whole duty will be well done. If the new provisions for the watch can be established by the Commissioners remaining where they are, it will save trouble; for then the money may be raised by them as it now is, and every parish may pay and clothe their own watchmen; so that the appointment, distribution, direction, wages, number, and punishment of the watch, may be in the Magistrates by a new commission, and the paying and clothing be in the present Commissioners.

"The words 'A Constable of the City and Liberties of Westminster,' to be placed over the Constable's doors; the words 'Ward-officer,' over the Ward-officers' doors. Beadles by name to be discharged; and the necessary part of their duty they now do, to be performed by the Ward-officers. That it would be right to confine the intended improvement and constables to Westminster only, as the watch in the adjoining parishes of Middlesex remain on the same footing as originally settled by the Statute of Winchester."

Second Paper. "The watch of Westminster is extremely defective; the number ought to be increased, their pay augmented, and the whole direction of them put under one Commission, and that Commission should be Magistrates of the City and Liberty of Westminster; the watch should be attended by ward-officers and relieved in the night, a whole night's duty being too hard. The round-houses should be capacious, no liquor should be sold in them; publicans should be punished for permitting watchmen to tipple during their duty, and watchmen should be particularly rewarded for diligence, and punished for neglect, by the civil power. High Constables should not quit their office at the end of three years. Constables should be increased, half the number only discharged annually. The constable of the night should be considered for his attendance on that duty, and punished for neglect.

"The power for raising money at present for the watch is too confined; it should be enlarged, raised by the present Commissioners, the watchmen paid by them, but their number, direction, and appointment, be by the new Commission of Magistrates. Receivers of stolen goods, especially of those taken by burglary or highway-robbery, should be made principals, with a power of mitigation in the Judge."

James Sayer, Esq. being again examined, approved of Sir John Fielding's plan; and added, that the beadles are an unnecessary set of men, advanced in years, and servants to the Churchwardens and Overseers, are forty in number over the whole City and Liberty; they have an allowance of 20*l. per annum* apiece, which they make up 30*l.*; that he apprehends, if the number was increased to sixty, and the City and Liberty divided into so many divisions, a beadle to each division, and the object of their duty to take up vagrants, they might be of great service: that, if the beadle was to have two shillings for every vagrant he took up, and four shillings was given to any other person who should apprehend one, the one-half to be deducted out of the beadle's salary of that district where the vagrant was apprehended, it would have a good effect.

Mr. T. Rainsforth, High-constable of Westminster, being examined, said, he had been in office twelve months; that he had visited the different night watch-houses in the City and Liberty of Westminster frequently from twelve to three in the morning, found many of the peace-officers upon duty, some were not. That there is a general complaint of peace-officers neglecting their duty, to which neglect it is owing, that the watchmen and beadles are not present; and this general neglect he apprehends is the reason why so many houses are robbed; that he has frequently found seven or eight watchmen together in an alehouse; he thinks, that the High-constable should visit the round-house in the night-time, once a month at least, or oftener if required.

James Sayer, Esq. being again examined, said, that Constables are appointed under Acts 29 and 31 George II. which Acts are in many articles defective; that 80 constables, which is the number limited, are not sufficient; that they are appointed by the Leet-jury, which has been attended by great partialities; for the Leet jury being composed of the Overseers of the several parishes of the preceding year, they protect each other from serving the office of Constable; that in general opulent inhabitants are excused, and young tradesmen returned; that, if a rich man is now and then returned, he is generally got off by pleading age and infirmities; that deputies are generally hired men, and though they cannot be appointed unless approved of by the Deputy High Steward, yet, as it is impossible for him to get a true character of the person nominated, he finds many unfit persons are appointed, who, he is informed, make a trade of serving the office; for remedy of which he proposed, that the number of constables should be increased to 120. He thinks the burthen of serving the office of constable should not lay wholly on the trading inhabitants, as it does by the late Act; that, by common law, every person able and fit is liable to serve: that the fine for not serving the office should be enlarged from 8*l.* to 20*l.* which fine should be distributed among those that do serve: and he added, that twelve being obliged to attend daily during the Session of Parliament, as long as either House sits, the duty comes round to each individual every sixth day, eight being excepted, who may be sick, or kept in reserve; during which attendance the constables must necessarily neglect their own business. With respect to the High-constable, he said, it is an office of great burthen and trust; that, by law, he the witness is obliged to appoint a substantial tradesman to that office; that the person appointed is not to continue in office above three years, and is liable to a penalty of 20*l.* for refusing to serve, which penalty goes to the poor of the parish; upon which he observed, that the High-constable should not be a tradesman, because his power enables him to oblige the keepers of public-houses to deal with him, or those with whom he is concerned in his way of trade; that the penalty on persons refusing to serve the office should be increased; that the High-constable should have a reward for his service, and that the constables of the night should have a reward also.

Sir John Fielding being again examined, said, that ballad-singers are a greater nuisance than beggars, because they give opportunity to pick-pockets by collecting people together; that the songs they sing are generally immoral and obscene; the people themselves capable of work, and of the lowest and most abandoned order of people; for remedy of which, he proposed that all ballad-singers should be considered as vagrants, and made liable to the same punishments, no person being a vagrant now but who comes within some one of the descriptions of vagrancy in the Vagrant Act. And the High-constable being again examined, informed the Committee that he has often had warrants for taking up ballad-singers; that he has apprehended a great many, notwithstanding which their numbers increase, and they are become a very great nuisance; that they have often been dispersed, but still continue the practice.

Sir John Fielding, being again examined, said, that the City of Westminster is a franchise under the Dean and Chapter of Westminster; that the common gaol thereof is called the Gatehouse, to which offenders of every kind, apprehended within the Liberty of Westminster, have been usually committed for several years back, to the number of 600 or 700 annually; that in this gaol there is little or no allowance or provisions for the prisoners but what arises from the charity of passengers, seldom amounting to more than five or six shillings a-week, the greatest part of which is given to the beggar at the window for the day. That the said gaol appears, from experience of the Magistrates, to be too small for the number, and too weak for the safe custody of prisoners; that to this gaol persons for execution in debts recovered in the Court of Conscience, are committed; and he said, he believed this is the only gaol in England where there is not some provision for the poor and distressed prisoners; and he added, that when a Magistrate commits a man to that gaol for an assault, he does not know but he commits him there to starve. For these reasons, as well upon the principles of humanity as of civil policy, this ought to be remedied; and that, on account of the vast increase of inhabitants, property, and number of offenders, there ought to be in Westminster a strong, capacious, and useful gaol, and there is no such thing at present; that the said gaol, called the Gatehouse, is a very old building, subject to be repaired by the said Dean and Chapter, who appoint the Gaoler; that the supposed original use of this gaol was for the purposes of committing Clerks convict. The commission of Magistrates is not later than Charles the First's reign; they began first to commit offenders to this gaol, rather by sufferance than by right; and he observed that, however proper it may have been for its original purposes, it is unequal to the present occasions, and, as he apprehends, cannot be altered without a Law. And he further informed the Committee, that the Magistrates of Westminster have represented this matter to the Dean and Chapter, who acknowledge it, are willing to pull it down, and to give a piece of ground in their Royalty in Tothill-fields to build a new gaol upon, and to subject the same, with every thing thereunto belonging, to the Magistrates of Westminster, under such regulations as the Legislature shall think proper, provided a sum be granted by the publick for building the same; and he added, that estimates have been made, by which it appears that a very effectual gaol may be built for the sum of 2500*l*. In order, therefore, to remedy the inconveniences above-mentioned, he proposed that such gaol should be built and kept in repair out of the County rate, which he said may be done without injury to the County at large, for this reason, that there is but one rate at present for Middlesex and Westminster, near one-third of which is paid by the latter since the increase of buildings there; that this proportion is much greater than the expences required by the Act for County rates would subject Westminster to; and he added, that the gaol, called the House of Correction, Westminster, is repaired by the Magistrates of Westminster, and the expence is paid by virtue of their orders on the County Treasurer; that the same thing, if allowed by Parliament for the repairs of the proposed new gaol, will answer the purpose without separating the rate.

James Sayer, Esq. being again examined, concurred with Sir John Fielding in every particular.

Sir John informed the Committee, that about six or seven years ago the Magistrates of Westminster had no other Court-house but a place at the bottom of the stairs leading to the House of Commons, called *Hell*, to keep their Sessions in. The increase of business and of offences in Westminster made it impracticable to carry on the business there. The nuisance was represented by the Magistrates to the Lord Lieutenant, Lord Northumberland, who said, he had then applied for redress, and told the Chairman it could not be taken up by Government then, but would be in future considered: in the mean time, at his own expence, amounting to 800*l.* he directed the Chairman to prepare a large house in King-street Westminster, which was formerly a tavern, to be made proper for a Courthouse; that the Magistrates for their Sessions, the Burgesses for their Courts, the Lieutenancy for the Militia, Commissioners of Sewers for their business, Grand Juries for the County of Middlesex, Writs of Enquiry for the Sheriffs, and meeting of inhabitants for nominating their Representatives, should use the said building; for all which purposes it has been constantly, effectually, and conveniently used; that it is scarce possible for the above business to be transacted without it, and the establishment of it is as essential to the Civil Power as any thing that has been mentioned. That the purchase of the said building and fitting it up, cost the Duke of Northumberland near 4000*l.*; and he added, that this building also might be kept in repair by the County rate, at an average of 30 or 40*l.* a year.

Sir John Fielding said, he thinks the acting part of the Magistrates in Westminster is in as good a state as it ever was, and more free from imputation of or neglect of duty; that it would be useful to have some persons of rank and condition in the Commission of the Peace for Westminster, who would attend at the Quarter Sessions, where they would become acquainted with the conduct of the Magistrates in general, give a dignity to the Commission, support the acting Magistrates on great occasions, and give encouragement to such of them as discharged their trust becoming the honour of the Commission, and discountenance those who did not; and he added, that for the last two or three years the Magistrates of Westminster have gone through very painful duty, and have been very diligent in it; and having been sensible of the necessity of their attendance, have mutually agreed to attend at any time or place upon the least notice from their Chairman.

James Sayer, Esq. being again examined, admitted that the Magistracy at present is composed in general of persons of character, and that justice is administered with activity, diligence, and skill, but alledged that it has been otherwise formerly, and may be the case hereafter; and therefore, he was of opinion that a regulation in the Magistracy of Westminster is necessary. That there should be a qualification of Justices, that they should have a reward for acting, as the most part of their time will be devoted to the public service; that the fees to be taken by their clerks should be devoted to some public service; such as a vagrant hospital; that there should be certain Rotation-offices established by Law; that, as he apprehends, one such office might be sufficient if properly regulated; that the Rotation-office should do all the business except in emergent cases, and that the private office of Justice of the Peace should be abolished, because it sometimes happens, that a man committed for a notorious bailable offence is carried to another Justice, who bails him without knowing the enormity of his offence; and Sir John Fielding said, that in criminal offences, that nearly regard the publick, it is impracticable to use a Rotation-office as there are many things necessary to be kept secret; and, though the whole of the circumstances must be known to the acting Magistrate, yet they cannot be known by a fresh Magistrate who attends in rotation; and he added, that the great number of brothels and irregular taverns carried on without licence from the Magistrates, are another great cause of robberies, burglaries, and other disorders, and also of neglect of watchmen and constables of the night in their respective duties. That these taverns are kept by persons of the most abandoned characters, such as bawds, thieves, receivers of stolen goods, and Marshalsea-court and Sheriffs officers who keep lock-up houses. The principal of these houses are situate in Covent-garden, about thirty in St. Mary-le-Strand, about twelve in St. Martin's, in the vicinity of Covent-garden, about twelve in St. Clement's, five or six at Charing-cross, and in Hedge-lane about twenty; that there are many more dispersed in different parts of Westminster, in Goodman's-fields, and Whitechapel, many of which are remarkably infamous, and are the cause of disorders of every kind, shelters for bullies to protect prostitutes, and for thieves, are a terror to the watchmen and peace-officers of the night, a nuisance to the inhabitants in the neighbourhood, and difficult to be suppressed by prosecution for want of evidence, and, in short, pregnant with every other mischief to Society; that any person desirous of gaining a livelihood by keeping a place of public entertainment, who is of good reputation, can obtain a licence with ease from the Magistrates to keep such house, when a public-house in any neighbourhood happens to be vacant that has been licensed before; the Magistrates of Middlesex and Westminster having long held it to be a rule essential to the public good, rather to diminish than increase the number of public-houses. That persons of abandoned characters, by applying to the Commissioners of the Stamp-office, may obtain a licence for selling wine; by virtue of such licences it is that the taverns above described are kept open, for the aforesaid Commissioners are impowered by law to grant such licences to whom they shall think fit; that licences for selling spirituous liquors by retail are not granted by the Commissioners of Excise, unless the parties produce to them a licence under the hands and seals of two Justices of the Peace to sell ale. That Magistrates cannot by Law authorise any person to sell ale, without a certificate of such person's being of good fame and sober life and conversation, so that producing this licence to the Commissioners establishes their character with them, and takes away the necessity of any enquiry; for remedy of which, he proposed that Wine-licences should be placed by Law under the same restraint as the licences for selling spirituous liquors now are. This remedy, he apprehended, might probably reduce the Revenue of Wine-licences; if confined to the Bills of Mortality, it would in his opinion diminish it no more than 400*l.*; but if extended to Portsmouth, Plymouth, Chatham, and other Dock-yards, it might lessen it 200*l.* more; he added, that he thinks it more necessary to correct the evil in those parts, as it has a direct tendency to corrupt and destroy the very vitals of the Constitution, the lives of the useful seamen, who by means of these houses become the objects of plunder as long as they have any money, and are induced to become robbers when they have none; and he informed the Committee that there is another great evil which is the cause of these disorders, namely, the immense number of common prostitutes, who, mostly from necessity, infest the streets of the City and Liberty of Westminster and parts adjacent, attended by common soldiers and other bullies to protect them from the civil power; these prostitutes, when they have secured the unwary customers, lead them to some of the aforesaid taverns, from whence they seldom escape without being robbed. The cause of this evil, as he apprehends, is the great difficulty, as the Law now stands, to punish those offenders, they being, as common prostitutes, scarce, if at all, within the description of any Statute now in being; and he added, that this subjects watchmen, round-house keepers, constables, and even the Magistrates themselves to prosecutions from low Attorneys; that the remedy in his opinion should be to declare, that persons walking or plying in the said streets for lewd purposes after the watch is set, standing at the doors, or appearing at the windows of such taverns in an indecent manner for lewd purposes, shall be considered as vagrants, and punished as such. That as to the circumstance of street-beggars, it never came to his knowledge that they are under contribution to the beadles.

Mr. Rainsforth the High-constable being called, delivered in a paper called "The State of the Watch in Westminster;" which paper is hereunto annexed: and said, that all the watchmen being assembled at Guildhall on Saturday, March 24, to see the housebreakers, they appeared to him in general very infirm and unfit to execute that office.

Mr. Thomas Heath, a Burgess of the Duchy of Lancaster, being examined, said, that both the constables and watch within the said Duchy are very insufficient and defective."

The Committee concluded their Report with thirteen resolutions, exactly corresponding with the evidence received, which were all agreed to by the House, and a Bill or Bills ordered to be brought in for carrying them into effect.

The High Constable's remarks:

St. Margaret's.

"Three quarters past 11. Constable came after I was there, house-man and beadle on duty; 41 watchmen, with St. John's united, at eightpence halfpenny *per night*, with one guinea at Christmas, and one guinea at Lady-day, and great coats as a present; their beats large; was obliged to take a soldier into custody for being out of his quarters, and very insolent, with several more soldiers, in the streets at 12 o'clock; called out "Watch," but could get no assistance from them.

St. George's.

Half-past 12. Constable and four house-men on duty; 57 watchmen at one shilling *per night*, and great coats; two men had attempted to break into Lady Cavendish's house, but were prevented.

St. James's.

One o'clock. Constable and beadle on duty, streets very quiet, meeting with no disorders; 56 watchmen at one shilling *per night* for five months, and eightpence for seven months, with coats, lanterns, and candles.

St. Anne's.

Half-past 1. Constable gone his rounds; 23 watchmen at one shilling *per night* for six months, and nine-pence the other six, with candles; no disorders.

St. Martin's.

Two o'clock. Constable, regulator, and beadle on duty; 43 watchmen at 14*l. per ann.* candles and great coats, every thing quiet, beats large.

St. Paul's, Covent-garden.

Half-past 2. Constable, house-keeper, and beadle on duty; 22 watchmen at one shilling *per night*, down to eightpence halfpenny; no disturbance.

St. Clement's Danes.

Past 3. No constable on duty, found a watchman there at a great distance from his beat; from thence went to the night-cellar facing Arundel-street in the Strand, which is in the Dutchy, and there found four of St. Clement's watchmen drinking; St. Clement's watchmen 22 at one shilling each.

St. Mary-le-Strand.

No attendance, having only two constables which only attend every other night; 3 watchmen, Dutchy included, at one shilling each; a very disorderly cellar near the New-church for selling saloop, &c. to very loose and suspected persons."

The number of felons who had been imprisoned in Newgate during the year 1772, amounted to the amazing number of 1475; from 1747 to 1764, the number had never exceeded 1300; from the year 1763 to 1772, the greatest number of prisoners who died in Newgate within twelve months was 36, and the least 14.

Impressed with the melancholy consequences to Society from this shocking increase of depravity, Sir John Fielding thus emphatically addressed the Grand Jury at the Quarter-sessions for Westminster, October 12, 1773.

"Gentlemen of the Grand Jury,

"By virtue of the trust now reposed in you, as a Grand Jury for the City and Liberty of Westminster, you are become the temporary guardians of the lives, liberty, property, and reputation of your fellow-citizens; nor can a higher trust than this be placed in man. And in order that it may be discharged with a conscientious regard to truth, and a fidelity becoming its importance, you are bound by the solemn tie of an oath to execute this office without malice, without resentment, without favour, and without affection. Under this sacred obligation, your fellow-subjects have reason to hope and expect that you will hear with patience, enquire with diligence, judge with candour, and present with impartiality.

"I am sorry to inform you, Gentlemen, that it appears from our Calendar, that there are a number of persons in confinement charged with felonies of different degrees, but it is a melancholy truth; probably some of these unfortunate fellow-creatures may suffer ignominious punishments; but, as prevention is far superior to punishment, permit me to call forth to your attention some of those public offences which first corrupt, and then precipitate the unwary to infamy and destruction. I mean the keeping of gaming-houses, disorderly houses, bawdy-houses, for it is these seminaries of vice, these polluted fountains, that first poison the moral spring of our youth, and consequently make footpads, highwaymen, and housebreakers, of those who might otherwise have been useful, nay, perhaps honourable members of society; and although I am convinced it is in the power of many of the inhabitants of this City and Liberty to remove, by prosecution, some of these nuisances; yet I am aware that they are deterred from it by the hateful idea indiscriminately annexed to the name of an informer; and thus, gentlemen, the parties injured, by a criminal cowardice, neglect their duty to the publick, whilst the ignorant and abandoned slanderer unjustly reviles the Magistrate for the continuation of these evils; but, if public spirit should produce any prosecutors of the keepers of such houses, I hope you will do your utmost to bring such miscreants to condign punishment, that the publick may have a fair opportunity of judging in what a detestable light the Magistrates of this Bench consider such offenders and offences. Let the inhabitants but complain, and if the Justice neglect his duty, may contempt and confusion overtake him! But till then, place confidence, and pay respect to that authority where confidence and respect are due.

"And now, gentlemen, give me leave to take notice of one public offence, so alarming in its nature, and so mischievous in its effects, that, like a pestilence, it does not only stand in need of your immediate assistance, but that of all good men, to stop its corroding progress; I mean the exposing to sale, and selling such indecent and obscene prints and books as are sufficient to put impudence itself to the blush. Surely, gentlemen, Providence has placed too strong propensions in our nature to stand in need of such inflammatory aids as these; on the contrary, in this particular, we rather require restraints than encouragements; but, if at that period of life when our children and apprentices stand in need of a parent to advise, a master to restrain, or a friend to admonish and check the first impulse of passion, pictures like these are held forth to meet their early feelings, what but destruction must be the event? Indeed, by care, you may prevent youth in some degree from frequenting bad company; you may accustom them to good habits, afford them examples worthy imitation, and by shutting your doors early, may oblige them to keep good hours; but, alas! what doors, what bolts, what bars, can be any security to their innocence, whilst Vice in this deluding form counteracts all caution, and bids defiance to the force of precept, prudence, and example, by affording such foul but palatable hints as are destructive to modesty, sobriety, and obedience? But, what is still more shocking, I am informed that women, nay mothers of families, to the disgrace of their sex, are the cruel dispensers of this high-seasoned mischief; but, if duty or humanity should spirit up any one to prosecute such offenders, I conjure you as fathers, masters, and subjects, to afford them the best assistance in your power, to put a stop to this shameful and abominable practice.

"I am very sensible that I have already trespassed much on your time, but cannot take my leave without acquainting you that our Courts of Judicature of late have abounded with prosecutions for wilful and corrupt perjury— dreadful offence! But, as oaths are the foundation of all our judicial proceedings, and the negligent administration of these oaths is one great cause of perjury, I do earnestly recommend it to you, Mr. Foreman, not to permit any witness to give his testimony without reminding him that he is about to speak under the sacred influence of an oath, and that he has called the great God himself to witness that he is speaking truth."

An Act, passed in 1774, has operated through the following clause, in suppressing some of the enormities which lead to the crimes Sir John deprecated. "That every watchman, as well patroles as others, and every beadle, shall, during his respective time of watching, to the utmost of his power endeavour to prevent as well all mischiefs happening by fire, as all murders, burglaries, robberies, affrays, and other outrages and disorders; *and to that end*, during the time of watching, each and every of them shall and may, and are hereby authorised and impowered to arrest and apprehend *all night-walkers*, malefactors, rogues, vagabonds, and other loose, idle, and disorderly persons, and all persons lying or loitering in any street, square, court, mews, lane, alley, or elsewhere; to apprehend and bring them as soon as convenient before the constable of the night. And if any person or persons shall assault or resist any watchman in the execution of his office, they shall pay any sum not exceeding five pounds."

The publication of obscene prints and books (though so justly reprobated by Sir John Fielding) had proceeded with very little interruption, almost through the space of time which elapsed between his charge and the termination of the century. A few prosecutions were instituted, but nothing systematic in opposition took place, till the Society for the Suppression of Vice attacked the enemies of virtue and decency with vigour, and obtained almost a complete victory. For this essential service rendered to the community they deserve every praise; and, however the publick may be divided in opinion as to their methods of proceeding, and the propriety of some of their operations, all will agree that vending obscene books and prints, riotous and disorderly houses, lotteries, and little-goes, and cruelty to animals, ought to be finally prevented. I shall close this article with a summary of their convictions during the first year of their establishment, ending in April 1803.

Profanation of the Sabbath.

Offenders.	*Punishments.*	*No.*
Two hundred and twenty-two Shop-keepers, for pursuing their ordinary callings; and two hundred and eighteen Publicans, for suffering Tippling during Divine Service, (having disregarded the warning previously delivered them).	Some convicted in the full penalty, with costs, and others in costs only.—Before the Magistrates.	440

Vending Obscene Books and Prints.

Offenders.	*Punishments.*	*No.*
GAINER, an Itinerant Hawker.	Six Months Imprisonment.—Middlesex Sessions.	7
HARRIS, a Vender of Ballads and Obscene Books and Prints, at Whitehall.	Two Years Imprisonment and Pillory.—Westminster Sessions.	

BERTAZZI[*], an Italian Itinerant Hawker.	Six Months Imprisonment. Middlesex Sessions.
BERTAZZI, on two other Indictments.	Six Months Imprisonment for each offence, and twice Pillory.—Court of King's Bench.
ANN AITKIN, Printseller, Castle-street, Leicester-fields.	One Year's Imprisonment and hard Labour.—Court of King's Bench.
BAINES, Keeper of a Stall, Skinner-street, Snow-hill.	One Year's Imprisonment.—Old Bailey Sessions.

[*] *N.B.* This man, in connection with many others, went about the City selling obscene books and prints, at boarding-schools of both sexes.

Riotous and Disorderly Houses, &c.

Offenders.	Punishments.	No.
Four Keepers of Houses where unlawful Dances were held, two on Sundays; three Keepers of Public-houses, and two of Private Theatres—being all receptacles for disorderly and abandoned characters, and places for the seduction of youth of both sexes; and two Keepers of Brothels, where practices of the grossest prostitution were carried on.	All suppressed in a summary way.—Before the Magistrates.	11

Lotteries and Little Goes.

Offenders.	Punishments.	No.
Twenty-five Persons for illegal Insurances, &c. some principals, and some agents.	From Two to Six Months Imprisonment each.—Before the Magistrates.	26
SAMUEL BEST, a Fortune-teller and Impostor.	Committed as a Vagrant.	

Cruelty to Animals.

Offenders.	Punishments.	No.
Two Drovers.	Imprisonment One Month each.—Before the Magistrates.	3

Several persons guilty of Bear and Badger baiting, in Black-boy-alley, Chick-lane, where the most shocking scenes of barbarity had been practised for twenty-two years, even on Sundays.	Suppressed by the Magistrates.

Total Convictions.

Profanation of the Sabbath	440
Vending Obscene Books and Prints	7
Riotous and Disorderly Houses, &c.	11
Lotteries and Little Goes	26
Cruelty to Animals	3
	487

Mr. Carlton, Deputy Clerk of the Peace, and Clerk to the Justices for Westminster, stated to a Committee of the House of Commons in 1782, that E-O tables were very numerous; that one house in the parish of St. Anne, Soho, contained five, and that there were more than 300 in the above parish and St. James's; those were used every day of the week, and servants enticed to them by cards of direction thrown down the areas.

I have hitherto noticed those general circumstances of depravity, which ever have and ever will prevail in a greater or less degree in every Metropolis; and shall conclude the black list with mentioning the *monster*, who terrified the females of London in 1790, by cutting at their clothes with a sharp instrument, and frequently injuring their persons. Renwick Williams was at length apprehended, tried, and convicted, for cutting the garments and person of Miss Anne Porter; and the horrid acts were never repeated.

QUACKS—1700.

The man who, without experience or education, undertakes to compound drugs, and, when compounded, to administer them as remedies for diseases of the human body, may justly be pronounced a dishonest adventurer, and an enemy to life and the fair proportions of his fellow-citizens. Quackery is an antient profession in London. Henry VIII. despised them, and endeavoured to suppress their nostrums by establishing Censors in Physick; but I do not profess to meddle with them before 1700.

"At the Angel and Crown, in Basing-lane, near Bow-lane, lives J. Pechey, a Graduate in the University of Oxford, and of many years standing in the

College of Physicians, London; where all sick people that come to him may have, *for sixpence*, a faithful account of their diseases, and plain directions for diet and other things they can prepare themselves; and such as have occasion for medicines may have them of him at reasonable rates, without paying any thing for advice; and he will visit any sick person in London or the Liberties thereof, in the day-time, for 2*s*. 6*d*. and any where else within the Bills of Mortality for 5*s*.; and if he be called by any person as he passes by in any of these places, he will require but 1*s*. for his advice."

The ridiculous falsehoods of Quacks have long been detested by the sensible part of the Community; but every thing that has been said and written against them avails nothing: thousands of silly people are yet duped, nay, are bigoted in their belief of the efficacy of nostrums. Be it my task to shew the reader a few of the contrivances and schemes of a Century, and to bring before him *genuine* effusions of impudence which have daily insulted and deceived the inhabitants of London.

"April 12, 1700.

A satisfactory experiment for the curious.

"If you please to pour one part of *Sal volatile oleosum*, or any other oily salts into a narrow-bottomed wine-glass, and near the like quantity of Stringer's Elixir, *febrifugium martis*, there will be a pleasant conflict: the elixir will immediately make a preparation of and precipitate those oily volatile salts into a fixed armoniac salt in the bottom, and receive the spirituous aromatic oily parts into itself, and yet retain its own virtues, colour, and taste. There is no other true and genuine elixir but Mr. Stringer's that is exposed to sale; for those called *Elixir proprietatu* and *Elixir salutis*, &c. are mere tinctures drawn by brandy or nasty spirits; but this is a perfect elixir or quintessence, whose perfect principles of spirits, oil, and salt, are so inseparably united, that it can neither decay, putrefy, nor die, *no more than the glass that contains it*; and is so far from being a harsh corrosive, that it feels like oil, yet dries like a spirit, cleanses the skin like soap, and not only allays all putrefactive ferments in a moment, *but immediately cures the most malignant fevers*, takes away all *sorts of corns and hardness* in the skin, and makes the roughest hands smooth and white, only by anointing with it morning and night for a month together: which medicine with his other called Salt of Lemons, *in despite of all opposers*, will approve themselves nearest of affinity to an *universal medicine*."

In this admirable medicine the Londoner of 1700 had an internal and an external application, and materials to cleanse and soften the hands, which would at the same time enable him to walk the streets in comfort and ease, in defiance of corns and *horny* excrescences. Happy Londoners! possessing such men as Dr. Pechey and Mr. Stringer, aided by Dr. Case, whose *unguentum panchrestum*, prepared by the *Spagyrick art*, might justly be called the *Golden*

Mine. This wonderful preparation cured by its *sympathetical* powers; in short, the Doctor found "it more infallible than the *Zenexton* of *Paracelsus*." This great Doctor was the means of informing us that Quacks were then in the habit of employing persons to thrust bills into the hands of passengers in the streets. For example: "Your old friend, Dr. Case, desires you not to forget him, although he has left the *common way of bills*."

A *brother Quack* this year issued the following notice: "John Poley, at Broken-wharf, over-against the Water-mill in Thames-street, next door to the Bell, will undertake to cure any smokey chimneys. *No cure, no money.*"

I very much doubt whether even the lowest class of ignorants would be deceived at present by the ensuing impudent falsehood. "Whereas it has been industriously reported, that *Doctor* Herwig, who *cures madness* and most distempers by *sympathy*, has left England, and returned to Germany: This is to give notice, that he lives at the same place, *viz.* at Mr. Gagelman's, in Suffolk-street, Charing-cross, about the middle of the street, *over-against* the *green* balcony."

The reader will undoubtedly admire the modesty of Mr. Bartlett, who, in 1704, advertised, "Bartlett's inventions of Steel Trusses, Instruments, Medicines, and methods to cure Ruptures and other faults of those parts, and to make the weak strong, and crooked strait, most of which I could help with the twentieth part of the trouble and charge occasioned only by delay. I reduce desperate ruptures in a few minutes, though likely to be mortal in a few hours, and have made the only true discovery of cause and cure. Infants and others born so, and to men of fifty or sixty years, in a few weeks cured. I sell strait stockings, collars, and swings, and such like things. Advice and medicines to the poor *gratis*."

Of all the inventions for the amendment and recovery of the human frame from disease *and death*, none equals the Dutch stiptick, *seriously* mentioned in the Supplement, printed by John Morphew, April 27, 1709; but which I suspect proceeded from the waggish pen of Mr. Bickerstaff, or some other wit, who sent their effusions to the publisher of the Tatler. "There is prepared by a person of quality in Holland a stiptick water; for the receipt of which, exclusive of all others, the French King has offered 150,000 pistoles; but the proprietor refused to take the same. It was tried upon a Hen, before his Grace the Duke of Marlborough, on board the Peregrine galley. The feathers being all plucked from her head, a large nail was drove through her brains, gullet, tongue, &c. and fastened her head to a table, where it was left near a minute; after which, drawing out the nail and touching the part immediately with the aforesaid stiptick, she was laid upon the deck, and in half an hour's time recovered, and began to eat bread. Several as extraordinary experiments have been made upon dogs, cats, calves, lambs, and other animals, by cutting their guts in several places, the nut of the thigh, and other parts; and it is affirmed, that this stiptick cures any part of the body, except the heart or bladder."

John Marten, with his "Attila of the Gout," and specifick, seemed determined in 1712, to expel that disorder from every human body in the Kingdom. Those who in 1807 read his advertisement, and are not thenceforward converts, must be stubborn unbelievers indeed. "I should be wanting (saith Mr. Marten) as well to the publick as myself, did I not reveal the *stupendious* effects of my specifick in the gout, which daily experience more and more confirms. And whatever mean opinion any who are strangers to its excellency may entertain of it, either through unbelief, or being prejudiced by those whose interest it is to explode it; let them remember, *I tell* them (as will many reputable people I will refer them to who have tried it), that if they ever expect certain and speedy relief, without the least detriment to their healths, they *must* have it. I say they *must*, because the surprising benefit all receive by it indicates that nothing else *can* more intimately dilute, and friendly and instantly obtrude and subdue by its soft balmy alterative nature, the acrimony of the humours that distend and torture the joints, and gently lead them away by urine, the only sensible operation it has. And as it is a medicine that will make its own way, it cannot but come (by degrees) to be as universally used and approved of in that distemper, as the Jesuits' bark is for agues, if not more; for none that shall drink it in time will ever be confined a day with the gout, nor others continue in pain an hour after drinking it, though they have lain for weeks together upon the *wreck*. Any may be further satisfied, and have all objections answered, *by word of mouth*, or by consulting the book I lately published, intituled, "The Attila of the Gout," being a peculiar account of that distemper, in which *the vanity of all* that has hitherto been writ and practised to remove it, and an infallible method to cure it, are demonstrated; with ample testimonies of patients cured by John Marten, Surgeon, in Hatton-garden."

I have before observed, that every profession has its Quacks, or persons who deviate from established rules. Such was the *Quack writer* who inserted the ensuing advertisement in the Evening Post of January 22, 1717. "Whereas a certain pretender to Penmanship has, in an illeterate manner, *fell* upon my late performance, let him know *I look down upon him*, yet thus give him his answer: if I did keep monsters for my diversion, that does not affect me in my art; and it is well known that I have not now a deformed creature in my house, which is more than he can say *while he is within doors*. I pass by the unworthy reflections on my N and O, which I could return upon his R and T; but his own ink will blacken him enough, while it appears in his own irregular scrawls.

While Cross of Paul's shines in the middle sky,

Thy name shall *stink*, but *mine* shall never die."

The above elegant production has a parallel in the following modest notice of August 1717. "This is to give notice, that Dr. Benjamin Thornhill, sworn servant to his Majesty King George, *seventh son* of *the seventh son*, who has kept a stage in the Rounds of West-Smithfield for several months past, will continue to be advised with every day in the week, from eight in the morning till eight at night, at his lodgings at the Swan Tavern, in West-Smithfield, till Michaelmas, for the good of all people that lie languishing under distempers, he knowing that *Talenta in agro non est abscondita*, that a talent ought not to be hid in the Earth; therefore he exposes himself in public for the good of the poor. The many cures he had performed has given the world great satisfaction, having cured 1500 people of the King's evil, and several hundreds that have been blind, lame, deaf, and diseased. God Almighty having been pleased to bestow upon him so great a talent, he thinks himself bound in duty to be helpful to all sorts of persons that are afflicted with any distemper. He will tell you in a minute what distemper you are troubled with, and whether you are curable or not; if not curable, he will not take any one in hand, if he might have 500*l.* for a reward.

"N. B. The Doctor has an infallible cure for the Gout, which in a few hours gives ease, and in a short time makes a perfect cure; likewise a never-failing remedy for the wind colic in the stomach and bowels."

The Original Weekly Journal of December 28, 1723, contains a set of queries, which seem better suited to the ideas of a person despising Quacks than to have been written by one. "An appeal to the judicious part of mankind, if it is not the grossest imposition imaginable to cram the public prints in so fulsome a manner with infallible specificks, arcana's, Italian boluses, and innumerable Quack-medicines put to sale at Toy-shops and other places, only to hide the shame, and screen from the resentment of injured people, the preparers of such notorious cheats. Are the best physicians or most eminent surgeons ashamed of their prescriptions? Can men of sense be gulled out of their money by the severe affliction of another's pocket (though, in his own words, of their body), because his pretended charity to their deplorable circumstances has induced him to publish what he does not own? Are not the degrees of distempers and the constitutions of men various? Was ever any one thing infallible? Can all people eat the most innocent food with equal advantage? Have we not ingenious Physicians and Surgeons, who act in public, not only to their own honour, but that of their country, and are, by their transcendant skill, become inimitable in all the world? Are not some disappointed in the success of a prescription from the most judicious hand? and will they depend upon what has no known author, and who refers them to the advice of some able Surgeon after cheating them himself? Shall any man's misery prevail upon his credulity to make him more miserable? or will any Surgeon expose his patient? For your *own sake*, apply to some man of ingenuity and probity, who appears to justify his practice by his success; *one of which invites you to his house*, at the Golden-heart and Square-lamp, in Cranecourt, near Fetter-lane. Ask for the Surgeon, who is to be advised with every morning till 11 o'clock, and from two till nine at night, in any distemper."

After the above interrogatories, it would be absurd to attempt the application of any argument against Quackery. The queries of this extraordinary Quack are absolutely unanswerable; but it will be necessary to add, for the *information of posterity*, that the daily papers are still filled with false advertisements and false testimonies of cures performed; and that the angles of the streets, walls, and fences of London, are covered with bills issued by Quacks, while, perhaps, upwards of an hundred persons obtain a livelihood by handing them to passengers in every street.

This method of proceeding may be pronounced one of the customs which distinguish London; and, as I purpose tracing those, the reader will forgive my entering upon the subject without any other preliminary observation, than that I am afraid he will find some of the number trench very closely upon the rights of the articles under the head of Depravity.

FOOTNOTES:

[90:A] The gentleman who reviews this work in the European Magazine, mentions 'the Royal Oak Lottery,' on the authority of Congreve's "Love for Love," as particularly ruinous.

[92:A] Mark the regularity of the gradations.

[92:B] Gazette.

[96:A] Original proposals.

[97:A] The artist against whom this advertisement was levelled, "was Bat Pigeon, whose sign of a Bat and a Pigeon once attracted much attention, and of whom honourable mention has been made both by Steele and Addison. Honest Bat had a very handsome house and shop on the North side of the Strand, a few doors from St. Clement's Church Yard." European Magazine.

[104:A] Newspapers.

[118:A] A writer in the European Magazine says, he could add *sixty other schemes* to my list; I should however imagine my readers are already satisfied.

[141:A] This amount seems impossible; but the authority from which it was taken is correctly copied.

[170:A] Poems for Children six feet high, 1757.

[185:A] In other words a Ventriloquist.

[191:A] The worthy Magistrate was right in his conjecture, for highway robbery is very uncommon at present in the neighbourhood of London.

CHAPTER. III.
MANNERS AND CUSTOMS OF THE INHABITANTS OF LONDON FROM 1700 TO 1800.

A Weekly Paper, intituled "The Dutch Prophet," was published at the commencement of the Century. The Author, in one of those, gives the outlines of each day in the week as employed by different persons; it is a filthy publication, and the following is almost the only decent part. "Wednesday, several Shop-keepers near St. Paul's will rise before six, *be upon their knees at chapel* a little after; promise God Almighty to live soberly and righteously before seven; *take half a pint of Sack and a dash of Gentian before eight*; tell fifty lies behind their counters by nine; and spend the rest of the morning over *Tea and Tobacco* at Child's Coffee-house."

"Sunday, a world of women, with *green aprons*, get on their pattens after eight; reach Brewers-hall and White-hart court by nine; are ready to burst with the Spirit a minute or two after, and delivered of it by ten. Much sighing at Salters-hall about the same hour; great frowning at St. Paul's while the service is singing, tolerable attention to the Sermon, but no respect shewn at all to the Sacrament," &c. &c.

These extracts inform us that Tradesmen were in the habit of attending Matins, which is certainly not the case at present; that they breakfasted upon sack and the root Gentian, and drank tea and chewed tobacco at the Coffee-house. Mark the change of 100 years: they now breakfast upon tea, and never chew tobacco; nor do many of them enter the Coffee-house once in a year.

The Halls of the different Companies appear to have been used at the above period for almost every public purpose, but particularly for the sighings of grace and over-righteousness, and to reverberate in thrice dissonant thunder the voices of the Elect, who saved themselves, and dealt eternal misery to all around them. Here again is a change: I believe not one Hall is now used for such purposes. The Cathedral service is admired, the Sermon neglected, and the Sacrament received with awe and devotion.

The effect of the Queen's proclamation against Vice and Debauchery in 1703 is thus noticed by Observator in his 92d number; some of the customs of the lower classes may be collected from the quotation. He says, the Vintners and their wives were particularly affected by it, some of the latter of which "had the profit of the Sunday's claret, to buy them pins, and to enable them every now and then to take a turn with the Wine-merchant's eldest 'prentice to *Cupid's*[231:A] garden, or on-board the *Polly*[231:B]. The Whetters are very much disobliged at this Proclamation, who used on Sundays to meet on their parade at the Quaker's meeting-house, in Gracechurch-street, and adjourn from thence through the Tavern back-door to take a whet of white and wormwood, and to eat a bit of the Cook-maid's dumpling, and then home to their dinner with their dear spouses, and afterwards return to the Tavern to take a flask or two for digestion. They tell me, all the Cake-houses at Islington, Stepney, and the suburbane villages, have hung their signs in mourning: every little kennel of debauchery is quite dismantled by this Proclamation; and the beaux who sit at home on Sundays, and play at piquet and back-gammon, are under dreadful apprehension of a thundering prohibition of stage-playing."

The Grand Jury, impanneled July 7, 1703, renewed their presentment against the Play-houses, Bartholomew-fair, &c. and clearly demonstrated that the elasticity of Vice had recovered from its temporary depression by the weight of Justice. Upon this presentment, *Heraclitus Ridens* made the following observations, which will point out a new scene in the customs of the Londoners:

"*Earnest*. But the Grand Jury tell you, in their presentment, that the toleration of these houses corrupts the City youth, makes them dissolute and immoral, and entices them to take lewd courses.

"*Jest*. I am sorry to hear the Citizens' instructions bear so little weight with them, and am apt to think they are not so exemplary in their lives and conversations as they have been supposed to be. Would their masters keep a strict hand over them, there would be no reasons for complaints; and I dare be persuaded, there is more debauchery *occasioned by pretending to eat Custards* towards Hampstead, Islington, and Sir George Whitmore's[232:A], in a week, than is possible to be brought about by a Playhouse in a twelvemonth."

The reader of this work who has visited St. Paul's or Westminster-abbey within the present Century, will subscribe to the faithful representation of the manners of a certain class of Citizens, that seem to have survived the usual period of life, or have scrupulously transmitted them to their posterity, in a dialogue between Jest and Earnest, 1703[233:A].

"*Jest*. Certainly you have never been at St. Paul's. The flux of people there would cause you to make use of your handkerchief; and the largest Meeting-house in London bears no proportion to it.

"*Earnest*. And what should I do there, where men go out of curiosity and interest, not for the sake of religion? Your shop-keepers assemble there as at full 'Change, and the buyers and sellers are far from being cast out of the Temple. *The body of the Church every Lord's-day contains three times the number of the choir*; and when *the organ* has done playing *an adieu to devotion, the greatest* part of the audience give you their room rather than their company."

If an advertisement frequently published about this time may be credited, Dram-drinking prevailed rather more than a sound moralist would have approved of. Mr. Baker, a bookseller at Mercers Chapel, offered his Nectar and Ambrosia, "prepared from the richest spices, herbs, and flowers, and done with right French Brandy;" and declares that, "when originally invented, it was designed only for ladies' closets, to entertain visitors with, and for gentlemen's private drinking, *being much used that way*;" but, becoming more common, he then offered it in two-penny dram glasses, which were sold, inclosed in gilt frames, by the gallon, quart, or two-shilling bottles.

One of the *customs* of the Police of 1708, was the sending a Constable through the streets at night, with proper assistants, to apprehend offenders of all descriptions, but particularly idle men, who were immediately dispatched to the receptacles of *this species* of recruits for her Majesty's service; but it was a hazardous employment; and one of those peace-officers, named Dent, lost his life in endeavouring to convey a woman to Covent-garden watch-house, by the cuts and stabs of three soldiers, who were all seized, and committed to Newgate. The above Mr. John Dent was buried at St. Clement's Danes, March 24, 1708-9, when a Sermon was pronounced by Thomas Bray, D. D. Minister of St. Botolph, Aldgate, and afterwards published under the title of "The good Fight of Faith, in the cause of God, against the Kingdom of Satan," by desire of the Justices and the Societies for the Reformation of Manners, who were present at the solemnity.

Mrs. Crackenthorpe, the Female Tatler of 1709, justly reprehends the practice of pew-opening for money during Divine service; and thus describes "A set of gentlemen that are called Sermon-tasters: They peep in at 20 different churches in a service, which gives disturbance to those united in devotion; where, instead of attention, they stare about, make some ridiculous observations, and are gone." And the same lady informs us that the fashionable young men were quite as much at a loss how to *kill* time as those of the present day; they played at quoits, nine-pins, threw at cocks, wrestled, and rowed upon the Thames. Nor were ridiculous wagers unknown: they betted upon the Walking Dutchman; and Mrs. C. adds, that "four worthy Senators lately threw their hats into a river, laid a crown each whose hat should swim first to the mill, and ran hallooing after them; and he that won the prize was in a greater rapture than if he had carried the most dangerous point in Parliament."

To this voluble Tatler I am indebted for an illustration of the manners of the *male* shopmen of 1709; and I will consent to be accounted an *ignoramus* if it can be proved that the shopmen of 1809 are not an improved race. "This afternoon some ladies, having an opinion of my fancy in clothes, desired me to accompany them to Ludgate-hill, which I take to be as agreeable an amusement as a lady can pass away three or four hours in. The shops are perfect gilded theatres, the variety of wrought silks so many changes of fine scenes, and the Mercers are the performers in the Opera; and, instead of *vivitur ingenio*, you have in gold capitals, 'No trust by retail.' They are the sweetest, fairest, nicest, dished-out creatures; and, by their elegant address and soft speeches, you would guess them to be Italians. As people glance within their doors, they salute them with—Garden-silks, ladies Italian silks, brocades, tissues, cloth of silver, or cloth of gold, very fine mantua silks, any right Geneva velvet, English velvet, velvet embossed. And to the meaner sort—Fine thread satins both striped and plain, fine mohair silk, satinnets, burdets, Persianets, Norwich crapes, anterines, silks for hoods and scarves, hair camlets, druggets, or sagathies, gentlemen's night-gowns ready made, shallons, durances, and right Scotch plaids.

"We went into a shop which had three partners: two of them were to flourish out their silks; and, after an obliging smile and a pretty mouth made, Cicero like, to expatiate on their goodness; and the other's sole business was to be gentleman usher of the shop, to stand completely dressed at the door, bow to all the coaches that pass by, and hand ladies out and in.

"We saw abundance of gay fancies, fit for Sea-captains' wives, Sheriffs' feasts, and Taunton-dean ladies. This, Madam, is wonderful charming. This, Madam, is so diverting a silk. This, Madam—my stars! how cool it looks! But this, Madam—ye Gods! would I had 10,000 yards of it! Then gathers up a sleeve, and places it to our shoulders. It suits your Ladyship's face wonderfully well. When we had pleased ourselves, and bid him ten shillings a-yard for what he asked fifteen; 'Fan me, ye winds, your Ladyship rallies me! Should I part with it at such a price, the Weavers would rise upon the very shop. Was you at the Park last night, Madam? Your ladyship shall abate me sixpence. Have you read the Tatler to-day?' &c.

"These fellows are positively the greatest fops in the Kingdom; they have their toilets and their fine night-gowns; their *chocolate in the morning*, and their *green tea two hours after*, turkey-polts for their dinner; and their perfumes, washes, and clean linen, equip them for the Parade."

It is not improbable that many of those effeminate drivelers composed part at least of the various Clubs held at different Taverns: the *Beaux* was an attractive title for them; and if they were not *Virtuoso's*, the *Beefsteak* had irresistible charms; besides, they had the choice of many others, such as the Kit-cat, Knights of the Golden-fleece, Florists, Quacks, &c. &c. which were supplied by no less than fifty-five newspapers weekly.

The Fashionables of 1709 dined by candle-light, and visited on Sundays; and their footmen announced them in the same ridiculous manner upon the doors of their friends as at present. A quotation from the Tatler will confirm this assertion: "A very odd fellow visited me to-day at my lodgings, and desired encouragement and recommendation from me for a new invention of knockers to doors, which he told me he had made, and professed to teach rustic servants the use of them. I desired him to shew me an experiment of this invention; upon which he fixed one of his knockers to my parlour-door. He then gave me a complete set of knocks, from the *solitary* rap of the dun and beggar, to the *thunderings* of the saucy footmen of quality, with several flourishes and rattlings never yet performed. He likewise played over some private notes, distinguishing the familiar friend or relation from the most modish visitor, and directing when the reserve candles are to be lighted. He has several other curiosities in this art. He waits only to receive my approbation of the main design. He is now ready to practise to such as shall apply themselves to him; but I have put off his public licence till next Court-day.

"N. B. He teaches *under ground.*"

It appears from the lucubrations of Mr. Bickerstaff, that the idea of obtaining a wife by advertisement was not unknown in 1710; there is a specimen in the Tatler of September 23. It will be remembered that the hint has been pretty well improved upon.

There was a paper published in 1711, called The Growler. True to the assumed character, this modern Diogenes snarled at the vices and follies of the day. One of his subjects was the Mercers, who are thus introduced: "Alas! a handsome young Mercer cannot carry on his business with any reputation without an embroidered coat to stand at the shop-door in, instead of a sign or a footman in a laced livery, to invite in his customers."

The Tatler of May 1, 1711, speaks of the strange infatuation then and at present prevalent, of walking in the Park during the Spring. He says that "No frost, snow, nor East wind, can hinder a large set of people from going to the Park in February; no dust, nor heat in June. And this is come to such an intrepid regularity, that those agreeable creatures that would shriek at an hind-wheel in a deep gutter, are not afraid in their proper sphere of the disorder and danger of seven rings."

Perfumes scented the air, and rendered the paths of fashion delightful and inviting, long before the period at which I date my review. The votaries of this fickle Goddess distributed their money so liberally amongst the inventors and combiners of sweets, that they had become very conspicuous persons by the reign of Queen Anne; as Mr. Charles Lillie will serve to prove, who had the good fortune to be celebrated by Sir Richard Steele in his Tatlers, and by the authors of the original numbers of the Spectator. But, that this gentleman may not monopolize all the fame of his day, I shall proceed to exhibit the flowing periods of another retailer of essences, who points out in which way they were generally used by the belles and beaux of the time.

"Incomparable perfuming drops for handkerchiefs, and all other linen, clothes, gloves, &c. being the most excellent for that purpose in the Universe; for they stain nothing that is perfumed with them any more than fair water; but are the most delectable, fragrant, and odoriferous perfume in nature, good against all diseases of the head and brain. By their delicious smell, they comfort, revive, and refresh all the senses, *natural, vital,* and *animal,* enliven the *spirits,* cheer the heart, and drive away melancholy; they also perfume rooms, beds, presses, drawers, boxes, &c. making them smell surprizingly fine and odoriferous. They perfume the hands excellently, are an extraordinary scent for the pocket, and, in short, are so exceeding pleasant and delightful, so admirably curious and delicate, *and of such general use,* that nothing in the world can compare with them. Sold only at Mr. Payn's Toy-shop, at the Angel and Crown in St. Paul's Church-yard, near Cheapside, at 2*s.* 6*d.* a bottle, with directions."

One of the most inconsiderate and provoking customs prevalent in the lower classes of the community was the peal rattled in the ears of a new-married pair on the morning after their nuptials. The Spectator mentions drums on such occasions; those, though they were continued till within these very few years, are not now used; and I believe the practice is confined to the procession of Butchers' men and boys, who ring their discordant cleavers with leg-bones of oxen in a sort of chime, which may be prevented by a few pence, and is always a *day-light* operation.

Another of the customs of the Londoners is thus accidentally noticed in the British Mercury, October 1712, "who plied there to be hired, like Chimney-sweepers, at Cheapside Conduit."

The Peace of 1713 gave great satisfaction to the Citizens; and the Proclamation of it was honoured with the usual State ceremonies, the responses of shouts and bonfires, and with general illuminations. Although many eccentric methods may have been taken by individuals to express their joy, one only of those has been recorded, which was the thought of the keeper of the Spread Eagle Inn, in Gracechurch-street, who advertized one shilling tickets for a *Peace* Pudding, nine feet in length, twenty inches in breadth, and six inches deep.

The ingenuity of Mr. Winstanley, exhibited at his Winter Theatre by his widow on the same occasion, may be worthy notice. That lady advertised, as a specimen of their skill in Hydraulicks, "six sorts of wine and brandy coming out of the famous barrel, to drink the Queen's health, and Peace. Being enlarged, there will be an addition of claret, pale ale, and stout, playing out of the head of the barrel when it is in the pully, and water at the same time, &c. &c."

"A Coach-maker, of Long-acre, actuated by mistaken zeal, provided the effigies of Dr. Burges, just then deceased, which he placed in an old chariot, with a pipe in the mouth, and two tapers before him. Thus represented, as if in his pulpit, he gave the whole to the mob to burn, which they did in due time, much to his shame."

The tenth number of the Lover, published March 18, 1714, treats on the absurdity of filling the best rooms of the houses of fashionable females with china. The author says, that the venders of articles of this description usually bartered them for rejected clothing, a custom now faintly discernible amongst certain Jews, who exchange with servants glass, earthen-ware, and a little china, for old clothes. Mr. Addison, who wrote the paper, adds, that he remembered when the largest article of china was a coffee-cup; but that it had then swelled to vases as large as a half-hogshead, and that those useless jars were accompanied by a variety of absurd representations, arranged, I suppose, in cupboards and on mantle-pieces, as the reader may have seen in some *old-fashioned* apartments of the present day: indeed, I believe some of the jars may be found in corners yet; but it would perhaps puzzle the owners to designate their use, or to prove in what respect they are even ornamental.

The year 1714 gave rise to the practice of a contrariety of customs. The Queen died, and the Nation outwardly mourned in black habits. Custom was thus complied with in relation to Death. But the joyful entry of George the First required the gayest apparel and the appearance of happiness. Surely the publick must have been puzzled how to express these opposite feelings; to-day all grief and sables, to-morrow all splendour, laces, scarlet, gold, and jewels; and the third, a recurrence to mourning.

As the public entry of this King undoubtedly secured the succession in the Protestant line, I shall be diffuse upon the ceremonies attending it; and those will be best explained by the ensuing original orders, published by the Earl of Suffolk.

"A Ceremonial for the Reception of his most sacred Majesty GEORGE, by the grace of God, King of Great Britain, &c. upon his arrival from Holland to his Kingdom of Great Britain.

"The King being arrived at Greenwich, and the day fixed for his Majesty's Royal Entry; public notice thereof is to be given by the Lord Marshal of the times and places where the Nobility, the Lord Mayor, Aldermen, and Citizens of London, &c. are to meet, in order to attend his Majesty. And some of the Officers of Arms, being appointed by the Lord Marshal, to go to Greenwich early that morning, to rank the coaches of the Great Officers, the Nobility, and others, in order, the juniors first, which are to assemble by ten of the clock in the morning in the Park there, in order to precede the King's coach: And notice being given to the Officers of Arms when his

Majesty is ready to set out: His Majesty, preceded as aforesaid, and attended by his *guard du corps*, is to proceed from thence in his coach towards London, in the following order; *viz.*

Four of the Knight Marshal's Men on Horseback.

Coaches[244:A] of Esquires with six horses each.

Coaches of Knights Bachelors.

Baronets of Ireland, Nova Scotia, and Great Britain.

The King's Solicitor. The King's Attorney.

Younger Sons of Barons of Ireland and Great Britain.

Younger Sons of Viscounts of Ireland and Great Britain.

| Barons of the Exchequer and Justices of both Benches | — | according to their Seniority. |

Lord Chief Justice of the Common-Pleas (may go as a Baron.)

| Master of the Rolls, Lord Chief Justice of the King's-bench, | — | may go as Privy Counsellors. |

Privy Counsellors not Peers.

Eldest Sons of Barons of Ireland and Great Britain.

Younger Sons of Earls of Ireland and Great Britain.

Eldest Sons of Viscounts of Ireland and Great Britain.

The Speaker of the House of Commons.

Barons of Ireland and Great Britain.

Bishops of England.

Younger Sons of Marquisses.

Eldest Sons of Earls of Ireland and Great Britain.

Viscounts of Ireland and Great Britain.

Younger Sons of Dukes of Great Britain.

Eldest Sons of Marquisses of Great Britain.

Earls of Ireland and Great Britain.

Earl Poulet Lord Steward of the King's Household.

Earl of Suffolk and Bindon, as exercising the Office of Earl Marshal of England.

Eldest Sons of Dukes of Great Britain.

Marquisses of Great Britain.

Marquis of Lindsey, Lord Great Chamberlain of England.

Dukes of Ireland and Great Britain.

The Lord Chamberlain (who appears as Treasurer.)

The Great Officers, *viz*.

The Lord Privy Seal.

The Lord President of the Council.

The Lord High Treasurer.

The Lord Archbishop of York.

Lord Chancellor.

Lord Archbishop of Canterbury.

His Royal Highness the Prince, (if not in the Coach with his Majesty.)

The KING's Majesty in his Coach.

The King's Guards of Horse, commanded by the Captains of the Guards.

In this manner his Majesty, preceded by the Nobility and others in their Coaches as aforesaid, is to be attended from the Queen's House in the Park through Greenwich and Deptford to Kent-street end, and from thence to St. Margaret's-hill in Southwark, where the Lord Mayor of London and others wait his arrival.

And upon notice that the Nobility, &c. are arrived near to St. Margaret's-hill in their coaches, the Officers of Arms are to begin to draw out the grand proceeding, in the following order; viz.

A detachment of the Artillery Company
in buff-coats, &c.

The two City Marshals on Horseback, with their
men on foot to make way.

Two of the City Trumpets on horseback.

The Sheriffs' Officers on foot, with javelins in
their hands.

The Lord Mayor's Officers in black gowns, on
foot, two and two.

Two more of the City Trumpets on horseback.

The City Banner borne by the Water-bailiff on horseback, with a servant on foot in a coloured livery.

Then the City Officers on horseback, in their proper gowns, each attended by a servant on foot in coloured liveries.

The four Attorneys, two and two.

The Solicitor, and the Remembrancer.

The two Secondaries.

The Comptroller.

The four Common Pleaders.

The two Judges.

The Town-clerk.

The Common Serjeant, and the Chamberlain.

Two more of the City Trumpets on horseback.

The King's Banner, borne by the Common Hunt on horseback, with a servant on foot in a coloured livery.

The Common Cryer in his gown, and the City Sword-bearer in his black damask gown and gold chain, both on horseback, each having a servant on foot in coloured liveries.

Then those who have fined for Sheriff or Alderman, or served the office of Sheriff or Alderman, in scarlet gowns on horseback, according to their seniorities, two and two, the juniors first, each attended by two servants on foot in coloured liveries.

The two Sheriffs in scarlet gowns on horseback, with their gold chains, and their white staves in their hands, each attended by two servants on foot in coloured liveries.

The Aldermen below the Chair on horseback in scarlet gowns, two and two, each attended by his beadle and two servants on foot in coloured liveries.

Then the Recorder in a scarlet gown on horseback, attended by two servants on foot.

Then the Aldermen above the Chair in scarlet gowns, on horseback, wearing their gold chains, attended by their beadles, and two servants each, in coloured liveries.

Then the coaches of the Nobility, Great Officers, &c. in the order they come from Greenwich.

The Knight Marshal's Men on horseback,
two and two.

The Knight Marshal, or his Deputy, on horseback.

The King's Kettle-drums.

The Drum-major.

The King's Trumpets, two and two.

Serjeants at Arms with their Maces, bare-headed.	The Serjeant Trumpet with his mace. Pursuivants of Arms uncovered, two and two. Heralds of Arms, as before. Kings of Arms, as before.	Serjeants at Arms with their Maces, bare-headed.

The PRINCE in his Coach.

Gentleman Usher of the Black-rod, on his left-hand, uncovered.	The Lord-mayor of London in his Crimson Velvet Gown on horseback, wearing his rich collar and jewel, uncovered, bearing the City-sword by his Majesty's permission, with only four servants on foot, bareheaded, in coloured liveries.	Garter King of Arms, or his Deputy, on the right hand, uncovered.
Yeomen of the guard, Footmen, Equerries.	The KING in his Coach.	Yeomen of the guard, Footmen, Equerries.

His Majesty's Horse-guards as before, to close the proceeding.

Thus the KING is to pass from St. Margaret's-hill (after the Recorder has made his speech, and the Lord Mayor received the City sword from his Majesty) to his Royal-palace of St. James's.

The Trained-bands of Southwark, by order of the Lord-Lieutenant of Surrey, are to line the way from Kent-street end, to the foot of London-bridge.

Three regiments of the City Trained-bands are to make a guard from the Bridge to the Stocks-market.

The several Companies of London, with their Ensigns, are to line the streets on both sides, from the Stocks-market to St. Paul's Church-yard; at the East-end whereof, the Children of Christ's-hospital are to stand, and one of the King's boys makes a speech to his Majesty.

And the other three regiments of the City Trained-bands are to guard the way from St. Paul's Church-yard to Temple-bar. From Temple-bar, the Steward, High-bailiff, and Burgesses of Westminster, in their gowns, attended by all the Constables and Beadles with their respective staves: and the High-bailiff's officers, with their ensigns of office, are to line the way: and next to them the Militia of Westminster make a guard, leaving a space between them and his Majesty's Foot-guards (who line the way from St. James's into the Strand) for the Artillery-company to draw up in.

Against St. Alban's-street in the Pall-mall, the Sheriffs' officers and Lord Mayor's officers are to make a stand on the right-hand.

Those who have served, or fined for Sheriffs or Aldermen of London, are to make their stand between the passages into St. James's-square.

The Sheriffs and Aldermen make their stand towards the upper-end of the Pall-mall, on the right-hand leading to St. James's-gate.

The Nobility, and others who go in their coaches, are to alight at St. James's-gate; and the coaches to pass by St. James's Meuse into St. James's-park, and go out again at the upper gate by Hyde-park.

The Knight-marshal's men, kettle-drums, trumpets, and serjeant-trumpet, are to make a stand on the right-hand side from the end of the Pall-mall, by the Gloucester-tavern.

The Officers of arms and Serjeants at arms are to pass on to the second gateway, and there alight.

The Lord-mayor, with Garter, and the Gentleman-usher of the Black-rod, are to attend his Majesty into St. James's, to the foot of the stairs leading up to the Guard-chamber; where they alight, and the Lord Mayor humbly takes his leave of his Majesty.

During the whole proceeding from St. Margaret's-hill, the Conduits at Stocks-market and other parts of the City are to run with wine as usual. And the great guns at the Tower are to be twice discharged: first, at his Majesty's taking coach at Greenwich; and secondly, after his passing over London-bridge. And at his Majesty's arrival at his Royal Palace, the foot-guards in the Park fire three volleys, and the cannon in the Park are to be discharged."

Such was the eagerness evinced on this occasion, that seats were erected in every situation where it was possible the King could be seen, and the balconies in Cheapside, Cornhill, &c. were let for 20 and 30 guineas each. It must, however, be acknowledged to have been a superb spectacle, to grace which the publick provided prudently and amply. Coaches, carts, &c. were forbid to enter the streets, and those were lined by six regiments of Trained bands; the Conduits ran with wine; the Charity-children, assembled on a vast range of seats, sung Hymns; the Livery Companies exhibited their persons and costume; and a number of aged gentlemen, whose hairs were silvered by time, determined to invite others to join them in white camblet cloaks, and seated on white horses to form part of the procession; but some unforeseen obstacles intervening, they were compelled to substitute a stand at the East-end of St. Paul's, erected over another appointed for a boy from Christ's-hospital to pronounce an oration to the King, where a considerable number appeared to shew their loyalty.—One of the newspapers of the day observes, that the weather was uncommonly fine, and that the cavalcade of the procession and volunteers reached from Greenwich to St. Paul's. Exclusive of the usual evening demonstrations of joy, a fire-work was exhibited in St. Paul's church-yard, representing two flaming dragons on one side, and on the other the Crown accompanied by the motto, "*Floreat Civitas.*" Cockades of ribband, and ribbands decorated with mottos and devices in gold and silver, were very generally worn on this occasion, and at the subsequent Coronation; previous to which, the Envoys of Sicily and Venice had a warm dispute on precedency in the box prepared for the Ambassadors in Westminster-hall; this the Marshal of the Ceremonies adroitly parried, by declaring all precedency ceased *in* the box. Every description of utensils and table-linen were purloined from Westminster-hall, as at the preceding Coronation.

Dreadful accidents occurred during the procession, by the fall of over-loaded scaffolds in Old Palace-yard and the Broad Sanctuary: nineteen persons were killed and wounded, amongst whom was Lady Burton, far advanced in pregnancy; this unhappy lady died in a few minutes. Every recompence was made to the survivors, by the King's orders, that pecuniary assistance could afford.

The King soon after witnessed the Lord Mayor's annual ceremony from Mr. Taylor's balcony in Cheapside. This gentleman was a Quaker and a Linen-draper, to whom the Monarch offered the honour of Knighthood in return for his civility; but the wary Friend declined the tempting bait, which would have procured him the less acceptable ceremony of being read out of Meeting.

The Proprietors of Sion gardens advertised the following singular method of selling deer from their park, in May 1715. They appointed the afternoons of Mondays, Thursdays, and Saturdays, for killing those animals; when the publick were admitted at one shilling each to see the operation, or they might purchase tickets from four to ten shillings, which entitled them, I suppose by way of Lottery, to different parts of the beast, as they say the quantity killed was to be divided into sixteen lots, and the first choice to be governed by the numbers on the tickets; a ten shilling ticket was entitled to a fillet; eight a shoulder; seven a loin, &c. If the full price of the Deer was not received on a given day, the keeper held the money till that sum was obtained. They offered to sell whole deer, and to purchase as many as might be offered.

A singular wedding occurred in November 1715, *secundum usum Tremulorum*, between a rich Quaker Apothecary, and a daughter of Daniel Quare, the celebrated watch-maker in Exchange-alley. The place of entertainment was Skinners-hall, "where 300 persons were present, amongst whom was the Duchess of Marlborough, &c. The Princess of Wales was invited, but did not go."

However unpleasant the yells of Barrow-women are at present, no other mischief arises from them than the obstruction of the ways. It was far otherwise before 1716, when they generally carried Dice with them, and children were enticed to throw for fruit and nuts, or indeed any persons of more advanced age. However, in the year just mentioned, the pernicious consequences of the practice beginning to be felt, the Lord Mayor issued an order to apprehend all retailers so offending, which speedily put an end to street-gaming; though, I am sorry to observe, that some miscreants now carry little wheels marked with numbers, which being turned govern the chance by the figure a hand in the centre points to when stopped.

The first notice of coloured lamps for illuminations that I have met with is in the year 1716, when Dr. Chamberlain displayed 200 on the front of his house in Surrey-street, in honour of the King's birth-day.

The same year produced the annual rowing-match by six young watermen who have just completed their apprenticeship, which was founded by Mr. Doggett, the Comedian, who left a certain sum in trust for the purchase of the prize, an orange-coloured coat with a silver badge, representing the Hanoverian horse, as I take it; but the papers of the day will have it to represent *the wild unbridled horse* Liberty.

The reader will find in the following advertisement a singular method of invitation to a public-house and gardens; and I think he will agree with me, that this custom of our predecessors is better honoured in the breach than in the observance.

"Sion Chapel, at Hampstead, being a private and pleasant place, many persons of the best fashion have been lately married there. Now, as a Minister is obliged constantly to attend, this is to give notice, that all persons, upon bringing a licence, and who shall have their wedding-dinner at the house in the gardens, may be married in the said Chapel without giving any fee or reward; and such as do not keep their wedding at the gardens, only five shillings will be demanded of them for all fees."

A grand aquatic procession occurred in July 1717. The King, accompanied by the Dutchess of Newcastle, Lady Godolphin, Madam Kilmanseck and the Earl of Orkney, went in the evening in an open barge to Chelsea. As they floated up the tide, surrounded by thousands of boats, fifty performers in a City-barge serenaded his Majesty with the strains of Handel, composed expressly for this occasion, with which he was so enraptured that they were thrice repeated. At eleven o'clock the boats had reached Chelsea; there the Monarch landed, and, proceeding to the mansion of Lady Catharine Jones[257:A] he supped, was entertained by a concert, and returned at two in the morning. The Princess of Wales frequently hired the common watermen, and glided about the same part of the river; and once honoured a West-country barge with a visit, partaking with the men their homely fare of salt-pork and bread, and distributing a tenfold equivalent of guineas. This honour was so acceptable to the Master of the vessel, that he immediately gave her a

Royal title, and expended great part of the money in purchasing a splendid cockade as a *distinguishing vane* for his head, vowing to *renew it when decayed*.

Such were the happier moments of Royalty! Thanks to our Constitution, happiness reigns in gradations from the Throne to the Cottage; and while George I. solaced in his Gondola, fanned by the evening breeze, and lulled by the sweet notes of Handel, his peasants were celebrating their Florists' feast at Bethnal-green, with a Carnation named after him, the King of the Year; the Stewards bearing gilded staves, crowned with laurel, and bedecked with flowers, and 90 cultivators in their rear, each bearing his blooming trophy, traversed the fields to the sound of musick, happy in themselves, and rendering the numerous spectators not less so. Why is this pleasing custom neglected and forgotten?

It would have been well if the Society for the Reformation of Manners had attempted the reform of a class of people whose manners were extremely provoking and very disgusting.

I beg leave to introduce a paragraph from the Medley of May 16, which will explain my meaning, and support my assertion, that in this particular the watermen of our day are greatly improved, though still very rough in their actions and conversation.

"On Monday last, being the day King George set out for Hanover, several of his lower domesticks went before; and while they were upon the Thames, a brisk bold lass, that was perfectly well versed in water-language, gave them several plaguy broadsides; certain it is, she made use of several odd, comical, out-of-the-way expressions, at which, though at the same time they were heartily vexed, they could not forbear laughing. The phrases she made use of should be repeated here, but only they were of such a rude nature, that, though they did not fall under the cognizance of the law by water, yet they would be perfectly punishable by land; and I question whether if they would not even be deemed treasonable. The Thames seems to have a charter for rudeness; and the sons of Triton and Neptune have not only a freedom of, but a licence for, any sort of speech. The privilege, by being so antient, is grown incontestible; and scandal there is as it were a law by prescription. Crowned heads in former times did not go scot-free, and yet no punishment ensued; so that Majesty then seemed, by conniving in silence at the abuse, to give the Royal assent to those rough water-laws. Several bitter jests were cast on our good Queen Catharine; and people told her Majesty merrily of the several children King Charles had by his concubines, and made it a matter of ludicrous wonder and surprize, that the constant bedfellow of so mettlesome a Prince should not give the world one token of their mutual love."

Such were the manners of watermen; and, without doubt, their passengers frequently bore a part in the low *amusement of abuse*. Mr. Mist, well known as one of the heroes of the Dunciad, enables me to shew those of some of the landsmen of the same period. He introduces them in very good advice to parents and masters previous to the holidays of May; and observes, that many coaches were in a state of requisition for the conveyance of journeymen, apprentices, and their masters' daughters, to the churches of St. Pancras and Mary-le-bon, for private marriage.

He conjures all sober honest tradesmen who love their wives to walk abroad with them and their children. "And whereas Mr. Mist has been informed, that in holiday times divers persons of distinction and figure *transform themselves into the shapes of journeymen, apprentices*, and other mechanical habits, to trepan young wenches out of their modesty; he therefore requires of all viceroys and governors of families to give the strictest orders for their female children and servants to repair to their respective habitations before candle-light.

"All journeymen Drapers, Mercers, Lawyers-clerks, *and other ten or twelve-shilling workmen*, are strictly forbid to cause riots and routs in the streets *concerning precedency*, as they return from their carouses in the night-time.

"N. B. Bullies and Gamesters, who have an indisputable right to make disturbances every night in the year, are not meant in this article.

"Journeymen Shoemakers are desired to take notice, that by an antient statute, yet unrepealed, any of their function going sober to bed on the night of Whitsun-Monday forfeits 5*s.*; upon non-payment to be levied by distress, one moiety to the informer, and the other to the poor alehouse-keepers of the Parish where the fact was committed."

The horrid custom of Duelling never was at a greater height than at the above date. The newspapers from 1700 to 1719 appear to have preserved their progression faithfully; every gaming-table, despicable brothel, tavern, coffee-house, masquerade, the theatres, and even festive meetings, produced its duellist; and the universal fashion of wearing swords allowed no time for passion to subside, or reason to reflect; a walk into the street or into an adjoining room, enabled the parties to wound each other in an instant; revenge and pain maddened them; and death frequently ensued to both. Government at length interfered; but duelling has again recovered from *temporary* interruption!—Doctors Mead and Woodward fought like a pair of butchers, in June 1719, at the very gates of Gresham-college; and every drunken rake who staggered through the streets had it in his power to plunge a sword into an unoffending breast, or to *wound* where he now *dare* not *strike*. Dead bodies were frequently found; and the thief and the duellist seemed emulous which should furnish the Diaries of the time with the greater number of victims. Robberies, attended with monstrous cruelty, were dreadfully frequent; and such was the general profligacy of the age, that the paragraph-writers endeavoured to convey horrid facts with a levity of expression suited to the coarseness of their style, which was truly vulgar throughout all the newspapers. Let one instance speak for me: "People sicken and die at an uncommon rate in and about this city and suburbs; and there is a sad outcry raised (especially by antient females) of a plague, pestilence, and what not, which has occasioned abundance of people to leave the town, and fly to the *countries* for refuge, whilst horse and foot physicians, mountebanks, *dead-mongers*, parish-clerks, and other lesser *ministers of dust and ashes*, are continually in motion in one part or other to perform their several offices; and we hear that in some parishes the sexton or grave-digger can afford to employ two or three journeymen."

Original Weekly Journal, May 22, 1719.

It must, however, be allowed that frequent attempts were made to resist the progress of vice, and many of the Justices concurred in warning the people of the illegality of their conduct; ten of them, at a special Session held for the division of the Tower, in pursuance of an order made at the General Quarter Sessions for Middlesex, on the 19th of January 1719, for putting in execution the Statute of 33 Henry VIII. Cap. 9, directed authentic copies of the order to be given to all victuallers, &c. whom it concerned, and also to be affixed in all public places within that Division; "That none shall keep or maintain any house or place of unlawful games, on pain of 40*s.* for every day, of forfeiting their recognizance, and of being suppressed; that none shall use or haunt such places on pain of 6*s.* 8*d.* for every offence; and that no artificer, or his journeyman, husbandman, apprentice, labourer, servant at husbandry, mariner, fisherman, waterman, or serving-man, shall play at tables, tennis, dice, cards, bowls, clash, coiting, loggating, or any other unlawful game, out of Christmas, or then out of their master's house or presence, on pain of 20*s.*"

But, though it was sometimes possible to prevent the depravity of the lower order of people, there were others, that moved in the sphere of gentlemen, who set the worst of examples to their inferiors. Such were those that had assembled on the evening of a Court drawing-room at the Royal Chocolate-house in St. James's-street; where disputes at hazard produced a quarrel, which became general throughout the room; and, as they fought with their swords, three gentlemen were mortally wounded; and the affray was at length ended by the interposition of the Royal-guards, who were compelled to knock the parties down with the butt-ends of their muskets indiscriminately, as intreaties and commands were of no avail. A footman of Colonel Cunningham's, greatly attached to his master, rushed through the swords, seized, and literally carried him out by force without injury.

This horrid rencontre was the effect of sudden passion, roused by disappointment and avarice; there was nothing of depravity prepense, except the act of gaming. Weak as this palliative may be, the members of two other clubs had them not to plead for their infamous profligacy. The wretches who associated under the titles of the "*Bold Bucks*" and the "*Hell-fires*," are described in a paper of February 20, 1720, as deliberate abandoned villains. "The principles of the first are to come up to the flaming lust of their worthy patrons, from whom they take their denomination, by their examples; they attempt all females of their own species promiscuously—grandmothers and mothers, as well as daughters; even their own sisters fear their violence, and fly their privacies. Blind and bold Love is their motto, and their soul's faculties strictly terminated in a participation of entertainment and judgment with brutes."

"The Hell-fires, you may guess by the appellation, aim at a more transcendant malignity; deriding the forms of Religion as a trifle with them, by a natural progression from the form they turn to the substance; with Lucifer they fly at Divinity. The third person of the Trinity is what they peculiarly attack; by the following specimen you may judge of their good will: *i. e.* their calling for a Holy Ghost-pye at the Tavern, in which, by the bye, you may still observe the propriety and justice of God's judgment on them, that blasts the advantages of their education, so as to make this shocking stupidity to be the poignancy of their wit, and the life they lead, the sublimity of their genius. Such is their disposition; the next things to be remarked are their education and usual place of conference. Their education then, after the care of tender parents, and their initiation into the liberal arts, is proposed to be finished in an academy; (do not mistake me) not a scholastic schismatical one, but a riding one; where obsceneness, curses, blasphemy, exclamations, with revolving regularity, meet each curvet of the more rational animal. Their usual place of conference in full council, is a diminutive Tavern not very far from thence; where the master and cook may perhaps in time hear something from a Magistrate for striking in with the rakes' blasphemous jests, and supplying them with cards and dice on Sundays."

As a further illustration of the manners of the times, the following paragraph is of importance: "On Wednesday night last, about twelve, there was such a great riot in Windmill-street, near the Haymarket, that near 100 gentlemen and others were all engaged at one time, some with swords, and others with sticks and canes, wherein abundance were dangerously wounded; the watchmen that came to put an end to the affray were knocked down and barbarously used; at last the patrole of Horse-guards came, and finding them obdurate, rode through them cutting all the way with their swords; yet we hear of none that were killed upon the spot, though many, it is thought, cannot recover of their wounds. When they saw their own time, they gave over; and, upon summing up the matter, the quarrel began at first by two chairmen only[266:A]."

On the evening of May 28, Captain Fitzgerald and three young men his companions met a lady in the Strand, returning from St. James's, conveyed in a sedan-chair. They immediately endeavoured to force her out, but were opposed by the chairmen, upon which they drew their swords, and proceeded to demolish the vehicle. The noise brought a watchman to the spot, who instantly received a deadly wound through the back, and as instantly expired. This mighty son of Mars was secured; but the others fled from their foul deed, like true cowards.

It may be supposed that this laxity of manners influenced all ranks, when inroads upon the paths of decorum prevailed even in the Church. In order that this fact may not rest upon my mere assertion, I shall quote the concluding lines of a letter to the Author of the London Journal, dated December 21, 1720, and signed "A. A. a lover of decency and order." He speaks of an impropriety, *now* become quite common, in the Stewards of the Sons of the Clergy permitting persons from the Theatres to perform in their annual celebration at St. Paul's; and then proceeds: "There are other things truly blameable to be observed, when the *Te Deum* or Anthem hath been performing, yes, when the parson hath been preaching, (viz.) *persons eating, drinking wine*, laughing and talking; a conduct much more becoming those who attend the performances of Drury-lane or the Haymarket, than the Temple of the Lord.

"What is here taken notice of, as it is fact, so it is abominable, and ought to be exposed; the doing of which may tend to reform such irregularities for the future, and keep those disorders from the House of God, which cannot admit of a justification unless by those who may think the same liberties may be taken in places set apart for devotion, as are in the Synagogue of Satan."

The progress of the shocking Clubs already noticed became so alarming, that the King found it necessary to issue his proclamation for their suppression, in April 1721, which establishes their existence beyond all dispute.

"At the Court of St. James's, the 28th day of April 1721.

Present, the King's most excellent Majesty in Council.

"His Majesty having received information which gives great reason to suspect that there have been lately, and still are, in and about the Cities of London and Westminster, certain scandalous Clubs or Societies of young persons, who meet together, and in the most impious and blasphemous manner insult the most sacred principles of our Holy Religion, affront Almighty God himself, and corrupt the minds and morals of one another; and being resolved to make use of all the authority committed to him by

Almighty God to punish such enormous offenders, and to crush such shocking impieties, before they increase, and draw down the vengeance of God upon this nation: His Majesty has thought fit to command the Lord Chancellor, and his Lordship is hereby required, to call together his Majesty's Justices of the Peace of Middlesex and Westminster, and strictly to enjoin them in the most effectual manner, that they and every of them do make the most diligent and careful inquiry and search for the discovery of any thing of this and the like sort, tending in any wise to the corruption of the principles and manners of men, and to lay before his Lordship such discoveries as from time to time may be made, to the end that all proper methods may be taken for the utter suppression of all such detestable practices. His Lordship is further directed to urge them to the due execution of their office, in detecting and prosecuting with vigour all profaneness, immorality, and debauchery, as they value the blessing of Almighty God, as they regard the happiness of their country, which cannot subsist if things sacred and virtuous are trampled upon; and, as they tender his Majesty's favour, to which they cannot recommend themselves more effectually than by shewing the utmost zeal upon so important an occasion; to which end his Lordship is to acquaint them, that as his Majesty, for himself, has nothing more at heart than to regard the honour of God so impiously struck at, and is determined to shew all marks of displeasure and discouragement to any who may lie even under the suspicion of such practices; so he shall always account it the greatest and substantial service they can do to his Majesty or his government, to exert themselves in discovering any who are guilty of such impieties, that they may be openly prosecuted and punished with the utmost severity and most public ignominy which the laws of the land can inflict.

"EDWARD SOUTHWELL."

"His Majesty has been pleased to give orders to the principal officers of his Household, to make strict and diligent enquiry whether any of his Majesty's servants are guilty of the horrid impieties mentioned in the Order of Council inserted above, and to make their report to his Majesty."

The dreadful consequences of this attempt to set aside all virtue and all religion were conspicuously observable, even at the moment, in the sudden deaths of four members of these dreadful clubs; not that I mean to insinuate the Almighty interfered by miracles to shew his displeasure; on the contrary, the event was produced by natural causes inherent in each diabolical act. The hurry of the spirits, occasioned by ardent liquors and the terrors of conscience, were sufficient; Nature shrunk from the contest; and he that drank a toast too shocking to repeat fainted under the recollection; and she that had assumed the character of the Mother of Christ fell a victim to the keen horrors of remembrance in her lucid moments of repentance. It was said, that one of the clubs met at Somerset-house, where they celebrated their infamous orgies to the sound of musick during the hours of Divine service, which will account for the concluding paragraph of the Proclamation. The number of Justices who attended the Lord Chancellor's summons exceeded 100; they received his most strenuous recommendation to exert themselves in the execution of the order, but I find no recorded effects of its operation.

The mob carried the same brutality more brutalised to the feet of the gallows; and even while the miserable wretches, who afforded them a spectacle, were supplicating that forgiveness which the laws of morality denied on earth, they were interrupted by shouts and execrations, and injured by stones, dirt, and filth, thrown with violence in every direction. At an execution, June 1721, several persons had their limbs broken, others their eyes almost beaten out; and Barbara Spencer, carried to Tyburn to be strangled and burnt, was beaten down by a stone when beseeching on her knees the mercy of Heaven. These wretches frequently robbed the Surgeons.

The wretched manner in which the lowest description of people lodged in 1721, may be gathered from the ensuing extract from an order of the Court at a General Quarter Session, October 4. "It is now become a common practice in the extreme parts of the town, to receive into their houses persons unknown, without distinction of age or sex, on their paying one penny or more *per night* for lying in such houses without beds or covering; and that it is frequent in those houses for 15 or 20, or more, to lie in a small room."

These miserable people, thus indiscriminately mixed, corrupted each other, and licentiousness reigned triumphant amongst them; in truth, the population of London always exceeded the means of subsistence; and I believe there are now, upon an average, three families to each house, and thousands of homeless wanderers. Fleet marriages were common in 1723; and the wonderful omissions of government at that period, in permitting so sacred an office to be celebrated, and registers of marriages kept at ale-houses and brandy-shops within the rules, where 32 couples are known to have been joined in three days, was one cause of the overgrown community. An author of the time alluded to says: "It is pleasant to see certain fellows plying by Fleet-bridge to take poor Sailors, &c. into the noose of matrimony every day throughout the week, and the clocks at their offices for that purpose *still standing at the canonical hour*, though perhaps the time of the day be six or seven in the afternoon."

Macky gives a good sketch of the manner of living in 1724. The following is extracted from his Journey through England, vol. I. p. 190.

"I am lodged in the street called Pall-mall, the ordinary residence of all strangers, because of its vicinity to the King's Palace, the Park, the Parliament house, the Theatres, and the Chocolate and Coffee-houses, where the best company frequent. If you would know our manner of living, it is thus: we rise by nine, and those that frequent great men's levees find entertainment at them till eleven, or, as in Holland, go to tea-tables. About twelve the *beau-monde* assembles in several chocolate and coffee-houses; the best of which are the Cocoa-tree and White's chocolate-houses, St. James's, the Smyrna, and the British coffee-houses; and all these so near one another, that in less than an hour you see the company of them all. We are carried to these places in chairs (or sedans) which are here very cheap, a guinea a-week, or a shilling *per* hour, and your chairmen serve you for porters to run on errands as your gondoliers (watermen) do at Venice.

"If it be fine weather, we take a turn in the Park till two, when we go to dinner; and if it be dirty, you are entertained at Picket or Basset at White's, or you may talk politics at the Smyrna and St. James's. I must not forget to tell you, that the parties have their different places, where, however, a stranger is always well received; but a Whig will no more go to the Cocoa-tree or Ozinda's, than a Tory will be seen at the coffee-house of St. James's.

"The Scots go generally to the British, and a mixture of all sorts to the Smyrna. There are other little coffee-houses much frequented in this neighbourhood, Young-man's for officers, Old-man's for stock-jobbers, pay-masters, and courtiers, and Little-man's for sharpers. I never was so confounded in my life, as when I entered into this last: I saw two or three tables full at Faro, heard the box and dice rattling in the room above-stairs, and was surrounded by a set of sharp-faces, that I was afraid would have devoured me with their eyes. I was glad to drop two or three half-crowns at Faro, to get off with a clear skin, and was overjoyed I was so got rid of them.

"At two we generally go to dinner: ordinaries are not so common here as abroad; yet the French have set up two or three pretty good ones, for the conveniency of foreigners, in Suffolk-street, where one is tolerably well served; but the general way here is to make a party at the coffee-house to go dine at the tavern, where we sit till six, then we go to the play; except you are invited to the table of some great man, which strangers are always courted to, and nobly entertained.

"I know abundance of French, that by keeping a pocket-list of tables, live so almost all the year round, and yet never appear at the same place above once in a fortnight. By looking into their pocket-book in the morning, they fix their place of dining, as on Monday with my Lord ———, and so for two weeks, fourteen Lords, Foreign Ministers, or men of quality; and so they run their round all the year long, without notice being taken of them.

"There are three very noble Theatres here: that for Opera's at the end of the Pall-mall, or Hay-market, is the finest I ever saw, and where we are entertained in Italian music generally twice a-week: that for History, Tragedy, and Comedy, is in Covent-garden (a Piazza I shall describe to you in the sequel of this letter), and the third for the same, is by Lincoln's-Inn-Fields, at a small distance from the other.

"The Theatres here differ from those abroad; in that those at Venice, Paris, Brussels, Genoa, and other parts, you know, are composed of rows of small shut-boxes, three or four stories in a semi-circle, with a Parterre below; whereas here the Parterre, commonly called the Pit, contains the gentlemen on benches; and on the first story of boxes sit all the ladies of quality; in the second, the Citizens wives and daughters; and in the third, the common people and footmen: so that between the Acts you are as much diverted by viewing the beauties of the audience, as, while they act, with the subject of the Play; and the whole is illuminated to the greatest advantage. Whereas abroad, the stage being only illuminated, and the lodge or boxes close, you lose the pleasure of seeing the company; and indeed the English have reason in this, for no nation in the world can shew such an assembly of shining beauties as here.

"The English affect more the Italian than the French music; and their own compositions are between the gravity of the first, and the levity of the other. They have had several great masters of their own: Henry Purcel's works in that kind are esteemed beyond Lully's every where; and they have now a good many very eminent masters: but the taste of the town being at this day all Italian, it is a great discouragement to them.

"No nation represents History so naturally, so much to the life, and so close to truth, as the English; they have most of the occurrences of their own History, and all those of the Roman Empire, nobly acted. One Shakespear, who lived in the last century, laid down a masterly foundation for this in his excellent plays; and the late Mr. Addison hath improved that taste by his admirable Cato, which hath been translated into several languages, particularly into Italian blank verse, and is frequently acted in Italy.

"Their comedies are designed to lash the growing follies in every age; and scarce a fool or a coxcomb appears in town, but his folly is represented. And most of their comedians, in imitation of Moliere, have taken that province; in which Mr. Cibber, an extreme good player, hath succeeded very well.

"They seldom degenerate into farce, as the Italians; nor do they confine their tragedies to rhyme and whining, as the French. In short, if you would see the greatest actions of past ages performed over again, and the present follies of mankind exposed, you must come here.

"After the Play, the best company generally go to Tom's and Will's coffee-houses, near adjoining, where there is playing at Picket, and the best of conversation till midnight. Here you will see blue and green ribbons and stars sitting familiarly with private gentlemen, and talking with the same freedom, as if they had left their quality and degrees of distance at home; and a stranger tastes with pleasure the universal liberty of speech of the English nation. Or, if you like rather the company of ladies, there are assemblies at most people of quality's houses. And in all the Coffee-houses you have not only the foreign prints, but several English ones with the Foreign Occurrences, besides papers of morality and party-disputes.

"My Bills of Exchange oblige me now and then to take a turn to the Royal-Exchange, in a hackney-coach, to meet my merchant. These coaches are very necessary conveniencies not to be met with any where abroad; for you know that at Paris, Brussels, Rome or Vienna, you must either hire a coach by the day, or take it at least by the hour: but here you have coaches at the corner of every street, which for a shilling will carry you any where within a reasonable distance; and for two, from one end of the City to the other. There are eight hundred of them licensed by Act of Parliament, and carry their number on their coaches; so that if you should chance to leave any thing in a coach, and know but the number of it, you know presently where to lay your claim to it; and be you ever so late at a friend's house in any place of this great City, your friend, by taking the number of the coach, secures your safety home.

"The Royal-Exchange is the resort of all the trading part of this City, foreign and domestic, from half an hour after one, till near three in the afternoon; but the better sort generally meet in Exchange-alley a little before, at three celebrated Coffee-houses, called Garraway's, Robin's, and Jonathan's. In the first, the people of quality who have business in the City, and the most considerable and wealthy Citizens, frequent. In the second, the Foreign Banquiers, and often even Foreign Ministers. And in the third, the buyers and sellers of Stock.

"When I entered into this last, I was afraid I had got into Little-man's Coffee-house again; for busy faces run about here as there, with the same sharp intent looks, with the difference only, that here it is selling of Bank-stock, East-India, South-Sea, and Lottery Tickets, and there it is all cards and dice.

"You will see a fellow in shabby clothes selling ten or twelve thousand pounds in stock, though perhaps he may not be worth at the same time ten shillings, and with as much zeal as if he were a Director, which they call selling a Bear-skin; and these men find bubbles enough to get bread by it, as the others do by gaming; and some few of them manage it so, as to get pretty large estates.

"Near this Exchange are two very good French eating-houses, the one at the sign of Pontack, a President of the Parliament of Bourdeaux, from whose name the best French clarets are called so, and where you may bespeak a dinner from four or five shillings a-head to a guinea, or what sum you please;

the other is Caveack's, where there is a constant ordinary, as abroad, for all comers without distinction, and at a very reasonable price.

"I am told, that while wagers were allowed to be made on taking of towns, and gaining of battles, during the last war, this Exchange-alley was the sharpest place in the World; but the abuse of intelligence, sham letters spread upon the Exchange, and private letters coming before the Mails, made that practice so notorious, that the Queen and Parliament wisely thought fit to put a stop to it by a seasonable provisional Act against it, as they have endeavoured to do by another Act against excessive gaming, being both equally looked on as a cheat and imposition upon the well-meaning subject. However, some great men have not disdained to be deeply concerned in both, and have got good estates: for tricking is not here reckoned so despicable a quality as abroad, when it is cleanly done; therefore, my friend, when you come here, play not in England, nor venture to lay wagers, except you know your company very well, or are sure of your fact. The fatal South-Sea scheme, and the wicked execution of it, proves what I foretold you to be too true."

The pernicious and general custom of wearing masks enabled half-repentant sinners to mix with the most profligate of the female sex undiscovered, and to indulge in excesses which they would not have dared to commit had their features been exposed as at present. This practice afforded opportunities of gratifying very improper curiosity, and of visiting places at unseasonable hours; an instance of this description occurred in May 1724. The White-lion[280:A], in Wych-street, had long been famed for riotous assemblies under the pretence of Concerts; and the neighbouring moralists waited with impatience for the hour when they should effectually transgress the Law: that hour at length arrived, and a posse of Constables, executing a warrant obtained for the purpose, discovered females even of some distinction, tradesmen's wives, their daughters, and many common prostitutes, a collection that really surprised each other; the vicious hardly crediting that they were in so much good company, and the noviciates frightened at the features of unmasked depravity. The latter received wholesome admonition, and were sent home; the former visited Bridewell.

The custom of walking and talking in the Nave of St. Paul's cathedral had become so very prevalent in 1725, that the Bishop of London found it necessary, at his visitation in that year, to declare his positive intention of enforcing the 18th Canon, and the Act of the First of William and Mary, by which transgressors forfeited 20*l*. for every offence.

A subscription was opened in 1727 for the relief of Mrs. Clark, the aged and only surviving daughter of Milton. An author, under the signature of Bruyere, in the London Journal, ardently recommended liberal contributions; and drew the following picture of the manners then prevailing. "At White's we see nothing but what wears the mask at least of gaiety and pleasure; powder and embroidery are the ornaments of the place, not to forget that *intolerable stink* of perfumes, which almost poisons the miserable chairmen that besiege the door. Conversation is not known here; the enquiries after news turn chiefly upon what happened last night at the Groom Porters. The business of the place is to promote some musical subscription; to make all possible court to some young man of quality that is next expected to take possession of a great estate; to take care to be very well with a knot of well-dressed people that meet here, and modestly call themselves *the world*; but, above all, to solicit a share in the direction of the moneyed interest, which is established here under the name of a Faro Bank.

"At Tom's Coffee-house, in Cornhill, there is a very different face of things. Plenty, the parent of Cheerfulness, seems to have fixed her residence on this spot; while Joy, which is the offspring of Folly, seems to be utterly unknown. Industry, the first principle of a Citizen, is an infallible specifick to keep the spirits awake, and prevent that stagnation and corruption of humours which make our fine gentlemen such horrible torments to one another and to themselves. Decency in dress is finery enough in a place where they are taught from their childhood to expect no honours from what they seem to be, but from what they really are. The conversation turns principally on the interests of Europe, in which they themselves are chiefly concerned; and the business here is to enlarge the commerce of their country, by which the publick is to gain much more than the merchant himself. For the rest I need not add, that there is a vein of strong sense and useful knowledge runs through their whole discourse, which makes them to wise men very desirable companions. If I should say that in this house I have met with Merchants of as liberal education and generous principles, of as exquisite taste in classical knowledge and polite learning, as are to be found at Court or in the College, I should be confident of every reader's credit when he knows that in this place was first projected the subscription for the relief of the sightless old age of Milton's daughter."

The Monarchs of this happy Island have frequently honoured the Citizens of London with their presence at Guildhall, when the Lord Mayor enters upon his office. On the 29th of October 1727, and in the Mayoralty of Sir Edward Becher, Knight, and afterwards Baronet, George II. his Queen, the Princess Royal, and the Princess Carolina, proceeded to Cheapside at three o'clock in the afternoon, attended by a great number of the Nobility and others, through a double line of the London Militia. A balcony near Bow-church had been prepared for their reception, whence they viewed the procession, and the houses decorated with carpet, and tapestry to do them honour. After the City-officers were disposed in due order for the reception of the King in Guildhall, the Sheriffs waited on him, and conducted him there; the Lord Mayor, kneeling at the entrance, presented the Sword of State to his Majesty, who returned it, and followed the Mayor to the Council Chamber, where Sir William Thompson (as Recorder) thus addressed the King:

"May it please your Majesty,

"The Lord Mayor, Aldermen, and Commons of this City, beg leave to offer their most humble acknowledgments for this great honour to the City, by the presence of your Majesty, your Royal Consort, the Princess Royal, and her Royal Highness. Their joy is inexpressible, to behold their Sovereign condescending to accept their good-will and affections, and in the most engaging manner vouchsafing here to receive their homage and duty.

"This day will be ever remembered by them with the highest satisfaction: this happy day, which gave birth to their most gracious King, who is pleased thus to honour them, and who protects them in the enjoyment of all their rights and privileges: a Prince who takes pleasure in promoting their happiness, and who thinks it gives the truest lustre to his Crown, to preserve the religion, the laws, and liberties of his people. Fortunate is their present condition, and delightful is their prospect while they have in view your Majesty, their most gracious and justly admired Queen, and the illustrious branches of your Royal Family. Permit, Sire, these your Majesty's most faithful subjects to take this opportunity of assuring your Majesty of their unalterable attachment to your Royal Person, and of their warmest zeal for the support of your government.

"The best, the only security of our excellent Constitution in Church and State, and of every thing which is dear and valuable to Englishmen, Gratitude and Interest, make these the unanimous sentiments of this your Majesty's most loyal and most dutiful City of London."

Their Majesties (preceded by the Lord Mayor bearing the Sword) went to the Hustings, where they dined in company with the Princesses and the Ladies of the Bed-chamber. The entertainment was of the most sumptuous description, and served at different tables, prepared for the Lord Mayor, Aldermen, and Common Council, the foreign Ministers, the Nobility, Privy Counsellors, the Judges, ladies, &c. &c. After silence had been commanded, the Common Cryer announced that the King drank to the health of the Lord Mayor, and prosperity to the City of London and the trade thereof, and, that her Majesty drank, confirming the same. He then proclaimed that the Lord Mayor, Aldermen, and Common Council drank health, long life, and a prosperous happy reign to our Sovereign Lord King George; and that they drank to the health, long life, and happiness of our most gracious Queen Caroline, and all the Royal family.

When the dinner was concluded, their Majesties returned to the Council Chamber, where they were seated till 11 o'clock during a ball in the area below. The City was illuminated on this occasion.

An author of this period, treating on the number of poor, and their manner of living, very justly observes: "If any person is born with any defect or deformity, or maimed by fire or any other casualty, or any inveterate distemper which renders them miserable objects, their way is open to London; where they have free liberty of shewing their nauseous sights, to terrify people, and force them to give money to get rid of them; and those vagrants have for many years past been moved out of several parts of the three Kingdoms, and taken their stations in this Metropolis, to the interruption of conversation and business.

"The Quaker workhouse is an example for each parish: the poor orphans among them, as well as the children of such poor as are unable to subsist them, are put to their workhouse, where they are taught to read and write certain hours of the day, and at other times are put to spin, or other employments. And as the Nation has found great advantage by those workhouses, which have been established by Act of Parliament, it is a great pity that so profitable an Institution was not made general through the Nation, that so there might be no pretence for any beggar to appear abroad. Their example is very pernicious, for what they get by begging is consumed commonly in Ale-houses, Gin-shops, &c.; and one drunken beggar is an inducement to a great many to follow the same trade.

"But, as to those creatures that go about the streets to shew their maimed limbs, nauseous sores, stump hands or feet, or any other deformity; they are by no means objects fit to go abroad; and considering the frights and pernicious impressions which such horrid sights have given to pregnant women, should move all tender husbands to desire the redress of this enormity."

I have frequently observed, in the course of my researches, the strange methods and customs peculiar to gaming, horse-racing, dice, and wagers; the latter are generally governed by whim and extreme folly. We have already noticed Noblemen running their coaches and footmen. In 1729, a Poulterer of Leadenhall-market betted 50*l*. he would walk 202 times round the area of Upper Moorfields in 27 hours, and accordingly proceeded at the rate of five miles an hour on the *amusing pursuit*, to the infinite improvement of his business, and great edification of hundreds of spectators.—Wagers are now a favourite custom with too many of the Londoners; they very frequently, however, originate over the bottle or the porter-pot.

A curious exhibition distinguished the anniversary of the Queen's birth-day, March 3, 1730; 100 wool-combers assembled in their shirts, with various coloured woollen caps on their heads, in Bishopsgate-street, from whence they went in procession to St. James's Palace, preceded by the Steward of their company and a person on horseback, representing Bishop Blaze, in wigs of wool neatly curled; the Bishop carried a wool-comb in one hand, and a Prayer-book in the other. They arranged themselves in the Park facing the Palace; and their leader addressed the King and Queen, who appeared at a window, thanking his Majesty for the encouragement they had received, and intreating his future protection.

A writer in Read's Weekly Journal of January 9, 1731, has obliged us with a concise and pleasing description of Christmas customs prevalent at that period, which I shall transcribe for the reader's information.

"My house, Sir, is directly opposite to a great Church; and it was with great pleasure I observed from my window, last Christmas-day, the numerous poor that waited at the doors very liberally relieved; but my joy was soon over, for no sooner were the charitable congregation dispersed, but these wretches, who before appeared the very pictures of misery, forgot their cant, and fell to quarrelling about the dividend; oaths and curses flew about amongst them, very plentifully, and passion grew so high that they fell hard upon one another's faults. In short, Sir, I learned from their own mouths that they were all impostors, both men and women; and that amongst their whole number, which was very large, there was not one object of charity. When they had tired themselves with scolding, they very lovingly adjourned to a neighbouring brandy-shop, from whence they returned in a condition neither fit for me to describe nor you to hear.

"The next day I met with another wonder; for, by that time I was up, my servants could do nothing but run to the door. Enquiring the meaning, I was answered, the people were come for their Christmas-box; this was logick to me; but I found at last, that, because I had laid out a great deal of ready-money with my brewer, baker, and other tradesmen, they kindly thought it my duty to present their servants with some money for the favour of having their goods. This provoked me a little; but, being told it was the custom, I complied. These were followed by the watch, beadles, dust-men, and an innumerable tribe; but what vexed me the most was the Clerk, who has an extraordinary place, and makes as good an appearance as most tradesmen in the parish; to see him come a-boxing, *alias begging*, I thought was intolerable; however, I found it was the custom too, so I gave him half-a-crown; as I was likewise obliged to do to the bell-man, for breaking my rest for many nights together.

"Having talked this matter over with a friend, he promised to carry me where I might see the good effects of this giving box-money. In the evening away we went to a neighbouring ale-house, where abundance of these gentry were assembled round a stately piece of roast-beef and as large a plumb-pudding. When the drink and brandy began to work, they fell to reckoning of their several gains that day; one was cursed for a stingy dog for giving but sixpence; another called an extravagant fool for giving half-a-crown, which perhaps he might want before the year was out; so I found these good people were never to be pleased. Some of them were got to cards by themselves, which soon produced a quarrel and broken heads. In the interim came in some of their wives, who roundly cursed the people for having given them money, adding, that instead of doing good it ruined their families, and set them in a road of drinking and gaming, which never ceased till not only their gifts, but their wages, were gone. One good woman said, if people had a mind to give charity, they should send it home to their families; I was very much of her opinion; but, being tired with the noise, we left them to agree as they could.

"My friend next carried me to the upper-end of Piccadilly, where, one pair of stairs over a stable, we found near an hundred people of both sexes, some masked, others not, a great part of which were dancing to the musick of two sorry fiddles. It is impossible to describe this medley of mortals fully; however, I will do it as well as I can. There were footmen, servant-maids, butchers, apprentices, oyster and orange-women, common w——s, and sharpers, which appeared to be the best of the company. This horrid place seemed to me the very sink of hell, where, however virtuous young people may be before, they will not come often thither before they learn to be both w——s and thieves. It is a notable nursery for the gallows. My friend informed me, it was called a three-penny hop; and while we were talking, to my great satisfaction, by order of the Westminster Justices, to their immortal honour, entered the constables and their assistants, who carried off all the company that was left; and, had not my friend been known to them, we might have paid dear for our curiosity.

"I believe I have almost tired you as well as myself with an account of the lower sort of diversions. I come next to expatiate on the entertainment and good cheer I met with in the City, whither my friend carried me to dinner these holidays. It was at the house of an eminent and worthy merchant; and though, Sir, I have been accustomed in my own county to what may very well be called good house-keeping, yet, I assure you, I should have taken this dinner to have been provided for a whole parish, rather than for about a dozen gentlemen. It is impossible for me to give you half our bill of fare; so you must be content to know that we had turkeys, geese, capons, puddings of a dozen sorts, more than I had ever seen in my life, besides brawn, roast-beef, and many things of which I know not the names; mince-pies in abundance, and a thing they call plumb-pottage, which may be good for aught I know, though it seems to me to have 50 different tastes. Our wines were of the best, as were all the rest of our liquors; in short, the God of Plenty seemed to reign here. And, to make every thing perfect, our company was polite, and every way agreeable; nothing but mirth and loyal healths went round.

"I allowed myself now but one day more to finish my ramble and my curiosity; and that was last Wednesday, being Twelfth-day. The preparations which were made for the keeping this day, which is reckoned the conclusion of the holidays, were reported to me to be so great, and the cheerfulness and good humour with which most persons spoke of its approach appeared so remarkable, that my expectation was not a little impatient for the sight of this last scene of the Jubilee. And as I had the honour of having been several times invited by a person of quality, with whom I had transacted some affairs since my being in town, to take the freedom of his table; I determined with myself that I could not choose a more agreeable time for the acceptance of his courtesy than this. Accordingly, I dressed myself in a manner as suitable as I could to the place where I proposed to make my visit, and took coach for the Court end of the town; in my passage to which, from the extreme part of the City, I was highly entertained with almost one continued subject of wonder and amusement. All the trades in town seemed to be suspended for a while, and to yield to that single one of the pastry-cooks; and no other manufactories were thought on but the grocery and confectionary wares, that were taken up in the incredible number of cakes prepared for this night's revel. The pomp and pageantry with which the several pastry-shops were set out, the fancy, richness, and number of their flags and streamers, and the contention which appeared in every one to outdo his neighbour in splendor and delicacy, were pleasingly remarkable; and failed not of attracting the eyes of successive crowds of admirers.

"Having passed through this diverting scene, I was set down at last at my nobleman's door, who, being at home, gave me a free, noble, and generous reception. There was a pretty deal of company besides, but all perfectly easy and cheerful, without stiffness or ceremony. I need not, I believe, inform you that we had a very elegant and sumptuous entertainment; and that one article of it was the reigning topick of the day, an immense rich twelfth-cake. The sight of this immediately introduced the ceremony of choosing King and Queen, a custom, whose rise or antiquity very few I believe are able to give us. Through the extraordinary bounty of my stars, the election of King fell upon me; whereupon, I instantly received the compliments of the company upon my new dignity. The title of Queen came to a beautiful lady who sat opposite to me. There were inferior characters, which fell amongst others of the company. In short, after having supported my mock Royalty with a great deal of innocent and decent mirth for some hours, till the night was pretty far wasted, making my profoundest respects to his lordship and company, and rewarding the servants, according to the rank I had borne that night, I very contentedly drove home, and having taken a hearty sleep, I found myself in the morning entirely divested of all Royalty, and no more than your plain humble servant,

THOMAS NORTH."

An attempt was made, at the commencement of 1731, to suppress some of the most considerable gaming-houses in London and the Suburbs, particularly one behind Gray's-Inn walks. The Editor of the St. James's Evening-Post, observed upon this occasion: "It may be matter of instruction as well as amusement, to present our readers with the following list of officers which are established in the most notorious gaming-houses.

"A *Commissioner*, always a proprietor, who looks in of a night; and the week's account is audited by him and two others of the proprietors.

"A *Director*, who superintends the room.

"An *Operator*, who deals the cards at a cheating game called Faro.

"Two *Crowpees*, who watch the cards, and gather the money for the Bank.

"Two *Puffs*, who have money given them to decoy others to play.

"A *Clerk*, who is a check upon the Puffs, to see that they sink none of the money given them to play with.

"A *Squib* is a Puff of a lower rank, who serves at half-salary, while he is learning to deal.

"A *Flasher*, to swear how often the bank has been stripped.

"A *Dunner*, who goes about to recover money lost at play.

"A *Waiter*, to fill out wine, snuff candles, and attend in the gaming-room.

"An *Attorney*, a *Newgate* solicitor.

"A *Captain*, who is to fight any gentleman that is peevish for losing his money.

"An *Usher*, who lights gentlemen up and down stairs, and gives the word to the Porter.

"A *Porter*, who is generally a soldier of the foot-guards.

"An *Orderly-man*, who walks up and down the outside of the door, to give notice to the Porter, and alarm the house at the approach of the Constables.

"A *Runner*, who is to get intelligence of the Justices meetings.

"Link-boys, watchmen, chairmen, drawers, or others, who bring the first intelligence of the Justices meetings, or of the Constables being out—half a-guinea reward.

"Common-bail, affidavit-men, ruffians, bravoes, *cum multis aliis*."

To characterise the follies of the day, it will be necessary to add to the account of the *walking* man, in a preceding page, another of a *hopping* man, who engaged to hop 500 yards in 50 hops, in St. James's-park, which he performed in 46. This important event occurred in December 1731.

The Lord Mayor issued a notice in December 1732, observing, that vagrant children were suffered to *skulk* about the streets and lanes, and sleep upon bulks, stalls, and other places, "whereby many of them perish by the extremity of the weather." In order to prevent this, he commanded constables, &c. to apprehend them, and to have them properly taken care of according to Law.

The Citizens of London have been particularly distinguished for their loyalty since the Revolution of 1688; this they have evinced by public rejoicings or respectful mourning on any great event occurring in the domestic concerns of their Sovereigns; thus it has become an established custom to celebrate the marriages of the respective branches of the Royal family. When that of the Prince of Orange and the Princess Royal took place in March 1734, the City was brilliantly illuminated; but, as that of Ludgate exhibited on each front, at the expence of Henry Vander Esche, surpassed every other, I shall present the reader with a minute description.

"First, A pyramid, whose base and perpendicular were 25 feet each, on each side of which was placed an obelisk, standing upon a pedestal, supported by the arms of the most noble and antient City of London.

"Secondly, A little higher on the face of the plan, were interwoven the cyphers of Prince William of Nassau, and her Royal highness the Princess Anne of Great-Britain.

"Lastly, At the extreme height of the building, were the Royal arms, over a large transparent semicircle, on which were delineated the several hieroglyphicks following. In the middle stood his Highness the Prince of Orange, hand-in-hand with his illustrious bride, the Princess Royal.

> "For these bless'd nuptials, loyal hearts contend
>
> Which shall the most with ardent joy transcend.

"On the left-hand of his Highness was represented Prudence, by a woman with two faces, having a helmet on her head, a looking-glass in one hand, and in the other a remora, which retards the motion of a ship.

> "Whilst others court applause by feats of arms,

> The fair, 'tis Nassau's wit and prudence, charms.

"Behind, on the right hand of his Highness, appeared the emblem of Fortitude, a virtue which enables us to overcome the greatest difficulties, and frequently rewards with riches and glory those who are happily endowed with it.

> "'Tis this which bears aloft on the wings of fame,
>
> Great Cæsar's, and royal William's greater name.

"Farther forward on the right-hand near his highness stood Hymen, the God of Marriage, with a burning torch, the emblem of ardent love, in one hand, in the other a flame-coloured veil, the emblem of modesty, called *flammeum*, with which the bride used to be covered to conceal her blushes.

> "Patron of marriage! bless the Royal pair,
>
> Nor veil, nor burning torch are wanting there.

"Near Hymen's right-hand was pourtrayed Religion, a woman with her face veiled, fire in her left hand, and in her right a book with a cross; veiled because she is always secret; the cross is the victorious banner of the Christian religion; the book the Holy Scriptures.

> "True piety ne'er so lovely does appear,
>
> As when conspicuous in the great and fair.

"Over the Prince near the sweep of the circle was the figure of Fame, holding a trumpet in her right-hand, with which she celebrates the glorious actions of heroes; now flying abroad with this joyful motto:

> "Happy Union!
>
> Happy, thrice happy, may this Union be,
>
> And prove the firm support of Liberty!

"On the right-hand of Fame was represented Diana, the goddess of chastity and sister of Apollo, with a crescent on her forehead and lance in her hand; her dress, though careless, yet decent, and behaviour modest and unaffected.

> "As amongst the rural nymphs her beauties shine,
>
> Amidst the British fair, so Anna, thine.

"On the other side of Fame, is seen the figure of Divine Justice, a winged woman with a crown on her head, her hair dishevelled, a sword in the right-hand, and a shield in her left, from which shines the piercing eye of Justice; she flying thus to the assistance of Hercules, the emblem of heroic Virtue, who is chasing away faction, envy, malice, and tyranny, in the defence of Britannia, who is seated leaning upon the British arms, holding those of Nassau in her right hand.

"Thrice happy Isle, where Peace and Plenty reign;

Whose Royal fleets give laws unto the main.

"On the fore-ground, on the left-hand of the circle, stood Peace, a young woman winged, crowned with olive and ears of corn; having seated by her on the ground, Plenty crowned with a garland, holding a cornucopiæ in her right hand, denoting the affluence of all things necessary for human life.

"What by those joyful emblems are design'd,

May Britain in abundance ever find;

May Peace and Plenty still join hand-in-hand,

And unanimity spread o'er the land!

"Lastly, on the left-hand and on the foremost ground were Thame and Isis, whose united streams, as they flow with a long and easy course

"So may great Nassau and his Royal Dame,

In blended love, glide with a gentle stream,

Nor ebb 'till sweet repose of night they know,

At day's return, fresh tides of transport flow."

2000 lamps were used for the above transparencies: the monument was singularly ornamented with lamps suspended on the urn and flame, and the Duke of Newcastle caused a large bonfire to be lighted before his door in Lincoln's-inn-fields, where he regaled the populace with strong-beer.

The humane Act for the transportation of felons had saved 6000 lives in the Metropolis alone, from the date of its commencement till 1734.

The Beau of 1734 "was like the cinnamon-tree; his bark is worth more than his body. A creature of the doubtful gender, masculine in habit, and feminine in manners; one who has so little manners, that he himself doth not regard it half so much as his body. All his reading has been the academy of compliments; and his heels have profited as much by it as his head. The cut of his clothes he learnt at Paris, the tone of his voice in Italy, and his affectation every where. In his dressing he shews his industry; for he spends four hours a day constantly in it without being fatigued or out of patience. His genius appears in the variety of his suits, and his generosity in his taylor's bills; his delicacy in not so much as bearing a breath of wind to blow on him, and his innocency in being seen with ladies at all hours, and never once suspected of doing an uncivil thing. When he is dressed, the business of the day is over; when he is undressed, he grows invisible, for his clothes are all that is seen of him; when he dies, they are his only valuable remains, and hung up as trophies in Monmouth-street."

The customs and manners of a part of the community of 1735 are satirically detailed in a "Covent-garden Eclogue:"

>"The *midnight* Justice, now devoid of care,
>
>Began to slumber in his elbow-chair;
>
>Long had he wak'd, but now his trade was o'er,
>
>Nor could expect a single shilling more:
>
>The watch had cry'd *Past one*, with hollow strain,
>
>And to their stands return'd to sleep again;
>
>Grave cits and bullies, rakes and squeamish beaux,
>
>Came reeling with their doxies from the Rose;
>
>Jephson's and Mitchell's hurry now was done,
>
>And now Tom King's (so rakes ordain'd) begun;
>
>Bright shone the Moon, and calm around the sky,
>
>No cinder-wench, nor straggling link-boy nigh,
>
>When in that *garden*, where with mimic pow'r
>
>Strut the mock-purple heroes of an hour;
>
>Where by grave *matrons* cabbages are sold,
>
>Who all the live-long day drink *gin* and *scold*;" &c.

The St. James's Evening Post of August 21, 1735, contains the following paragraph: "Yesterday the antient company of Archers of this City met at the Pied Horse, at the Artillery-ground, where a grand entertainment was provided for them, after which they performed their exercise with bows and arrows. This company is of several hundred years standing, and used formerly to muster at this time of the year in the Artillery-ground, as our Trained Bands do now. Some time after the invention of fire-arms the City voted them useless; but they have ever since kept up the company and their annual meeting, having a Marshal handsomely equipped in a green livery with a large silver badge."

Michaelmas or Mile-end fair was presented as a nuisance by the Grand Jury of Middlesex in 1735, which had been extended to seven days continuance beyond the original grant.

Another Royal marriage was celebrated in 1736, which is so amply described by Read in his Weekly Journal of May 1, that I cannot do better than give it in his own words:

"Monday between one and two in the afternoon his Royal Highness the Prince of Wales set out from St. James's, and crossing the water at Whitehall, went on horseback to Greenwich, where he dined with the Princess, and returned in the evening to St. James's in his barge.

"The crowd of people at Greenwich was the greatest that had ever been seen; it is thought there was not less than 10,000 persons at one time in the Park: and her Highness had the goodness to shew herself for upwards of half an hour from the gallery of the Palace, which drew the loudest acclamations.

"On Tuesday the King's leading coach, followed by his Majesty's body coach, drawn by his cream-coloured horses, brought her Highness and her retinue to Lambeth, where the King's barge waited, and carried her over to Whitehall, and from thence in the King's own chair through the Park to St. James's house, where the Court was in the Drawing-rooms, and appeared in their new clothes to receive her with all imaginable splendor.

"When her Royal Highness the Princess came to St. James's, she was dressed in a suit of rich silk; deep ground, trimmed with gold; and embroidered with green, scarlet, and purple flowers: in which manner her Highness was so condescending, that she shewed herself in several of the windows of the Prince of Wales's apartments, to gratify the curiosity of the people, who expressed their joy and satisfaction with the loudest acclamations.

"About four o'clock her Highness dined with the Prince of Wales and the Princess Amelia and Caroline, in his Royal Highness's apartment.

"Between six and seven o'clock her Highness, dressed in her wedding-clothes, which were of silver tissue, and all over white, with her hair curled and stuck with jewels, after the German fashion, was presented to her Majesty, who presented her to the Prince; whose clothes were of silver tissue, with white shoes and stockings.

"In the evening the ceremony of the marriage was performed; and the procession from the King's apartments down the great stairs, under the Piazza, to the Chapel Royal, was as follows: Four drums, drum-major, eight trumpets, four and four. Kettle-drum. Serjeant-trumpeter in his collar of SS. bearing his mace. The master of the ceremonies, with the Right Honourable the Lord Carnarvon, Gentleman Usher, between the two senior heralds. The Prince of Wales in his nuptial apparel, invested with the collar of the garter, conducted by the Lord Chamberlain and Vice Chamberlain, and supported by two Lords Bachelors. The officers attendant upon the Prince followed by pairs.

"Upon the entry into the Chapel, the Master of the Ceremonies, with the Gentleman Usher, went to the seats assigned them; and the Bridegroom was brought to the stool placed for his Highness, fronting his Majesty's Throne.

"The Lord Chamberlain and Vice Chamberlain returned to conduct the Bride; and the two Heralds returned with them to perform other functions, as did the Drums and Trumpets.

Procession of the Bride.

"Gentleman Usher to the Bride, between two Provincial Kings at Arms. The Bride, in her nuptial habit, with a coronet, conducted by the Lord Chamberlain and Vice Chamberlain, and supported by the Duke of Cumberland; her train borne by ten young ladies.

"Upon the entry, the Bride was conducted to her stool, below her Majesty's Chair of State, opposite to the Prince; the Duke sat on a stool near the Altar; and the ladies who bore the train stood near the Bride, to perform their duties while the Marriage was solemnizing.

"The Lord Chamberlain and Vice Chamberlain returned, with the Provincial Kings, to wait upon his Majesty.

His Majesty proceeded in this manner.

"Knight Marshal. Pursuivants. Heralds. Sir Robert Walpole, Knight of the Garter, with his collar. The Comptroller of the Household. The Bishop of London, &c. Two Provincial Kings at Arms. Lord Privy Seal. Lord Chancellor. Garter Principal King at Arms, between two Gentlemen Ushers. The Earl Marshal with his gold staff. The Sword of State carried by the Duke of Portland. His Majesty in the Great Collar of the Garter. The Lord of the Bed-chamber in waiting.

"Her Majesty, preceded by Mr. Coke, Vice Chamberlain, and supported by the Earl of Grantham, her Lord Chamberlain, and the Earl of Pomfret, her Master of the Horse.

"The Princesses Amelia, Carolina, Mary, and Louisa, supported severally by two Gentlemen Ushers.

"The Ladies of her Majesty's Bed-chamber, Maids of Honour, and Women of the Bed-chamber.

"Upon the entry into the Chapel, none of the persons in this procession remained upon the Hautpas, except the Lord of the Bed-chamber in waiting behind the King, the Lord who bore the Sword, who continued holding it erect upon his Majesty's right-hand, and the Lord Chamberlain, who stood upon the left-hand of his Majesty, having the Vice Chamberlain next to him.

"His Majesty was seated in his Chair of State in the upper angle of the Hautpas, on the right side.

"Her Majesty was seated in her Chair of State, on the other side of the Hautpas.

"And the four Princesses on stools placed next the Duke at the side of the Altar.

"Her Majesty's Lord Chamberlain, Master of the Horse, and Vice Chamberlain, stood upon the Hautpas behind her.

"The Ladies of the Bed-chamber, &c. went to the places assigned them.

"During all this time the organ played; but, as soon as the persons were thus seated, the organ ceased, and Divine Service began.

"After the Bishop of London and Dean of the Chapel had given the Blessing, their Majesties removed to the Throne, erected on the right-hand of the Altar of crimson velvet, richly laced with gold.

"Then the Prince of Wales, leading the Princess of Wales, went up to the Altar, and kneeled there.

"When the Dean had finished the Divine Service, the married pair rose, and retired back to their stools upon the Hautpas; where they remained while an Anthem composed by Mr. Handel was sung by his Majesty's band of musick, which was placed in a gallery over the Communion-table.

The Return was in the manner following.

"The drums, &c. as before.

"The Prince of Wales, supported by two married Dukes, &c.

"The Princess, supported as before.

"Then their Majesties and the Princesses, in the same manner as they went to the Chapel.

"As soon as the Procession came back to the door of the latter Drawing-room, the company stopped; but their Majesties, the Prince and Princess of Wales, the Duke and the Princesses, went in, when the Prince and Princess received their Majesties' blessing.

"About half an hour after ten the Royal Family supped in public, in the Great State Ballroom. Their Majesties were placed at the upper end of the table under a canopy: on the right-hand the Prince of Wales and the Duke; and on the left the Princess of Wales, and the Princesses Amelia, &c.

"The first course consisted of fifteen dishes cold and fifteen hot, the second of thirty dishes hot; and then came the dessert, which formed a fine garden rising to a terrace, the ascent to which was adorned with the resemblance of fountains, grottoes, groves, flowers, &c. In the middle was the Temple of Hymen, the dome of which was supported on transparent columns three foot high. As the meats were the most exquisite and rare that could be procured, so the dessert contained a profusion of the finest fruits, amongst which were cherries in great perfection, apricots, pine-apples, &c. At the end of the first course, their Majesties drank to the Bride and Bridegroom; and soon after, the Prince and Princesses rising up, drank the healths of their Majesties, during which the Duke and Princesses stood likewise. When the Royal Family rose from table, the sweetmeats were distributed amongst the Quality.

"Their Majesties retired to the apartments of his Royal Highness the Prince of Wales; the Bride was conducted to her bed-chamber, and the Bridegroom to his dressing-room, where the Duke undressed him, and his Majesty did his Royal Highness the honour to put on his shirt. The Bride was undressed by the Princesses; and being in bed in a rich undress, his Majesty came into the room, and the Prince following soon after in a night-gown of silver stuff, and cap of the finest lace, the Quality were admitted to see the Bride and Bridegroom sitting up in the bed, surrounded by all the Royal Family.

"His Majesty was dressed in a gold brocade turned up with silk, embroidered with large flowers in silver and colours, as was the waistcoat; the buttons and star were diamonds. Her Majesty was in a plain yellow silk, robed and laced with pearl diamonds, and other jewels of immense value.

"The Dukes of Grafton, Newcastle, and St. Alban's, the Earl of Albemarle, Lord Hervey, Colonel Pelham, and many other noblemen, were in gold brocades of 3 to 500*l.* a suit. The Duke of Marlborough was in a white velvet and gold brocade, upon which was an exceeding rich Point d'Espagne; the Earl of Euston, and many others, were in cloths flowered or sprigged with gold; the Duke of Montague in a gold brocaded tissue. The waistcoats were universally brocades, with large flowers. It is assured that most of the rich cloths were the manufacture of England; and it must be acknowledged, in honour of our own Artists, that the few which were French did not come up to these in richness, goodness, or fancy, as may be seen by the Royal Family, which are all of the British Manufacture.

"The ladies were principally in brocades of gold and silver, with large flowers, and wore their sleeves much lower than had been done for some time.

"Some worthy Citizens, on this further strengthening the Protestant Succession, a truly joyful occasion, finely illuminated the Monument (as was indeed the whole City), to shew their regard to his Majesty, and his most illustrious Family, the great protectors of it.

"At the Drawing-room on Wednesday morning his Royal Highness saluted all the ladies, and afterwards the Princess Amelia presented them to her Royal Highness, to kiss her hand; when the Honourable Colonel Townshend informed her Royal Highness of the names of every particular lady as they came up.

"His Royal Highness presented all his chief officers and servants himself to his Royal Consort; and they had severally the honour of kissing her Royal Highness's hand.

"Wednesday at noon there was the greatest appearance of the Nobility, Quality, and Gentry at Court, that has been known in the memory of man, to congratulate their Royal Highnesses on their nuptials.

"The ladies were variously dressed, though with all the richness and grandeur imaginable; many of them had their heads dressed English of fine Brussels lace, of exceeding rich patterns, made up on narrow wires, and small round rolls, and the hair pinned to large puff caps, and but a few without powder; some few had their hair curled down on the sides: pink and silver, white and gold, were the general knots wore. There were a vast number in Dutch heads, their hair curled down in short curls on the sides and behind; and some had their hair in large ringlets behind, all very much powdered, with ribbands frilled on their heads variously disposed, and some had diamonds set on ribbands on their heads; laced tippets were pretty general, and some had ribbands between the frills; treble-laced ruffles were universally worn, though abundance had them not tacked up. Their gowns were either gold stuffs, or rich silks, with gold or silver flowers, or pink or white silks, with either gold or silver nets, or trimmings; the sleeves to the gowns were middling (not so short as formerly) and wide, and their facings and robings broad; several had flounced sleeves and petticoats, and gold or silver fringe set on the flounces; some had stomachers of the same sort of the gown, others had large bunches of made flowers at their breasts; the gowns were variously pinned, but in general flat, the hoops French, and the petticoats of a moderate length, and a little sloped behind. The ladies were exceeding brilliant likewise in jewels, some had them in their necklaces and ear-rings, others with diamond solitaires to pearl necklaces of three or four rows; some had necklaces of diamonds and pearls intermixed, but made up very broad; several had their gown-sleeves buttoned with diamonds, others had diamond sprigs in their hair, &c. The ladies' shoes were exceeding rich, being either pink, white, or green silk, with gold or silver lace and braid all over, with low heels, and low hind-quarters, and low flaps, and abundance had large diamond shoe-buckles.

"The gentlemen's clothes were generally gold stuffs, flowered velvets, embroidered or trimmed with gold, or cloth trimmed, the colours various. Their waistcoats were also exceeding rich silks flowered with gold, of a large pattern, all open sleeves, and longer than formerly, and the cuff broader; the clothes were longer waisted than of late, and the plaits of the coat were made to stick out very much (in imitation of the ladies hoops) and long. The wigs were of various sorts; the tyes, higher foretops than formerly, and tied behind with a large flat tye; the bag-wigs, &c. as usual. White stockings were universally worn by the gentlemen as well as the ladies.

"Her Royal Highness the Princess of Wales left 100 guineas to be distributed among Sir John Jennings's servants at Greenwich.

"The officers of the horse and foot-guards that mounted on Tuesday at St. James's wore Ramellie periwigs by his Majesty's order."

The now almost obsolete practice of giving strong-beer to the populace on public rejoicings always occasioned riots instead of merriment. This assertion is supported by the behaviour of the mob in August 1737, when the present Duchess of Brunswick was born. The Prince of Wales ordered four loads of faggots and a number of tar-barrels to be burnt before Carleton-house as a bonfire, to celebrate the event; and directed the Brewer to his household to place four barrels of beer near it, for the use of those who chose to partake of the beverage, which certain individuals had no sooner done, than they pronounced the liquor of an inferior quality: this declaration served as a signal for revolt, the beer was thrown into each other's faces, and the barrels into the fire, "to the great surprize of the spectators; it being perhaps the first instance of Sir John Barleycorn's being brought to the stake, and publicly burnt by the rabble in Great Britain."

The Prince had the good-nature to order a second bonfire on the succeeding night, and procured the same quantity of beer from another brewer, with which the populace were pleased to be satisfied. Such was the strange disposition of the collected mind of the lower classes; a mind compounded of insensibility of kindness, pride, and independence, that condescended to accept of an entertainment, and that had the ill-nature to condemn the provision even in the presence of their Prince, who must have been ignorant that the beer was bad—*if it really was so.*

An instance of blind folly arising from a better motive occurred very soon after, during the exercise of an antient custom practised by the mob at that period, though now discontinued.

Two loose women had seized upon an inebriated gentleman, and were conveying him to their lodgings at noon-day: the populace concluded he would at least be robbed, and determined to rescue him immediately; which they did, and severely ducked the women in the Chequers Inn yard. Thus far justice proceeded in its due channel; but an unfortunate journeyman cutler happened to exert himself rather too outrageously, and attracted notice: he was observed to hold the woman or women in a manner that might be supposed real efforts of anger, or as efforts intended to mask an intention to release them; the word was instantly given to duck him as *their bully*—the women were released, and escaped; the cutler was thrown into the horse-pond in defiance of his protestations of innocence; and when his wife endeavoured to rescue him, she underwent the same discipline.

Many of the follies committed in this wanton manner must doubtlessly have originated from the excessive use of beer and gin; to suppress which, every possible effort was then making; but such was the demand for the latter, that no less than 587 persons were convicted, and paid a penalty of 100*l.* each, between September 1736 and August 1737, for retailing it, besides 127 committed to Bridewell.

Practical jokes sometimes distinguished the manners of the Citizens of London: those were generally innocent, and generally very silly; but one of a contrary description marked the Autumn of the year just mentioned. A well-dressed man rode down the King's road from Fulham at a most furious rate, commanding each turnpike-gate to be thrown open, as he was a Messenger, conveying the news of the Queen's sudden death. The alarm instantly spread into every quarter of the City; the Trained-bands, who were on their parade, desisted from their exercise, furled their colours, and returned home with their arms reversed. The shop-keepers began to collect sables; when the jest was discovered, but not the author of it.

The following ballad gives a pleasant review of the customs, or, if you please, fashions of the Citizens, previous to 1737, in care of their health:

> "On fashions a ditty I mean to indite,
>
> Since surely you'll own, 'tis the fashion to write:
>
> And, if you don't like it, then e'en lay it down,

The fashion is not to be scar'd with a frown.

To fashion our healths, as our figures, we owe;
And, while 'twas the fashion to *Tunbridge* to go,
Its waters ne'er fail'd us, let ail us what wou'd;
It cemented crack'd bones, and it sweeten'd the blood.

When Fashion resolv'd to raise *Epsom* to fame,
Poor *Tunbridge* did nought: but the blind or the lame,
Or the sick or the healthy, 'twas equally one,
By *Epsom's* assistance their business was done.

Bath's springs next in fashion came rapidly on,
And out-did by far whate'er *Epsom* had done;
There the gay and the sullen found instant relief,
And the sighing young widow was eas'd of her grief.

Unrival'd by any, *Bath* flourish'd alone,
And fail'd not to cure in gout, colic, or stone,
Till *Scarborough* waters, by secret unknown,
Stole all the fam'd qualities *Bath* thought her own.

Ev'n *Islington* waters, *though close to the Town,*
By Fashion one Summer were brought to renown;
Where we flock'd in such numbers, that for a supply,
We almost had tippled the *New-river dry*.

It late was the fashion by *Ward* to be cur'd;
And his pill mov'd the cause on't, whate'er we endur'd;
While every eye saw on which *Taylor* laid hand,
And no cripple *Mapp* touch'd, but could instantly stand.

But since 'tis the fashion to banter their skill,
Our eyes are relaps'd, and we're worse for the pill;

Our joints are contracted, our anguish so sore,

We fly to the Doctors we laugh'd at before."

One of the strange and perverse customs practised by the Society of Quakers is, their determination to open their shops on those days held sacred by other classes of Religion. On the Fast-day of February 1757, the Lord Mayor sent the proper officers to close their windows *per* force, which they did to the number of 70: yet a person of this persuasion had the presumption to wait on the Chief Magistrate with an anonymous letter he had received, threatening to destroy his house if his windows were opened, at the same time soliciting him to go there and read the Riot Act; thus demanding protection from the vengeance he provoked, by insulting the piety of others, exclusive of the impiety of opposing respect and supplication, directed to the same Divinity he worships.

Curiosity may be said to have become so prevalent throughout all classes of the inhabitants of London, that it is actually a distinguishing trait in their general character; nor is it by any means a new one, an assertion that might be supported by many proofs. An essayist of 1757 says: "I have that opinion of the ladies and gentlemen of the present age, that if the French were in full march along the New-road, and they had no engagement of pleasure on their hands, they would go out to see a *new* army, as, indeed, there would be a variety in it; the clothes, standards, &c. being different; nor do I believe that any one person would put off their intended pleasure, even though they heard the enemy's drums beating."

PORTRAIT OF A BEAU, 1757.

"Would you a modern beau commence,

Shake off that foe to pleasure, sense;

Be trifling, talkative, and vain;

Of ev'ry absent friend complain.

Their worth contemn, their faults deride,

With all the insolence of pride.

Scorn real unaffected worth,

That claims no ancestry by birth:

Despise the virtuous, good, and brave,

To ev'ry passion be a slave.

Let not sincerity molest,

Or discompose your tranquil breast;
Barter discretion, wit, and ease,
As idle things, that seldom please
The young and gay, who laugh and wink
At senseless drones who read and think;
Who all the fleeting hours count o'er,
And wish the four-and-twenty more;
Furnish'd with volumes in their head,
Above all fire, below all lead.
Be it your passion, joy, and fame,
To play at ev'ry modish game,
Fondly to flatter and caress;
A critick styl'd in point of dress;
Harangue on fashions, point, and lace,
On this one's errors, t'other's face;
Talk much of Italy and France,
Of a new song and country-dance;
Be vers'd in politicks and news;
All Statesmen, Ministers, abuse;
Set public places in a blaze:
Loudly exclaim 'gainst Shakspeare's Plays;
Despise such low insipid strains,
Fitted for philosophic brains:
But modern Tragedies extol,
As kindling rapture in the soul.
Affect to know each reigning belle,
That throngs the Playhouse or the Mell,
Declare you're intimate with all
You once have met with at a ball;

At ev'ry female boldly stare,

And crowd the circles of the fair.

Tho' swearing you detest a fool,

Be vers'd in Folly's ample school:

Learn all her various schemes, her arts,

To shew your merit, wit, and parts.

These rules observ'd, each foppish elf

May view an emblem of himself."

London Chronicle.

TERMS—VACATIONS.

The reader who has waded through my *Londinium* will find that several thousands of our vast community are of that profession which might furnish matter for a very considerable number of pages—*Lawyers*; but what can I say of their manners or customs, without incurring a charge of fixing upon a *single class*, and of thus appearing particular in praising or censuring? In this dilemma I have very fortunately met with the "Long Vacation, by Jemmy Copywell, of Lincoln's-Inn;" which the writer and the editor of the London Chronicle, *foreseeing* the use I should make of it, have kindly preserved for the present purpose.

"My Lord now quits his venerable seat,

The Six-clerk on his padlock turns the key,

From bus'ness hurries to his snug retreat,

And leaves vacation and the town to me.

Now all is hush'd, asleep the eye of Care,

And Lincoln's-Inn a solemn stillness holds,

Save where the Porter whistles o'er the Square;

Or Pompey barks, or basket-woman scolds.

Save, that from yonder pump, and dusty stair,

The moping shoe-black, and the laundry-maid,

Complain of such as from the town repair,

And leave their usual quarterage unpaid.

In those dull chambers, where old parchments lie,
And useless drafts, in many a mould'ring heap,
Each for parade to catch the client's eye;
Salkeld and Ventris in oblivion sleep.

In these dead hours, what now remains for me,
Still to the stool and to the desk confin'd:
Debarr'd from Autumn shades, and liberty,
Whose lips are soft as my Cleora's kind!"

"See Term appears to rule a passive world,
And awe the frighted rustick with its train
Of wigs and gowns, and bands. The jemmy clerk,
Close by his master's side, stands powder'd, while
His client at a distance cringes. Now,
Thou dear associate of my busy hours,
Whom (since Vacation in her sleepy lap
Lull'd me to indolence, Circæan queen,
Who poisons while she smiles) I have disdain'd,
Welcome to my embrace—once again
Thy presence let me hail—I greet thee well.
Now will I lead thee thro' the maze of law,
Perplexing and perplex'd. The knotty point,
And ev'ry quirk and quibble, will I shew:
And sometimes on huge folios shalt thou tread
With black-brow'd sections hideous. There, intent,
The puzzling clause shalt thou transcribe, until
Thy pilot sickens. Strait he shall revive,
And speed thy flight to equitable shores.

There shalt thou penetrate each deep recess,
And labour'd labyrinth of a Bill *in Canc.*
Daring to face tautology. How thick
Thy stream will run, respondent to each note
Of dull interrogation! Quickly thence,
As time may prompt, and active fancy flow,
Thy font I'll purify, and turn its course
O'er fairy mountains and poetic vales.
Say! hadst thou rather the Demurrer's bar
Erect invincible, than waft my sighs
To my Cythera's bosom, and direct
Her eyes, those lamps of beauty, where to shine?
When Cupid's messenger, how dost thou fly,
Swifter almost than thought! and as I touch,
In honour of my love, the Sapphic lyre,
Methinks thy feather dances to the tune.
But, when I bid thee up the heavy hill,
Where Bus'ness sits, to travel, how thy pace
Wants quick'ning! this and that way dost thou writhe,
Convolv'd, uneasy with the tiresome march.
Hold up awhile—for sure is the reward
That waits on labour—Bear, oh! bear me thou
Thro' long succeeding covenants, from sense
However devious. Spread thy black'ning cloud
O'er this fair face of parchment—Haste, dispatch
This cumbrous load of things. On, quicker on,
And rid me of the bus'ness of the Term.
Then in reward for all thy service past
(Tho' gratitude be held a crime) thy plume

> With gold shall blazon. Safe in silver case
>
> Shalt thou recline, from vulgar ken remote,
>
> Nor ever visit more the sons of care,
>
> Unless to win respect, and be admir'd."

The conduct of both sexes, when mixed in what are generally termed parties, can only be known by the person who actually views it. How then am I (who had not received the breath of life in 1758) to draw a faithful picture of the manners of that period? There is but one way, quotation from contemporary moralists. The Craftsman says, "A Frenchman has no more idea of a party of pleasure without ladies, than an Englishman can entertain the least conception of enjoying himself until they retreat. From those opposite dispositions it arises, that the first introduces himself with a becoming unconcern into company, and master of that *bienseance* which distinguishes the gentleman, and performs all offices of life without the least embarrassment; whereas nothing is more common among us, than to find gentlemen of family and fortune, who know nothing of the fair sex but what they have collected from the most abandoned part of it, and can scarce reckon a virtuous family within the scope of their whole acquaintance. It is not unpleasant to observe one of this class, when chance or necessity has brought him in a room with ladies of reputation. An awkward restraint hangs about him, and he is almost afraid to speak, lest he should inadvertently bolt out something, which, though extremely suitable to the dialect of Coventgarden, would be grossly offensive to those females who had not received their rudiments of education in that seminary. The gloom that hangs over an English company while the ladies remain, and the reciprocal restraint that each sex seems to be upon the other, has been frequently a subject of ludicrous observation to foreigners; and, indeed, the fair-ones themselves, *though natives, and to the manner born*, frequently express astonishment, what mysteries the men can have to celebrate, so opposite to those of the *bona dea*, that no female must be present at the ceremony.

"At the same time that I condemn my countrymen for separating themselves from those who have the art of refining every joy this world affords; I am sorry to be obliged to observe, that the ladies themselves do in some measure contribute to this great evil. The scandalous practice so prevalent at present of giving up their whole thoughts as well as time to cards, has made the company of women, pardon the expression, extremely insipid to those who would willingly consider them as rational creatures, and do not depend upon superior skill in the game of whist for a subsistence. Is it to be imagined that a man, whose mind is the least raised above the vulgar, will devote that time which he may employ in conversing agreeably, either with the dead or the living, to those assemblies, where no ideas enter beyond the respective excellences of Garrick and Cibber; and the several possible cases so profoundly calculated by the incomparable Mr. Hoyle? Yet, from declining these places, I know many intimate friends who have acquired the odious character of women-haters; though at the same time they entertain the highest esteem for that amiable sex, and sincerely regret that the tyrant Fashion has put it out of their power to enjoy more of their company than a bare view of their persons, agitated by the various and uncertain revolutions of Fortune's wheel."

EDUCATION OF YOUTH.

Foreigners very justly conceive that a double advantage may be accomplished in teaching their languages to youth and adults, by introducing them into their families; the latter pronounce nothing but what is to be acquired, and the teacher obtains a handsome sum for lodgings and board. It may be supposed that this was a modern invention. Who is there that doth not recollect the Advertisements of Monsieur Du M———d; but Monsieur Switterda precedes him a whole century; and proves that the rage for acquiring French was in full vigour when our grandfathers were infants. "Mr. Switterda has lately given, in the Postman, a very kind and candid invitation to the nobility and gentry to learn of him to speak Latin, French, and High Dutch fluently, with as good grace as if it were natural to them, and no wise *pednatick*, according to Grammar rules, and to explain any author, as Erasmus, C. Nepos, &c.; but few noblemen and ladies of quality have taken notice of his proposals, which, if he had sent them in any Country beyond Sea, had been well accepted, to his great advantage. He intends to dispose of two Copper-plates, containing the grounds of the Latin tongue. Those who will study in Divinity, Law, or Physick, may but come twice a-week to him to learn Latin. He can be aspersed by none, but by slanderous and interested persons, who have need to lodge a competent dose of hellebore in themselves. Youth may board with him at his house in Arundel-street, next to the Temple passage, where you may have the grounds of the Latin tongue in three sheets of paper, or grammatical, and Latin and French historical cards, and a packet to learn *Copiam Verborum* and *Syntaxim ornatam*. He teacheth also in Drury-lane, within two doors of the Dog-tavern, at Mr. Peache's house, or at any place where ladies and gentlemen will appoint him, if it be worth his acceptance. Thursdays and Saturdays, from five till eight, he teacheth at the Cock and Bottle in the Strand, next to Salisbury-street. *Invidiam solertia et virtute vincam*." 1699.

Ladies boarding-schools were in high reputation at the same period, and had been so for many years before. Mrs. Bellpine, daughter to Mr. La Marre, a French Minister, who had kept one for thirty years, hired Mary-le-bon house, near the church, where she professed to teach every thing then taught in boarding-schools, together with musick, dancing, and singing.

Observers frequently attacked the general system of female education, and as frequently exposed the frivolous pursuits taught in the various schools near the Metropolis; even in the year 1759, two or three houses might be seen in almost every village, with the inscription, "Young Ladies boarded and educated," where every description of tradesmen sent their children to be instructed, not in the useful attainments necessary for humble life, but the arts of coquetry and self-consequence—in short, those of a *young lady*. The person who received the children had then the sounding title of Governess; and French and Dancing-masters prepared the girl for the hour when contempt for her parents' deficiencies was to be substituted for affection and respect. Instead of reading their native language with propriety and just emphasis, it was totally neglected, and in place of nervous sentences and flowing periods, the vulgarisms of low life were continued; while the lady repeated familiar words of the French language with a sound peculiar to Boarding-schools, and quite unintelligible to a native of France: the pleasing labours of the needle were thrown aside, and the young lady soon became an adept in imitating laces and spoiling the beauty of coloured silks.

Such were the follies of 1759; and they so nearly resemble those of 1807, that I really dread I shall be supposed to criticise the moderns, when I am in truth repeating the animadversions of an author probably long since deceased.

"Jan. 29, 1759.

"At a meeting of the Society for Reformation of Manners, especially with respect to the Lord's-day: Ordered, that the thanks of the Society be returned to the worthy person, unknown, for his kind present of ten guineas. They also hereby give notice to all grocers, chandlers, butchers, publicans, pastry-cooks, and others whom it may concern; that they are resolved to put the laws in execution against all such as shall continue to offend, by exercising their callings on the Lord's day, in such a manner as may most effectually suppress that great and growing evil, whether by indictments or otherwise, of which they are desired to take this friendly public warning."

The reader will observe, that it has long been customary for tradesmen of the above description to sell on Sundays; but it should be recollected that the lowest classes of the community are sometimes paid very late on Saturday evenings, and that they have it not always in their power to arrange their time, so as to procure every necessary for the only holiday they have. When such wants are supplied by the tradesman *before the hour of Divine service*, he must be a rigid moralist indeed who would prosecute the offender. If persons in opulent circumstances were in the practice of purchasing on Sundays, it could be attributed to no other cause than mere indolence in themselves and servants, and they would deserve punishment; but I cannot help thinking a grocer or chandler would find very little account from opening his shop for such, as I do not believe there are five in each parish throughout London. For the pastry-cooks and publicans I have no excuse.

There were people in the middle of the last Century who had so little regard for decency, that they even interrupted those solemn hours of silence which are devoted, in our Courts of Justice, to ascertaining the guilt or innocence of persons whose lives are in question. Would it be credited that when an evidence was speaking, a Jury and a Judge listening, spectators should be seen in deep discourse upon some irrelevant subject, others quarrelling about places, and young ladies actually sewing each other's clothes together amidst titters and suppressed laughter—yet such *was* the fact. Surely this practice cannot *now* prevail.

Illegal concerts were held in 1759, and the conductors of them collected innocent young men and apprentices, by declaring that the receipts were intended for charitable purposes. When assembled, notorious Procuresses made their appearance, attended by the Cyprians, their progeny; and the consequence to the manners of youth may be imagined. Sir John Fielding, acting under the authority of the following clause in a very salutary Act of Parliament, and supported by a party of guards, dispersed one of those riotous assemblies in April of the above year, and sent the *ladies* to Bridewell:

"Any house, room, garden, or other place, kept for public dancing, music, or other public entertainment of the like kind, in London and Westminster, or within 20 miles thereof, without a licence had for that purpose, shall be deemed a disorderly house or place; and that it shall be lawful for any person, authorised by warrant from a Justice, to enter such house, and seize every person found therein; and that every person keeping such house, &c. without such licence shall forfeit 100*l.* and be otherwise punishable as the Law directs in case of disorderly houses."

Since Sir John Fielding's time, the publick have frequently had occasion to applaud the vigilance of the Police in their attempts to prevent illegal assemblies, whether under the title of concerts or dances; and instances might be related when dancing-masters and groupes of their pretended scholars have visited the watch-house; but the most obstinate places of vicious amusement were the Dog and Duck, and the Apollo-gardens, in St. George's-fields; the latter of which is not only now suppressed, but the site has become a mere level, and the Dog and Duck served for several years as a public kitchen for charitable purposes, after the keeper had been expelled.

At the latter place there was a long room furnished with tables and benches, and at the upper-end an organ. The company who assembled in the evening, consisted of some of the finest women of the town of the middle rank, their bullies, and such young men as could, without reflection, condescend to supply the thirsty palates of the women with inflaming liquids: the conversation was—Reader, imagine what!

The Apollo-gardens might *accidentally* receive decent visitors, but I presume their stay to have been short. These places flourished much too long; infinite injury was done by them. But we have now the consolation to reflect, that Vice is compelled to hide her fascinating visage; and though it is impossible to dive into all her haunts, we do not find them blazoned with large characters in the public ways, where her votaries however contrive intimations which are passed unobserved by the virtuous, but understood by the vicious; and these Bagnio's, Seraglio's, or whatever else the reader pleases to term them, are in many instances large and handsome houses.

The lady who trades upon her own account can never be at a loss for a sign to indicate her profession, as long as her own sweet person is permitted to appear at a window, either in *elegant disorder*, or habited fit for a drawing-room. How shall I number these signs, or the streets where they most abound? The Reader would disbelieve the enumeration.

When some concurring circumstances have prevented the rapid letting of new houses in parts of the parish of St. Mary-le-bon, I believe it might be safely asserted, that builders have admitted persons into them who had a girl in almost every room as a distinct lodger; but they are generally *dislodged* as respectable inhabitants approach, and they return to their previous haunts in more obscure situations. Exeter-street was dreadfully infested with wretched women and thieves in 1759, and great difficulty occurred in driving them from it; that it has been accomplished, may serve as a hint for some modern unfortunate neighbourhoods.

There are but few of our Essayists who have not reprobated the distribution of *vales* to the domesticks of those to whom visits were paid. When the custom was in full vigour, the office of a footman became very lucrative, and the division of the profits arising from the contributions of a large company, was a matter of no small importance to the parti-coloured mendicants; who arranged themselves in their Master's hall in double ranks, prepared to affront those who infringed their rights, and were barely civil when they received sums which would have procured meals for fifty poor families. Card-money, or money deposited under the candlesticks for the servants where card-parties were held, deserved less reprehension, as it was in every one's power to avoid gaming; but when a man in moderate circumstances was insulted for not giving that which was necessary for his own existence, or was compelled to decline an invitation to his injury, we cannot but wonder that such a custom should have prevailed for a year, much less a Century or more. It was meanness in the master to suffer such an exaction, and folly to comply with it when himself a visitor. Some serious attempts were made about 1760 to abolish Vales, which has been at length gradually accomplished, though there are still unthinking people who give where it is not expected.

Cock-fighting, Cudgel-playing, and Boxing, were practised in some parts of the Metropolis in 1761; and most of the promoters of those elegant customs escaped punishment. Higginson, master of the Tennis-court and Little Theatre in James-street, near the Haymarket, less fortunate, was tried at the bar of the King's-bench, and convicted of encouraging this species of brutality; however, Mr. Higginson contrived either to set the verdict at defiance, or to evade future penalties, for subsequent newspapers contained long accounts of a battle between Meggs, a collier, and the celebrated Nailor, at the Tennis-court, where the seats let at 5*s.* and 10*s.* 6*d.* to an overflowing audience. The reader will forgive me, if I at once proceed to notice this hateful custom of Boxing in its present state; he need not be informed that it has been encouraged by persons of the highest rank, who have been and are now known to disgrace their situation in life, by witnessing the infliction of blows which sometimes produce death, and always disfigure the human form, for the avaricious purpose of betting on either party, to the injury at least of their fortunes.

The Magistracy, well aware of the wiles and power of their antagonists in the race between Justice and Depravity, made but few movements for a considerable length of time, by which means they gained to their support all well-disposed persons; in consequence, their exertions have been so far successful, that when matches are made for battles, cavalcades of Lords, Knights, Commoners, dustmen, and the rabble in general, may be observed in motion, destined for an *arena*—they know not where, as the spot fixed upon for the scene of combat is frequently occupied by a party of Officers of the Police previous to their arrival. Thus defeated, they have been known to traverse the roads and fields for miles, to enter some jurisdiction independent of their persecutors. Cock-fighting is yet *permitted* to be publicly advertised, though but seldom; and Cudgel-playing has lately exhibited some strong symptoms of revival.

"HINTS BY THE COBLER OF CRIPPLEGATE, 1761[336:A].

"He could wish to see Butchers' boys, who gallop through the streets of London, punished for so doing, or at least their horses seized for the use of the poor of the parish in which they so offend; for, though a poor man's life may not be worth preserving, his limbs may be of use to him while he crawls upon earth.

"Brewers starting their butts in the day-time, he considers as an intolerable nuisance.

"Ruinous Houses ought to be pulled down, because they may as well tumble upon the head of an Alderman as upon that of a Cobler.

"A regulation in Smithfield-market, he thinks, ought to take place, because a mad Ox may as well gore the lady of a *Knight Banneret*, as a poor Oyster-wench.

"Worn-out Hackney-coaches should in a particular manner be looked into, because none but those in easy circumstances can be affected by their breaking-down in the streets. This regulation in no shape regards my family, because I never suffer my *Moll* to enter one till I have first properly surveyed it.

"That Cheesemongers should not set out their butter and cheese so near the edge of their shop-windows, nor put their firkins in the path-ways, by which many a good coat and silk gown may be spoiled; as by advertising in the papers his shop will be sufficiently known, without carrying home the shop-bill upon their clothes.

"Ladders, pieces of timber, &c. should by no means be suffered to be carried upon men's shoulders within the posts of this City, because, by a sudden stop, they may as well poke out the eye of a rich man as that of a poor one.

"Chairmen, as they are a kind of human nags, ought to amble without-side the posts as well as other brutes.

"It is needless for ladies of a certain cast to patrole the streets at noon-day with a bundle in one hand, as they carry an evident sign of their profession in their eye.

"Long swords are a nuisance in the City at Change-time, as the wearer may very well receive a bill without that dangerous weapon; and as it is not often he comes into it to pay one.

"Churches are no places to sleep in, because, if a person snores too loud, he not only disturbs the congregation, but is apt to ruffle the preacher's temper.

"Barbers and Chimney-sweepers have no right by charter to rub against a person well-dressed, and then offer him satisfaction by single combat.

"Splashing a gentleman with white silk stockings designedly is a breach of decency, and utterly unknown at Wapping or Hockley in the Hole.

"That reading these hints and not endeavouring to redress them, will be a fault somewhere, but not in

CRISPIN."

The whimsical manner in which the above customs are reprehended, was fairly matched by the following notice from the Publick Advertiser, issued in downright serious earnest.

"To the Inhabitants of the Parish of St. Faith.

"I have observed of late years, that the London meeting-houses of all Sectaries have crowded audiences, and that the Prayers of our established Church are read, and the Sermons of her Ministers preached, to empty seats, unless at places where some new-fangled doctrines are propagated to captivate weak minds. It becomes me as an honest man, and agreeable to the oath I have taken, earnestly to admonish you to attend the service of the Church on Sundays, unless prevented by occasions that are lawful.

"It requires I should give you this notice publicly, that no person may have reason to think me over-officious, if he finds his name among the presentments my oath obliges me to exhibit before the Ecclesiastical Court at the expiration of my office.

DAVID RICE, *Churchwarden.*"

CELEBRATION OF THE PRESENT MONARCH'S ACCESSION— MARRIAGE—AND VISIT TO GUILDHALL.

The spirits of the Community were never more exhilarated than at the auspicious period which gave England her present King and Queen. The Coronation was necessarily similar to those described in *Londinium Redivivum*; and the simplicity of our Church in the article of marriage admits of little more splendour than that of dress, at all times superb on such occasions in the British court. The fireworks, illuminations, and behaviour of the populace, who were in some instances regaled with beer round a bonfire, was generally decorous, and in some measure compels me to silence as to incidents, except in one particular case, when an odd scene of *midnight gratitude* was exhibited to Earl Temple and Mr. Pitt, who were returning *incog.* from Guildhall, where they had dined on the 9th of November 1761. The instant those Patriots were recognized, the multitude crowded round the carriage, impeded its progress, and shouted with so much ardour, that the sleeping neighbours were roused, and, when they had discovered the cause of the tumult, heartily joined in the shouts with nightcaps instead of hats in hand.

The report of the Committee appointed to provide the entertainment on the above day, will evince how well they performed their duty.

"At a Court of Common Council held June 17, 1762, the following Report was presented to the Court:

"*To the Right Honourable the Lord Mayor, Aldermen, and Commons of the City of London, in Common-Council assembled.*

"We your Committee, appointed by your order, of the third day of October last, to manage the entertainment for their Majesties at the Guildhall of this City, on the then ensuing Lord Mayor's Day, beg leave to report, that duly sensible of the great honour done us in this appointment, we cheerfully devoted our time and utmost endeavours to prepare and regulate the said entertainment, so as best to answer the intention of this honourable Court.

"In the preparations for the intended feast, your Committee omitted no expence that might serve to improve its splendour, elegance, or accommodation: whilst on the other hand they retrenched every charge that was not calculated to that end, however warranted by former precedents. Their Majesties having expressed their Royal inclinations to see the Procession of the Lord Mayor to Guildhall, the Committee obtained Mr. Barclay's house in Cheapside for that purpose, where proper refreshments were provided, and every care taken to accommodate their Majesties with a full view of the whole cavalcade.

"The great hall and adjoining apartments were decorated and furnished with as much taste and magnificence as the shortness of the time for preparation and the nature of a temporary service would permit: the Hustings where their Majesties dined, and the new Council Chamber, to which they retired both before and after dinner, being spread with Turkey carpets, and the rest of the floors over which their Majesties were to pass with blue cloth, and the whole illuminated with near three thousand wax tapers in chandeliers, lustres, girandoles, and sconces.

"A select band of music, consisting of fifty of the best hands, placed in a superb gallery, erected on purpose at the lower end of the Hall, entertained their Majesties with a concert during the time of dinner, under the direction of a gentleman justly celebrated for his great musical talents; whilst four other galleries (all covered with crimson, and ornamented with festoons) exhibited to their Majesties a most brilliant appearance of five hundred of the principal Citizens of both sexes.

"Their Majesties table was served with a new set of rich plate, purchased on this occasion, and covered with all the delicacies which the season could furnish, or expence procure, and prepared by the best hands.

"A proportionable care was taken of the several other tables provided for the Foreign Ambassadors and Ministers; the Lords and Gentlemen of his Majesty's most Honourable Privy-Council; the Lord Chancellor and Judges; the Lords and Ladies in waiting; the Lord Mayor, Aldermen, Sheriffs, and Common Council; and many others, both of the Nobility and Gentry: the whole number of guests within the Hall, including the galleries, being upwards of twelve hundred; and that of the Gentlemen Pensioners, Yeomen of the Guard, Horse and Horse-Grenadier Guards, and servants attendant upon their Majesties, and the Royal Family, and who were entertained at places provided in the neighbourhood, amounting to seven hundred and twenty-nine.

"And that this Court may form some judgment of the manner of the entertainment, your Committee have hereunto subjoined the bill of fare of their Majesty's table, and the totals of the several bills on this occasion, amounting to 6898*l.* 5*s.* 4*d.*; which, your Committee have the satisfaction to acquaint this Honourable Court, have been all ordered for payment.

"Your Committee, likewise, having provided a great variety of the choicest wines, took care that every guest should be supplied with plenty and dispatch; and yet the various services performed without hurry or confusion.

"For this purpose your Committee issued no more tickets for admission than what (considering the necessary number of attendants, amounting to two hundred and forty persons) would fill the Hall without incommoding the Royal Personages for whom the feast was intended.

"And to prevent as much as possible the intrusion of strangers (too frequent on such occasions) your Committee directed a temporary porch to be erected in the front of the Hall, where gentlemen of trust were placed at three several bars.

"Upon the whole, your Committee omitted no care or pains to render the entertainment as commodious and agreeable as possible to the Royal Guests, and in some measure expressive of the zeal and veneration of this Honourable Court for their august Sovereign, his most amiable Consort, and illustrious Family, and of their sense of his gracious condescension in honouring this City with his Royal Presence: happy if they have in any degree answered expectation, and are allowed to have done justice to the honourable trust reposed in them. Signed this 15th day of June, 1762.

- "*S. Fludyer,*
- *Robert Alsop,*
- *Richard Glyn,*
- *Francis Gosling,*
- *Thomas Long,*
- *Robert Wilsonn,*
- *Francis Ellis,*

- *Henry Kent,*
- *James Walton,*
- *Charles Meredith,*
- *John Rivington,*
- *Thomas Cogan,*
- *Edward Waldo,*
- *W. Reeves,*
- *Samuel Freeman,*
- *William Tyser,*
- *John Paterson."*

THE KING'S TABLE.

	FIRST SERVICE.*	£.	s.	d.
12	Dishes of Olio, Turtle, Pottages, and Soups	44	2	0
12	Ditto Fish; *viz.* John Dories, Red Mullet, &c.	44	2	0
7	Ditto roast Venison	10	0	0
3	Westphalia Hams consume, and richly ornamented	6	6	0
2	Dishes Pullets à la Royale	2	2	0
2	Ditto Tongues Espagniole	3	3	0
6	Ditto Chickens à la Reine	6	6	0
1	Ditto Tondron de Vaux à la Danzie	2	2	0
1	Harrico	1	1	0
1	Dish Popiets of Veale Glasse	1	4	0
2	Dishes Fillets of Lamba la Conte	2	2	0
2	Ditto Comports of Squabs	2	2	0
2	Ditto Fillets of Beef Marinate	3	0	0
2	Ditto of Mutton à la Memorance	2	2	0
32	Ditto fine Vegetables	16	16	0

* The orthography of the French words in the following items is wrong in almost every instance; but it must be remembered that it is *culinary* orthography!

	SECOND SERVICE.			
6	Dishes fine Ortolans	25	4	0
10	Ditto Quails	15	0	0
10	Ditto Notts	30	0	0
1	Ditto Wheat-ears	1	1	0
1	Goodevau Patte	1	10	0
1	Perrigoa Pye	1	10	0
1	Dish Pea-chicks	1	1	0
4	Dishes Woodcocks	4	4	0
2	Ditto Pheasants	3	3	0
4	Ditto Teal	3	3	0
4	Ditto Snipes	3	3	0
2	Ditto Partridges	2	2	0
2	Ditto Patties Royal	3	0	0
	THIRD SERVICE.			
1	Ragout Royal	1	1	0
8	Dishes fine green Morells	8	8	0
10	Ditto fine green peas	10	10	0
3	Ditto Asparagus Heads	2	2	0
3	Ditto fine fat Livers	1	11	6
3	Ditto fine Combs	1	11	6
5	Ditto green Truffles	5	5	0
5	Ditto Artichoaks à la Provincale	2	12	6
5	Ditto Mushroons au Blanc	2	12	6
1	Dish Cardons à la Bejamel	0	10	6
1	Ditto Knots of Eggs	0	10	6

1	Ditto Ducks Tongues	0	10	6
3	Dishes of Peths	1	11	6
1	Dish of Truffles in Oil	0	10	6
4	Dishes of Pallets	2	2	0
2	Ditto Ragout Mille	2	2	0
	FOURTH SERVICE.			
2	Curious ornamented Cakes	2	12	0
12	Dishes Blomanges, representing different figures	12	12	0
12	Ditto Clear Marbrays	14	8	0
16	Ditto fine Cut Pastry	16	16	0
2	Ditto Mille Fuelles	1	10	6
	The Centre of the Table.			
1	Grand Pyramid of Demies of Shell Fish of various sorts	2	2	0
32	Cold things of sorts; *viz.* Temples, Shapes, Landscapes in Jellies, savoury Cakes, and Almond Gothes	33	12	0
2	Grand Epergnes, filled with fine Pickles, and garnished round with Plates of Sorts, as Laspicks, Rolards, &c.	6	6	0

Total of the King's Table	374	1	0
Totals of the several BILLS.			
	£.	s.	d.
Mr. George Dance, Clerk of the Works	65	4	6
Mr. Richard Gripton, Coffee-man	56	10	0
Ditto, Coffee, Tea, &c. for the Committee	31	13	0
Mr. John Read, Carpenter	876	6	0
Mr. Kuhff, Confectioner	212	1	0
Mr. Wilder, ditto	121	14	0

Mr. Scott, ditto	91	14	0
Messrs. Kuhff, Wilder, and Scott, ditto	174	9	0
Mr. Baughan, Wax Chandler	31	0	0
Mr. Garrard, ditto	30	12	0
Mrs. Jones, ditto	30	12	0
Mr. Cotterel, Chinaman	30	11	0
Mr. Vere, ditto	18	12	0
Mr Wylde, Paul's-head Tavern	47	13	0
Mr. Edward Wix, Bricklayer	147	16	0
Mr. Charles Easton, Mason	6	4	0
Messrs. Alexander and Shrimpton, Smiths	300	11	0
Mr. Peter Roberts, Remembrancer	63	0	0
Messrs. Wareham, Oswald, Angel, Horton and Birch, Cooks	1600	0	0
Mr. Stanley, Band of Musick	115	0	0
Mr. Thomas Pattle, Hall-keeper	126	0	0
Messrs. Chesson, Saunders, and Woodroffe, Upholsterers	458	19	0
Mr. Allan, Wine	178	12	0
Mr. Francis Magnus, ditto	175	8	0
Mr. Frederick Standert, Hock	116	8	0
Messrs. Brown and Righton, Wine	48	5	0
Mr. Thomas Burfoot and Son, Woollen-drapers	258	5	0
Messrs. Pistor and Son, ditto	74	13	0
Mr. Thomas Gilpin, Plate	57	17	0
Mr. Deputy Samuel Ellis and Richard Cleeve, Pewterers	264	3	0
Mr. Christopher Dent, Butler	190	0	0
Mr. Robert Dixon, Baker	8	0	10
Mrs. Rachel Stephens, Brewer	8	8	0

Messrs. Barber and Shuttleworth, Fruiterers	100	0	0
Messrs. Mason and Whitworth, Ribbands	7	3	0
Mr. Charles Gardner, Engraver	23	13	0
Artillery Company	20	0	0
Mr. Charles Rivington, Printer	3	3	0
City Musick	13	3	0
Mr. Bromwich, Papier Maché	70	14	0
Mr. James Dobson, Bear Inn, Basinghall-street	42	15	0
Mr. John Handford, Swan with Two Necks, Lad-lane	20	15	0
Mr. John Greenhow, Castle, in Wood-street	29	5	0
Mr. Richard Overhall, Blossom's-inn, in Lawrence-lane	34	5	0
Mr. Thomas Whaley, Bell-inn, in Wood street	12	10	0
Mr. Richard Walkden, Stationer	6	15	0
City Marshal	100	0	0
Mrs. Mary Harrington, Glazier	15	16	0
Messrs. Willis and Machel, Plumber	63	12	0
Messrs. Pope and Son, Painters	27	18	0
Heron Powney, Esq. Sword-bearer's claim	5	0	0
Mr. William Palmer, Senior Attorney of the Mayor's Court, claim	2	0	0
Serjeants of the Chamber, for delivery of the Tickets, &c.	4	10	0
Yeomen of the Chamber's claim	4	0	0
Peter Denny, for lighting the Chandeliers	20	0	0
Sir James Hodges, Town-clerk, for attending the Committee	157	10	0
William Rix, Clerk to Sir James Hodges, for ditto	15	15	0
Andrew Boson, Hall-keeper's man	10	10	0
Six Marshal's-men	1	10	0

Six Necessary Women	6	6	0
Town-clerk's Servants	5	5	0
Chamberlain's Household Servants	5	5	0
Messrs. Chesson, Woodroffe, and Saunders, Extra Bill	10	10	0
Mr. Thomas Gilpin, for the use of Plate	20	0	0
Mr. Chamberlain's Clerks	5	5	0
Daniel Philpot, Esq. Cook to his Majesty	10	10	0
Thomas Denny, for attending the Committee	1	1	0
Total	6898	5	4

It was ordered that the said Report be entered in the Journal of the Court; and the following motion being made, was unanimously agreed to:

"That the thanks of this Court be, and are hereby given, to the Committee appointed to conduct the entertainment of their Majesties and the Royal Family at Guildhall, on Lord Mayor's day last, for their constant and spirited attention, in that service, to the honour of the Crown, and the dignity of this City."

A futile plan has long been in use, intended to lessen the number of women of the town; and particularly in 1762, when the Society for the Reformation of Manners followed an old and unprofitable example, by sending some of their constables through the streets to apprehend those miserable young persons; 40 were taken to Bridewell, eleven were whipped, one sent to the Magdalen, and the remainder are said to have been returned to their friends. Such has been the practice at long intervals ever since, perhaps with some variations in the punishment inflicted, and I am afraid an omission of enquiring for their friends. One need only pass through the Strand and Fleet-street late in the evening, to perceive how ineffectual this method of reformation has been.

It appears from a very solemn address to the publick inserted in the Newspapers for 1762, that the brutal custom of throwing at Cocks on Shrove Tuesday was not then so uncommon as it happily is at present.

When we are passing through the streets of London, it but too frequently happens that our ears are offended by hearing shocking oaths, repeated with an emphasis which indicates violent irritation; but, upon observing the parties thus offending against the laws of morality and of the realm more closely, it may be immediately perceived that nothing particular has occurred to produce anger, and that the vice has become so much a custom, that oaths are now mere flowers of rhetorick with the vulgar.

However *unpleasant* the reflection, we may console ourselves in the certainty that we are not more reprehensible than our predecessors have been; as a proof, I present the reader with an excellent Charge delivered by Sir John Fielding, April 6, 1763, at Guildhall, Westminster.

"A Charge delivered to the Grand Jury, at the General Quarter Session of the Peace, held at Guildhall, Westminster, on Wednesday, April 6, 1763, by Sir John Fielding, Knight, Chairman of the said Session. Published at the unanimous Request of the Magistrates then present, and the Grand Jury."

In order to remind the Grand Jury of their duty, rather than to inform them of it, Sir John Fielding considers, 1st, the object of the enquiry they are expected to make, and 2dly, the manner in which it might be made.

The object of it is, offences towards God, the King, to one another, and to the publick in general.

Speaking of the offences against God, "I cannot sufficiently lament (says this devout Magistrate) that shameful, inexcusable, and almost universal practice of prophane swearing in our streets: a crime so easy to be punished, and so seldom done, that mankind almost forget it is an offence; and, to our dishonour be it spoken, it is almost peculiar to the English nation! I beg, Gentlemen, you would use your utmost endeavours to suppress this dreadful evil wherever you can; but this you will best do by your own example, as the offence is punishable in a judicial way before a Magistrate. Nor should I mention it here, was I not sensible that I am speaking in the presence of a great number of peace-officers, whose immediate duty it is to apprehend such miscreants, and carry them before a Magistrate; and who are not only blameable, but punishable, for the neglect of this duty.

"The last offence I shall mention on this subject is, the breach of the Sabbath; a practice as shameful as it is common: but, as these are unworthy members of the Church, and not only disgraceful, but noxious members of society, they will therefore, I doubt not, meet with the detestation of all honest and pious men, and consequently with every punishment due to such an insolent crime, which it may be in your power to inflict; for this sort of impious neglect partakes of the deepest ingratitude from the creature to the Creator."

With regard to offences committed against the Publick in general; "Of these (says this diligent Magistrate) there are a great variety, but I shall confine myself to the three following, *viz.* public lewdness, bawdy-houses, gaming-houses. And first, as to public lewdness:

"It is the observation of a moral writer of eminence, 'That there is some degree of virtue in a man's keeping his vices to himself:' for, as example is allowed to be more efficacious than precept in recommendation of virtue, where men act as it were in opposition to the depravity of human nature, how must the open and public example of lewdness draw men into the tide of wickedness, when their own passions and inclinations serve as winds to carry them down the stream! Men like these deserve punishment as public as their crimes. But, as this offence belongs to none but the most abandoned mind, I thank God it is not common; and perhaps it would be much less seen, were those persons punished, who exposed to sale the most abandoned prints of lewdness, and the most infamous books of bawdry, which are considerably bought by curious youths, to the danger of their modesty, the hazard of their morals, and too often to the total destruction of their virtue.

"As to bawdy-houses, they are the receptacles of those who still have some sense of shame left, but not enough to preserve their innocence.

"These houses are all sufficiently injurious, and do great mischief. But those I would particularly point out to your attention, are the open, avowed, low, and common bawdy-houses, where vice is rendered cheap, and consequently within the reach of the common people, who are the very stamina of the constitution.

"These are the channels through which rottenness is conveyed into the bones of the artificer, labourer, soldier, and mariner; by this means weakness and distemper are entailed on their offspring, whose utility to the publick depends on their health and strength. These are the houses that harbour and protect undutiful children, idle servants, and disobedient apprentices. Let me then intreat you, as fathers, as masters, and as tradesmen, to put an end to these sinks of vice in your respective neighbourhoods.

"Let not that common vulgar error, of being afraid of these people, because they are litigious, desperate, and full of threats (for these fears are groundless, and should not, nay, I hope will not) deter you from this particular duty. You present; and we will punish.

"As to gaming-houses; such numbers of persons of all ranks have brought themselves, some to the greatest distresses, and others to most shameful and ignominious ends, by frequenting these houses, where gentlemen, sharpers, highwaymen, tradesmen, their servants, nay, often their apprentices, are mixed together; that, when I mention the very name of a gaming-house, I am persuaded that it conveys to your minds such ideas of mischief to society, that you will not suffer any of them to escape that come to your knowledge: and by a particular attention to the last-mentioned offences, you may be the happy means of preventing frauds, thefts, and robberies; most of which take their rise from these impure fountains of extravagance."

What the Justice, speaking of the manner of the enquiry, remarks with regard to the contempt of oaths, is but too just, and alarming:

"When I mention the word Oath; where shall I find language to express the hearty concern I feel, when I consider with what shameful insensibility this great defence of our lives, this barrier of our liberties, this security of our properties, an oath, is treated by the lower rank of the community! I too much fear, that one of the principal causes of this contempt is the slovenly manner in which this solemn obligation is administered; which does not only take off the awe, but even the very idea, of the presence of Almighty God."

A facetious writer presented the following observations to the Editor of the London Chronicle, in June 1765. I think the Reader will find they promote the object of this work.

"It is common with the old men to assert, that times alter for the worse, and that every age increases in ignorance and folly. At the Theatres, they will tell you, that Garrick and Mrs. Cibber are tolerable performers, but they will not allow them to be equal to Booth and Mrs. Oldfield. 'When I was a boy, things were otherwise,' is their common expression. Now, Mr. Printer, in despite of all this, I affirm, that instead of altering for the worse, we daily improve, not only in Commerce, but also in Manners and the Polite Arts. Think not by the Polite Arts I mean only the Exhibitions in Spring-gardens and Maiden-lane. No, Sir, my inference is a general one; I include artists of every denomination, from the genteel Mr. Pencil, the Portrait-painter, to honest Brush, the Sign-painter; both Mr. Heeltap, the Shoemaker of St. James's, and plain Crispin, the Cobler of London-house-yard. And that we only began to improve of late years, is evident from the sarcastic sneer of a shop-keeper at Epping, who, about ten years ago, had painted over his door, 'All sorts of Manchester stuffs sold here; also cardinals, nails, and hats.' The force of the witticism is too plain to need an explanation. This, I imagine, gave rise to the number of Dancing-masters, who have of late filled England; and that we are, since that time, greatly polished, no one, I dare say, will attempt to deny; but that it may not be thought that I assert what I am unable to prove, I will only remind your readers of the revolution that common things have undergone in their names. Have we now any shops? Are they not all turned into warehouses? Have we not the English warehouse, the Scotch warehouse, the Irish warehouse, the shirt warehouse, the stocking warehouse, the shoe warehouse, the hat warehouse, nay, even the buckle and button warehouse? In like manner our drinking-houses are refined: they no longer go under the vulgar denominations of gin-houses, purl-houses, ale-houses, and porter-houses, but are all turned into coffee-houses without coffee, taverns without wine, and inns without a stable-yard. Not content with this, they even left off the showy sign-post and exuberant sign, which formerly distinguished the best-accustomed houses: convinced of their own merit, they have come to a right understanding of the words *simplex munditiis*; and therefore only put up a black board with the name of their *quondam* sign upon it. But I would just hint to them, that it would be something more grammatical, if, instead of '*This is* the Boar's-head,' they were to say, '*This was* the Boar's-head.' Indeed I cannot help thinking, that a very great improvement might be made by one of these alehouse innkeepers on the Essex road, who has a board with a large punch-bowl painted on it, and under it these words: 'The Boar's-head Inn.' Surely he would have more custom, if (like the man at Bath, who changed his sign of the Royal Oak into that of the Owl in the Ivy-bush, and wrote under it, 'This is not the Royal Oak') he would say under his punch-bowl, 'This is not the Punch-bowl Inn.'"

The impropriety and folly of employing young and vigorous men to serve female customers with articles of dress, and those silly catch-pennies idly supposed ornaments to the person now so prevalent, is by no means a new trait in our customs; that it should be continued, though severely reprehended even so long since as 1765, is astonishing. At that time the antient sisterhood of *tire-women* were almost extinct; but now what head can be dressed fit to be seen without the assistance of a smart male hair-dresser? or what lady will purchase her bandeaus, her ribbands, gloves, &c. &c. from the hands of a young woman, when the same shop contains—a young *man*? Unfortunately this is a fatal custom to many fine blooming females, who, thus consigned to idleness and temptations, often fall victims to seduction.

A strange infatuation prevailed for many years in that class of the community which might be termed demi-fashionables, of sending their daughters to Convents in France for education; if that could be so termed, which amounted to nothing more than speaking the French language tolerably correct, cutting and pasting coloured paper together in silly shapes, and learning tambour, or working in imitation of lace. To mention the disadvantages attending the practice would be futile; the Revolution in France, the dissolution of Monasteries, and our endless wars, have totally abolished the custom, at least as far as relates to Convents; though I have no doubt that, should Peace ever again smile on us, French boarding-schools will be preferred to British.

Many of the pernicious customs which disgrace the populace of London may, and indeed must be continued, by their attendance at the various Fairs still held near the Metropolis; some that are now suppressed, and that of St. Bartholomew's London, will be noticed hereafter. As long as the Legislature think proper to permit the exhibition of wild beasts, and the anticks of human brutes, the wicked and the curious will attend them: thus the profligate receives legal authority to continue his baneful and licentious manners, and the curious innocent learns to imitate them without restraint as something very worthy of imitation. It is well known that the passions of human nature require the utmost coercion, even in families of undoubted honour and virtue: is it then prudent, much less wise, to send apprentices, youth from schools, girls the offspring of the lower classes, and servants, into these regular scenes of riot and systematic violations of order and decency, where customs must be acquired which will not bear repetition? The very tradition of the origin of *Horn* fair, held at Charlton and Blackheath, though ridiculously unfounded, was a sufficient cause for its abolition, when we recollect the absurd reference it had to a shocking offence against the laws of society. The frequenters of this fair went to it prepared to laugh at those injured by seduction; and the exhibition of articles made of Horn invited constant inuendos and vulgar *double entendre*.

Accident this very day afforded me other arguments against Fairs. Entering the Kingsland-road, I was astonished at the scene before me: the foot-paths and the carriage-way were crowded with pedestrians and vehicles, from the humble dung-cart to the hackney-coach; the two latter filled with every description of persons, and the whole rushing, impelled by one governing mind, to Edmonton fair. Hundreds of carts and waggons, provided with seats placed on the sides, and others lengthways in the midst, were stationed by the owners in the neighbourhood of Shoreditch church, where several principal streets communicate with the road to Edmonton; and were immediately filled by the infant, its sisters, brothers, parents, the journeyman, the apprentice, and the master, and the female servant, all dressed in their best clothing; many of the latter and the daughters of tradesmen in white muslin, silk spencers, and new straw bonnets, worth at least 30*s*. each. I would ask what the conversation of five-and-twenty persons thus assembled in a cart or waggon, some of whom consisted of the very dregs of society, could well be at noon-day, when sober; but what *at night* on their return, when some at least were intoxicated? We will say nothing of the *fun* of the Fair.

The succeeding letters which were published in 1768 require no comment.

"To the Inhabitants of the three united Parishes of St. Mary-le-Bow, St. Pancras, and Allhallows Honey-lane.

"Gentlemen,

"It is a pain and grief to me, after having been your Minister four-and-twenty years, to have any occasion to make any complaint of your behaviour; but complain of you I must, for suffering the subscription for the daily prayers to be so diminished, and reduced almost to nothing; a manifest sign that your Parishes are much poorer or less religious than they were, for either of which I should be very sorry, but more especially for the latter; for the former may be your misfortune, the latter must be your fault.

"The former Inhabitants were so convinced of the reasonableness, the propriety, the expediency, and necessity of the daily prayers, that they thought it just and fitting to make an extraordinary allowance for this extraordinary duty, and entered into a voluntary annual subscription for this purpose, which contributions have in some measure been continued from the first building and opening of your church till within these few years. And will you, Gentlemen, suffer so good a work, which hath been carried on so many years, to perish in your hands? Have you so little concern for the honour of your Church, one of the first and most conspicuous in the City, the principal of the Archbishop of Canterbury's peculiars, the chief Court of Arches, where so many Bishops are confirmed, and so much public business is transacted? And shall such a Church, that ought to be a pattern of regular devotion to others, be the first to set an example of irreligion? I hope you have too much sense of honour, too much sense of religion, to bring such a load of reproach and infamy upon your names and characters: for it would be an eternal reproach and infamy to you in this world and in the world to come; and the piety of your predecessors would 'rise up in the judgment against you, and condemn you.'

"You will say, perhaps, that you have not time to attend the daily prayers. But why have you not time? What are you doing better? Ask God and your own conscience. Scarce more than half an hour is taken up in the daily prayers: and depend upon it, you will find the time not lost, or ill employed; you will proceed to business with the greater cheerfulness, and prosper the better for it. But if you cannot or will not attend the prayers yourselves, yet why should you hinder others who would attend? Why not rather, to make some amends for your own deficiency, contribute something, that others may have opportunities for praying for a blessing upon the community? For what will avail all your care and attention, all your labour and pains, without the blessing of God to prosper them? And how can you ever expect the blessing of God upon your undertakings, if you neglect and despise, and in effect destroy and abolish his service? The neglect of public worship is soon followed by the neglect of other duties, and it behoves you seriously to consider, whether this may not be the first source and origin, the principal cause and occasion, of so many failures and bankruptcies among you.

"You will urge perhaps that other charges and taxes lie heavy upon you, the price of every thing is advanced, and you cannot afford to do as you have done. But of all charges and expences why must this of the daily prayers be the first to be retrenched? Retrench every vanity and folly, retrench every idle pleasure and diversion, retrench all your superfluous, all your unnecessary expences, rather than what you contribute to the public service of God. But no great matter is required or expected from you. As but a very short portion of your time is taken up in the daily prayers, so a very small part of your substance will be sufficient to support so pious and useful an institution. All that I desire of you is, that of the better sort, every one would subscribe ten shillings a-year, that is half a crown a quarter, and of those in lower circumstances every one would subscribe five or four shillings a year, that is, at least a shilling a quarter. Some few (to their honour be it spoken) have all along continued to do the very thing that I desire; but I wish the thing to be general, and every one of you to do the same. You cannot surely think so small and inconsiderable a sum any loss or burden to you. You may easily make it otherwise, by riding out a Sunday or two less in a year, or by going an evening or two less in a year to Vauxhall or Ranelagh, to the Tavern or the Play. This you will do, if you are not 'lovers of pleasure more than lovers of God;' and what you thus 'lend unto the Lord,' will be *paid* you in blessings *again*.

"But I would rather prefer another proposal to your consideration, which probably may be more easy and agreeable to you, as it would be taking nothing immediately out of your own pockets, and certainly would be more easy and agreeable to your Ministers, as it would be less precarious and uncertain, though perhaps not altogether so beneficial. Whatever may be the case of some few individuals, your parishes are in general very wealthy. Your poor's-rate is low in comparison to that of many other parishes, where it is nearly equal to that of the land-tax. You are in possession of several considerable estates left you by the piety and charity of former inhabitants, amounting to 300*l.* a year or more: and these estates being left without any appropriation but to the best uses of your parishes, how can any part of them be applied to a better use, or more agreeably to the intention of the pious and charitable donors, than for the public benefit of men in the public service of God? Let me therefore recommend it to you, out of these estates, or in any other method that you may think more proper, to allow to your Rector, that is, not to your Rector properly, but to your Rector for his Curate and Reader of the daily prayers, a salary of *five-and-twenty pounds* a year, which is no more than three shillings and three-half-pence in a year from every house: and surely you cannot refuse so small a boon for the honour and credit of your parishes, for your own character and reputation, for the good of your own souls and the souls of others. You see I am very moderate and reasonable in my demands, and I hope you will be as reasonable in your compliance. This is not making *godliness a gain*. Only *the labourer is worthy of his hire*: and you would not pay to a Clergyman for double service in a day, less than you would pay to a porter.

"Though I have now been your Rector, as I said, these four-and-twenty years, yet I have never in all that time asked any thing of you. I have not sent any person to collect your Easter offerings, as other City Rectors do, and I might also justly have done. I have received nothing from you but what is strictly my due, and what you are obliged by law to pay: and I shall think I have very little weight and interest with you, I shall think that either I have preached the word of God, or you have heard it, to very little purpose, if after all my services I cannot obtain this favour from you; not that it is any favour to me, but as it is a real benefit to yourselves, and may prove the happy means of your salvation. Your not complying with this request would be such a disparagement and discouragement to my ministry, that I should almost despair of ever doing any further good among you, and could only leave you to your own reflections upon that solemn commination of Christ unto the Angel of the Church of Ephesus, Rev. ii. 5: 'Remember from whence thou art fallen, and repent, and do thy first works; or else I will come unto thee quickly, and remove thy candlestick out of its place, except thou repent.' God forbid that this should ever be your case! On the contrary I wish to say with the Apostle, Heb. vi. 9, 10, 11: 'Beloved, we are persuaded better things of you, and things that accompany salvation, though we thus speak. For God is not unrighteous, to forget your work and labour of love, which ye have shewed towards his name, in that ye have ministered unto the saints, and do minister. And we desire that every one of you do shew the same diligence, to the full assurance of hope unto the end:' And with this trust and confidence in you, I remain, Gentlemen,

"Your loving Friend,
and faithful Servant in Christ Jesus,

THOMAS BRISTOL."

March 21, 1768.

"To the Right Reverend Father in God THOMAS Lord Bishop of Bristol, Rector of the Three United Parishes of St. Mary-le-Bow, St. Pancras, and Allhallows, Honey-lane.

"My Lord,

"The first sentence in your Address to our united Parishes gave us inexpressible concern, as we found ourselves charged with some behaviour which had been the occasion *of great pain and grief to your Lordship*; but we were happily relieved from this distress, as soon as your Lordship condescended to mention the nature of the crime with which we are charged; *viz.* 'That we had suffered the subscription for the daily prayers to be diminished, and reduced almost to nothing.'

"When we reflect for twenty-four years past you have laboured amongst us in the Lord, we can have no doubt but this endearing connection which has so long subsisted between us will occasion your Lordship to receive with *paternal candour* every plea we have to offer in our defence.

"Permit us then to remind your Lordship, that, though the attendance on the morning prayers has been generally omitted, and the subscription to them reduced, yet we have hitherto endeavoured to promote the honour and reputation of St. Mary-le-Bow, all that we could. We acknowledge with your Lordship, 'that it is one of the first and most conspicuous Churches in the City,' and we often view its lofty spire both with pride and pleasure; we are happy in 'its being the principal of the Archbishop of Canterbury's *peculiars*, the chief Court of Arches, where so many Bishops are confirmed, and so much public business is transacted;' and we have always endeavoured, at a great expence, to keep every part of the Church in such good order, as that it might both decently and conveniently accommodate the good company which frequently resort there on the above solemn occasions.—Surely, my Lord, this part of our conduct must convince the world, and your Lordship, that those motives which you have suggested to us *have already produced* every effect which ought to be expected from them.

"But to enter more particularly into our defence.—Our not attending these *subscription prayers* is not generally owing either *to the want of time*, or to *the desire of saving the expence*, but proceeds from a very different motive—a motive which we cannot urge, till we have again bespoke your Lordship's affectionate candour. It is this: That we are not convinced of 'the reasonableness, the propriety, the expediency, and necessity of having the daily prayers' at those hours, and under those circumstances, for which your Lordship so warmly recommends a subscription; and there are two reasons on which our doubts are founded.

"The first is, that as your Lordship has undertaken the care of our souls, and in consequence of this trust, receives at least three hundred pounds *per annum*, we think ourselves fully authorised to believe, that this *extraordinary duty*, as your Lordship properly calls it, cannot be essentially necessary to our salvation; for, if it was so, it would, and must have been, a part of your *Lordship's own duty*, and consequently have rendered any extraordinary allowance unnecessary: And we think ourselves assured, that the other high offices which your Lordship sustains in the Christian Church could by no means divert you from duly executing the prior engagements made with us,—even though you had been obliged to employ a Deputy to share with you the honour of attempting our salvation.

"Nor, secondly, is it possible that these services referred to should be omitted, if they were really so absolutely necessary to prevent 'the eternal reproach and infamy in this world, and the next,' of *us* who are committed to your care. Your Lordship, receiving 300*l. per annum* for watching over this flock, could never permit it to be involved in *eternal infamy*, when so small a boon (as your Lordship acknowledges) as 25*l. per annum* would prevent it. Far from us be such imaginary fears as these! The great *Apostles*, to whom your Lordship succeeds in an uninterrupted line, were inspired with such divine zeal to promote the salvation of men, that so far from their hesitating to part with twenty-five pounds out of three hundred pounds *per annum*, which is but 8*l.* 6*s.* 8*d. per cent.* deduction, they calmly received 'bonds and afflictions, neither counted they their lives dear unto themselves, so that they might finish their course with joy, and the ministry which they had received.' (Acts xx. 24, &c.) 'They gloried in having coveted no man's silver or gold' (neither for themselves nor their Curates); and were enabled to make this honourable appeal to their flock,—'Ye yourselves know, that these hands have ministered unto our necessities, and to those who were with us.'

"For our part, therefore, we shall rest assured, that as 'the line of the Apostolic Succession is uninterrupted,' so also is the 'Apostolic Zeal;' and that, 'as the labourer is worthy of his hire,' so also is 'the hire worthy of a labourer;' and therefore we hope your Lordship will permit us to conclude, that when a wise, a learned, and pious Minister of Christ receives *the hire*, he will conscientiously perform *the labour*, or cause it to be performed.

"Our dependance, therefore, on your Lordship's exact and devout views of this *awful* and *responsible connection* must necessarily calm every fear on our part concerning our *own* 'eternal infamy and reproach on this account;' for we are legally committed to your care, for the established outward *means of grace*;— and such means as are absolutely necessary for rendering your Lordship a good Shepherd, or us a well-fed flock, we are very confident we shall never want, whilst we have the pleasure of being under your spiritual guidance and instruction.

"We are, my Lord, your Lordship's

"Most respectful, affectionate,

"and obliged humble servants,

A B C D E F G."

St. Mary-le-Bow, April 12, 1768.

When the King of Denmark visited our Court in 1768, he observed the eagerness of the middle and lower ranks in their attempts to view his person; and politely ordered that they should be admitted while he dined. The consequent press and rudeness was such, that the permission was rescinded after *one* trial: that rudeness may be estimated by the following paragraph: "A correspondent observes, in the London Chronicle, that the crowds which follow after and so rudely press upon the King of Denmark, render his situation very disagreeable, as he is constantly obstructed in the gratification of his curiosity at any public place of diversion, or of seeing any thing curious in or near the Metropolis, for fear of being stifled. He adds, that he wishes the people would consider the great rudeness they are guilty of, by thus treating so very high and respectable a Personage: and let all who have once had a view of him in any public place pass on, and not stand staring in the King's face with such intolerable effrontery as too many have done, to the annoyance of his Majesty, as well as the hindrance of others from the pleasure of seeing him."

The hospitality with which this Prince was received by the superior ranks and all the public bodies, particularly the Corporation of London, deserves the highest commendation.

The practice of Betting is tolerably prevalent at present, and by no means confined to any particular class of the community. In short, I am afraid it might be traced very far back in the history of our customs; but it will be sufficient for the information of the reader, that I present him with an article from the London Chronicle for 1768, which I think will remind him of some recent transactions in the City.

"The introduction and amazing progress of illicit gaming at Lloyd's Coffee-house is, among others, a powerful and very melancholy proof of the degeneracy of the times. It is astonishing that this practice was begun, and has been hitherto carried on, by the matchless effrontery and impudence of one man. It is equally so, that he has met with so much encouragement from many of the principal Under-writers, who are, in every other respect, useful members of society: and it is owing to the lenity of our laws, and want of spirit in the present administration, that this pernicious practice has not hitherto been suppressed. Though gaming in any degree (except what is warranted by law) is perverting the original and useful design of that Coffee-house, it may in some measure be excusable to speculate on the following subjects:

"Mr. Wilkes being elected Member for London, which was done from 5 to 50 guineas *per cent.*

"Ditto for Middlesex, from 20 to 70 guineas *per cent.*

"Alderman B———d's life for one year, now doing at 7 *per cent.*

"On Sir J—— H—— being turned out in one year, now doing at 20 guineas *per cent.*

"On John Wilkes's life for one year, now doing at 5 *per cent.*—N. B. Warranted to remain in prison during that period.

"On a declaration of war with France or Spain in one year, 8 guineas *per cent.*

"And many other innocent things of that kind.

"But when policies come to be opened on two of the first Peers in Britain losing their heads within a year, at 10*s.* 6*d. per cent.* and on the dissolution of the present Parliament within one year, at 5 guineas *per cent.* which are now actually doing, and underwrote, chiefly by Scotsmen, at the above Coffee-house; it is surely high time for Administration to interfere, and by exerting the rigour of the laws against the authors and encouragers of such insurances (which must be done for some bad purpose) effectually put a stop to it."

There are certain wags who find great amusement in contriving wonderful stories for the publick, which are sometimes circulated verbally, and frequently inserted in the newspapers.—This waggery has recently received the elegant term of *hoaxing*. Twice very lately crowds have been sent to the ship-yards below London to witness the launching of men of war and Indiamen which were not ready to launch; and last winter *re-produced* an old story of a gardener digging a pit to receive the body of a servant he had seduced, *whom he intended to have murdered*, had not his master luckily discovered the plan by the intervention of a dream. Many of these inventions are so slightly contrived that persons of very little sagacity might detect the impostor; and yet numbers are deceived.

The newspapers of 1772 furnish a rare instance of this description, which take *verbatim*:

"At the house of one Mrs. Goulding, a single gentlewoman, at Stockwell, in the parish of Lambeth, in Surrey, about eleven o'clock in the forenoon on Monday last, there being no person except herself and servant (Ann Robinson, aged fifteen years or thereabouts) several earthen plates, and one dish, of what is called the Queen's-ware, which were placed on a shelf in one of the kitchens, fell down, and all broke except the dish, without any visible cause; in a little time after, several candlesticks, and other things, the furniture of a mantle-piece in the back kitchen, were thrown into the middle of the floor, though no person was in that room; then some china, &c. on the mantle-piece in the other kitchen was in like manner thrown into the middle of the floor, and broke, and as the pieces lay, they snapped and flew just as though they had been thrown on an exceeding hot fire; a glazed lanthorn, which hung on the staircase, was thrown down; a clock also was thrown down and broke; a red earthen pan, containing salt beef, flew in pieces, and the beef fell about; and many such like uncommon things happened; which causing an alarm, the people from the road, without distinction, ran into the house, some supposing it to be on fire, others thought the house had received a shock from the explosion of a powder-mill at Hounslow, which was blown up about an hour before. However, all concurred in moving the goods; and Mrs. Goulding, together with her maid-servant, went to Mr. Gresham's, a gentleman who lives in the next house to Mrs. Goulding's, whither the goods were carried, and particularly a tray full of china, an iron bread-basket japanned, two mahogany waiters, several bottles of different sorts of liquors, a gallipot of jelly, and a pier-glass worth about five pounds, which glass was taken down by one Mr. Saville (a neighbour to Mrs. Goulding) who handed it to one Robert Hames, and a part of the gilt-work on each side of the frame flew off before he could put it down in the garden; but when it was laid down, remained without farther damage till it was taken into Mr. Gresham's, and put under a side-board, where it flew to pieces. Mr. Saville and others going to drink of a bottle of rum and a bottle of wine, they both flew in pieces, though they were uncorked; the china in the tray flew in pieces, some while it was in the house, and the rest in the garden, whither it was removed by the affrighted spectators after it began to break; the bread-basket was thrown down and broke, as also were the two mahogany waiters, and the pot of jelly, together with bottles of liquors and jars of pickles, all of them the property of Mrs. Goulding. Mrs Goulding, being ill with the fright, was let blood by Mr. Gardener, a Surgeon of Clapham, who borrowed a pint china bowl of Mr. Gresham's people to receive the blood, which being afterwards set upon a side-board, near a bottle of rum, the property of Mrs. Goulding, both bottle and bowl jumped on the floor and broke, the bowl going into five pieces (a piece of which is now in the possession of Mr. Waterfield at the Royal Oak Inn, Vauxhall). Mrs. Goulding and her servant then went to Mr. Maylin's next door to Mr. Gresham's; but during their stay there (which was but very short) nothing extraordinary happened; from thence they went to the house of Farmer Payne (to whose wife Mrs. Goulding is related) on Rush-common, near the Wash-way, about half a mile distant from her own house, where they found Mr. and Miss Gresham, Mr. Payne and his family; it being about dinner-time, they all dined with Mr. Payne; some time after dinner Mrs. Goulding's servant was sent home to examine into the state of the house, and returned with an account that every thing there had been quiet from the time they left it. In a little time after the return of the servant, Mr. and Miss Gresham went home (nothing unaccountable having yet happened at Mr. Payne's); but Mrs. Goulding and her servant staid, and about seven o'clock in the evening the same kind of uncommon operations as had been seen at Mrs. Goulding's began at Mr. Payne's, by seven pewter dishes out of eight falling from the top shelf over a dresser in the kitchen, without any apparent cause, which was followed by an infinite number of examples not less strange, and particularly the following: a pestle and mortar jumped from the mantle-piece in the kitchen to the floor, about six feet; a row of pewter plates fell from the second shelf (over the dresser) to the ground, and being taken up, and put one in the other on the dresser, which is about three feet high, they were thrown down again, and lay in the same manner as plates are generally placed on a shelf; the pewter, china, earthen-ware, &c. were then almost all set upon the floors in the kitchen and parlour (to prevent being broke or bruised by falling), but four pewter plates were left on one of the shelves over the dresser, which plates did not move the whole night. While the things were putting on the ground, a stone tea-cup jumped out of a beaufet to the floor; on the floor a glass tumbler jumped about a foot and a half and broke; another that stood near it jumped also about the same distance, but remained whole for some hours after, then took another spring and broke also; a china bowl jumped from the floor in the middle of the parlour, and went behind the feet of a claw table, which was standing in the same parlour, at the distance of about eight feet, but did not break at that time, but being replaced by one Mr. Fowler, remained whole for a considerable time afterwards, and then flew to pieces; three china cups, which had been left on the dresser in the kitchen, flew slant-wise across the kitchen about twelve feet, by which two were broke: an egg flew from the lower shelf over the dresser, taking the same direction as the cups had done, and went nearly the same distance; there was another egg on the shelf, which did not move the whole night: a candlestick flew from the mantle-piece in the kitchen into the parlour door-way, about fifteen feet from the place where it stood; a tea-kettle under the dresser was thrown out about two feet: another tea-kettle, which stood on the side of the grate, was thrown off against an iron that is fixed to keep the children from the fire; a mustard-glass, which was a little broke by some natural accident, was thrown from a table into a pewter-dish on the floor, at about seven feet distance, but did not break, neither was it broke afterwards; the cup that had escaped when the other two were broke (as is before-mentioned) being set on a table in the parlour, flew off to the distance of nine feet, and broke; a tumbler, with a little rum and water in it, standing on a waiter upon a table in the same parlour, jumped about ten feet, and broke; the table then overset, and threw off a silver tankard of Mrs. Goulding's, a candlestick, and the waiter the tumbler had jumped from; two hams, which had been hung up in the chimney to dry, fell down, though the nail and strings on and by which they had hung were not broke or misplaced; a case-bottle of liquor, part of which they had just drank, flew into pieces; and, in short, about four o'clock in the morning of Tuesday, almost every thing in the parlour and kitchen were animated, and made such a racket, that Mr. Payne's maid-servant ran up stairs, and took a child out of bed, and carried it into the stable naked, thinking it was not safe longer to stay in the house. Mrs. Goulding then seeing the general confusion, went with her servant across the road to Mr. Fowler's (the same Mr. Fowler as is before-mentioned in this narrative) and were accompanied by Mrs. Payne and her son, about nine years of age; and the confusion at Mr. Payne's immediately ceased, when Mr. Fowler had let them into his house, he proceeded to light a fire in his back room, which done, he put the candlestick and candle he had used upon a table in his fore-room (through which Mrs. Goulding and her servant had passed), where also stood another candlestick with a tin lamp in it, but they did not stand long before they were knocked against each other, and thrown to the ground by some invisible agent; then a lanthorn in the back-room, that had been used in lighting Mrs. Goulding, &c. across the road, was thrown to the ground; and lastly a basket of coals, which was brought from Mr. Payne's, overset, and emptied itself upon the floor. Mr. Fowler upon this told Mrs. Goulding he feared she had been guilty of some bad act, as it was plain the cause of such wonderful events was carried with her; but Mrs. Goulding answered, that her conscience was clear from any extraordinary evil, and that she could not tell the cause why she was so troubled, or such like words; however, Mr. Fowler desired her to quit his house, as he could not afford to have his goods destroyed; whereupon Mrs. Goulding and her servant left his house, which has been quiet ever since, and returned to her own house; and, in a little time after their arrival, a cask with some beer in it was thrown from its stand, and a pail of water was moved from its place a little, and some of the water spilled, but nothing more happened; then she discharged her servant, and has remained quiet ever since."

Another account has the following additional circumstance:

"Some plates of Mr. Gresham's, by way of trial, were placed upon the same shelf with those of Mrs. Goulding's; the former stood unhurt, the whole of Mrs. Goulding's were broke in pieces.

"The servant girl is gone home to her father, the clerk of Lewisham parish; and what remains are now just as inanimate as the furniture of other houses."

The following extracts from Nugent's translation of M. Grosley's Tour to London are inserted as the means by which the reader may collect facts in proof of my opinion, that the manners of the populace are greatly improved since the above period.

"Amongst the people of London we should properly distinguish the Porters, Sailors, Chairmen, and the Day-labourers who work in the streets, not only from persons of condition, most of whom walk a-foot merely because it is their fancy, but even from the lowest class of shopkeepers.

"The former are as insolent a rabble as can be met with in countries without law or police. The French, at whom their rudeness is chiefly levelled, would be in the wrong to complain, since even the better sort of Londoners are not exempt from it. Inquire of them your way to a street: if it be upon the right, they direct you to the left, or they send you from one of their vulgar comrades to another. The most shocking abuse and ill language make a part of their pleasantry upon these occasions. To be assailed in such a manner, it is not absolutely necessary to be engaged in conversation with them; it is sufficient to pass by them. My French air, notwithstanding the simplicity of my dress, drew upon me, at the corner of every street, a volley of abusive litanies, in the midst of which I slipped on, returning thanks to God I did not understand English. The constant burthen of these litanies was, French dog, French b——: to make any answer to them, was accepting a challenge to fight; and my curiosity did not carry me so far. I saw in the streets a scuffle of this kind, between a Porter and a Frenchman, who spit in his face, not being able to make any other answer to the torrent of abuse which the former poured out against the latter without any provocation. The late Marshal Saxe, walking through London streets, happened to have a dispute with a scavenger, which ended in a boxing bout, wherein his dexterity received the general applause of the spectators: he let the scavenger come upon him, then seized him by the neck, and made him fly up into the air, in such a direction, that he fell into the middle of his cart, which was brimful of dirt.

"Happening to pass one day through Chelsea, in company with an English gentleman, a number of Watermen drew themselves up in a line, and attacked him, on my account, with all the opprobrious terms which the English language can supply, succeeding each other, like students who defend a thesis: at the third attack, my friend, stepping short, cried out to them, that they said the finest things in the world, but unluckily he was deaf: and that, as for me, I did not understand a word of English, and that their wit was of consequence thrown away upon me. This remonstrance appeased them; and they returned laughing to their business.

"M. de la Condamine, in his journey to London two or three years ago, was followed, wherever he went, by a numerous crowd, who were drawn together by a great tube of block-tin, which he had always to his ear; by an unfolded map of London which he held in his hand; and by frequent pauses, whenever he met with any object worthy of his attention. At his first going abroad, being frequently hemmed in by the crowd, which prevented his advancing forward, he cried out to his interpreter, 'What would all these people have?' Upon this, the interpreter, applying his mouth to the tube, answered by crying out to him, 'They are making game of you.' At last they became used to the sight; and ceased to crowd about him as he walked the streets.

"The day after my arrival, my servant discovered, by sad experience, what liberties the mob are accustomed to take with the French, and all who have the appearance of being such. He had followed the crowd to Tyburn, where three rogues were hanged, two of whom were father and son. The execution being over, as he was returning home through Oxford-road with the remains of the numerous multitude which had been present at the execution, he was attacked by two or three blackguards; and, the crowd having soon surrounded him, he made a sight for the rabble. Jack Ketch, the executioner, joined in the sport, and entering the circle, struck the poor sufferer upon the shoulder. They began to drag him about by the skirts of his coat, and by his shoulder-knot; when luckily for him, he was perceived by three grenadiers belonging to the French guards, who, having deserted, and crossed the seas, were then drinking at an ale-house hard by the scene of action. Armed with such weapons as chance presented them, they suddenly attacked the mob, laid on soundly upon such as came within their reach, and brought their countryman off safe to the ale-house, and from thence to my lodgings. Seven or eight campaigns which he had served with an officer in the gens-d'armes, and a year which he afterwards passed in Italy, had not sufficiently inured him to bear this rough treatment; it had a most surprising effect upon him. He shut himself up in the house a fortnight, where he vented his indignation in continual imprecations against England and the English. Strong and robust as he was, if he had had any knowledge of the language and the country, he might have come off nobly, by proposing a boxing bout to the man whom he thought weakest amongst the crowd of assailants: if victorious, he would have been honourably brought home, and had his triumph celebrated even by those who now joined against him. This is the first law of this species of combat; a law which the English punctually observe in the heat of battle, where the vanquished always find a generous conqueror in that nation. This should seem to prove, in contradiction to Hobbes, that in the state of nature, a state with which the street-scufflers of London are closely connected, man, who is by fits wicked and cruel, is, at the bottom, good-natured and generous.

"I have already observed, that the English themselves are not secure from the insolence of the London mob. I had a proof of this from the young Surgeon who accompanied me from Paris to Boulogne.

"At the first visit which he paid me in London, he informed me, that, a few days after his arrival, happening to take a walk through the fields on the Surrey-side of the Thames, dressed in a little green frock which he had brought from Paris, he was attacked by three of those gentlemen of the mobility, who, taking him for a Frenchman, not only abused him with the foulest language, but gave him two or three slaps on the face. 'Luckily,' added he in French, 'I did not return their ill language; for, if I had, they would certainly have thrown me into the Thames, as they assured me they would, as soon as they perceived I was an Englishman, if I ever happened to come in their way again in my Paris dress.'

"A Portuguese of my acquaintance, taking a walk in the same fields, with three of his countrymen, their conversation in Portuguese was interrupted by two Watermen, who, doubling their fists at them, cried, 'French dogs, speak your damned French, if you dare.'

"Happening to go one evening from the part of the town where I lived to the Museum, I passed by the Seven-dials. The place was crowded with people waiting to see a poor wretch stand in the pillory, whose punishment was deferred to another day. The mob, provoked at this disappointment, vented their rage upon all that passed that way, whether a-foot or in coaches; and threw at them dirt, rotten eggs, dead dogs, and all sorts of trash and ordure, which they had provided to pelt the unhappy wretch, according to custom. Their fury fell chiefly upon the hackney-coaches, the drivers of which they forced to salute them with their whips and their hats, and to cry *huzza*; which word is a signal for rallying in all public frays. The disturbance upon this occasion was so much the greater, as the person who was to have acted the principal part in the scene, which by being postponed had put the rabble into such an ill-humour, belonged to the nation which that rabble thinks it has most right to insult.

"In England, no rank or dignity is secure from their insults. The young Queen herself was exposed to them upon her first arrival at London: the rabble was affronted at her Majesty's keeping one window of her sedan chair drawn up.

"The politeness, the civility, and the officiousness of people of good breeding, whom we meet in the streets, as well as the obliging readiness of the citizens and shopkeepers, even of the inferior sort, sufficiently indemnify and console us for the insolence of the mob, as I have often experienced.

"Whatever haste a gentleman may be in, whom you happen to meet in the streets, as soon as you speak to him, he stops to answer, and often steps out of his way to direct you, or to consign you to the care of some one who seems to be going the same way. A gentleman one day put me in this manner under the care of a handsome young directress, who was returning home with a fine young child in her arms. I travelled on very agreeably, though I had a great way to go, lending an arm to my guide; and we conversed together as well as two persons could do, one of whom scarce understood a word spoken by the other. I had frequent conversations of this sort in the streets, in which, notwithstanding all the pains I took to make myself understood, and others took to understand me, I could not succeed: I then would quit my guide, and say to him, with a laugh, and squeeze of the hand, *Tower of Babylon*! He would laugh on his side likewise; and so we used to part.

"Having occasion to inquire for a certain person in Oxford-road, I shewed his address at the first shop I came to; when out stepped a young man, in white silk stockings, a waistcoat of fine cloth, and an apron about his waist. After having examined whether I was able to follow him, he made me a sign, and began to run on before me. During this race, which was from one end of the street to the other, I thought that my guide had interest in view; and therefore I got ready a shilling, which I offered him upon arriving at the proper place; but he refused it with generous disdain, and taking hold of my hand, which he shook violently, he thanked me for the pleasure I had procured him. I afterwards saw him at the tabernacle of the Methodists.

"To take a man in this manner by the arm, and shake it till his shoulder is almost dislocated, is one of the grand testimonies of friendship which the English give each other, when they happen to meet: this they do very coolly; there is no expression of friendship in their countenances, yet the whole soul enters the arm which gives the shake. This supplies the place of the embraces and salutes of the French. The English seem to regulate their behaviour upon these occasions by the rules prescribed by Alexander Severus to those who approached his person[390:A].

"I met with the same politeness and civil treatment at all the public and private assemblies to which I was admitted. At the House of Lords as well as at the House of Commons, a foreigner may take the liberty to address himself to any gentleman who understands his language; and those who are applied to upon these occasions think it their duty to answer his questions. At the first meeting of the House of Lords to try Lord Byron, I happened to be seated amidst a family as much distinguished by their high rank as their amiable qualities. They all shewed the utmost eagerness to satisfy my curiosity with regard to the several particulars of this extraordinary spectacle; to explain to me all that was said; to instruct me with regard to the origin of the most remarkable ceremonies; and, in fine, to share with me the refreshments, which the length of the trial made it necessary for them to provide.

"When the King came to the House of Lords to give the royal assent to Bills, one of the Bishops near whom I was seated offered to be my interpreter; and he took upon him to serve me in that capacity during the whole time I staid.

"At the courts of Common Pleas, King's Bench, and Exchequer, in Westminster, I seated myself amongst the Lawyers; and upon my speaking French to the two next me, neither of whom happened to understand that language, one of them rose, and brought a brother Lawyer, who, being acquainted with the French tongue, explained to me the best he could all that passed.

"At the play-houses and other public diversions, I had the same good fortune. Those that did not understand me, were eager to look for somebody that did; and my interpreter, who had taken a bottle of wine with him, never drank without afterwards presenting me with it: I made it a rule to drink, because having declined the first time it was offered, I was given to understand, that such a refusal was contrary to the laws of English politeness.

"It must, however, be observed, that this obliging behaviour is not accompanied with all those external demonstrations of civility, which are customary upon such occasions in France. If an English gentleman, who did not understand me, went in quest of an interpreter, he rose, and quitted me with an air, which seemed rather to be that of a whimsical humourist, than of a gentleman who was going to do a polite action; and I saw no more of him.

"I met with the same civility and complaisance amongst all the shop-keepers, whether great or little. The tradesman sent his son or his daughter to me, who often served me as guide, after having first acted as an interpreter: for some years past, the French language has been taught as universally as the English, in all the boarding-schools of London; so that French will soon be by choice the language of the people of England, as it was by constraint and necessity under the Norman Kings. This is a demonstration, that the antipathy of that Nation for every thing belonging to the French is not universal and without exception.

"The French are apt to imagine, that it is on account of their country they are pushed and shoved in the most frequented streets, and often driven into the kennel; but they are mistaken. The English walk very fast: their thoughts being entirely engrossed by business, they are very punctual to their appointments, and those who happen to be in their way are sure to be sufferers by it: constantly darting forward, they jostle them with a force proportioned to their bulk and the velocity of their motion. I have seen foreigners, not used to this exercise, let themselves be tossed and whirled about a long time, in the midst of a crowd of passengers, who had nothing else in view but to get forward. Having soon adopted the English custom, I made the best of my way through crowded streets, exerting my utmost efforts to shun persons who were equally careful to avoid me.

"We should be equally in an error, if we were to imagine that the English fashions, diametrically opposite to those of France, are contrived in the manner they are, in order to avoid all resemblance to those of our Nation: on the contrary, if the former are any way influenced by the latter, it is by the desire of imitating them. A mode begins to be out of date at Paris, just when it has been introduced at London by some English Nobleman. The Court and the first-rate Nobility immediately take it up: it is next introduced about St. James's by those that ape the manners of the Court; and by the time it has reached the City, a contrary mode already prevails at Paris, where the English, bringing with them the obsolete mode, appear like the people of another world. The little hats, for example, at present so fashionable in France, begin to be wore by the Nobility, who borrowed the model from Paris: by degrees the English will come at the diminutive size; but the great hats will then be resumed at Paris. This holds good in general, with regard both to men and women's apparel."

It has long been customary for the lower classes to hold a burlesque election at Wandsworth after a dissolution of Parliament for the choice of a Mayor of Garratt. To describe the strange proceedings of the candidates, who are always selected from the most ludicrous or most hideous of the community, or the riotous freaks of the mob, would be impossible. One vast wave of the populace rolls impetuous from London after the candidates and officers of the election; and, if there is but little taste in their dresses, there is always much "unreal mockery" of finery disposed in a manner which cannot but excite laughter, and the curiosity of those who are but little satisfied to witness the quarrels and intoxication that distinguish the electors of the borough of Garratt.

Many whimsical and satirical imitations of speeches and promises are made upon these occasions; but the electors, contrary to the customs of other elections, always *treat themselves*, though *tin* sixpences have sometimes been thrown amongst the mob *as bribes*.

The present member for Garratt is *Sir* Henry Dimsdale, Citizen and Muffin-seller, one of the oddest productions of injured nature, *and an idiot*. It is strange that the people who act these follies cannot perceive they are satirizing themselves. If they were not willing to be deceived, promises never meant to be performed would not be made; and, if they would neither receive bribes nor be treated, candidates would never offer the former, or furnish materials for the latter. When they chair a real member through Westminster, after having violated the freedom of election by deeds which deserve hanging, these wanton fools pull the hustings over their own heads, and frequently maim peaceable spectators.—Such are the electors of Garratt and . . . . !

FOOTNOTES:

[231:A] "This should be *Cuper's* gardens, formerly the Bear Garden." *European Magazine.*

[231:B] "This should be the *Folly*; a very large vessel, said to have been the hulk of a ship of war or frigate, which was moored on the Surrey-side of the Thames, nearly opposite Hungerford stairs, and, consequently, abreast of *Cuper's* gardens. It was used as a floating *tavern* and *bagnio*. The proprietors had an idea, that a licence was not necessary for a place of this *description on the river*, and it was continued many years unrestrained, till at length its enormities became so notorious, that its suppression was deemed a most necessary object of Police." *Ibid.*

[232:A] At Hoxton.

[233:A] Heraclitus Ridens.

[244:A] No Coaches to be admitted but with six horses, nor any Coach to come into the Park after ten of the clock in the morning.

[257:A] Daughter to the earl of Ranelagh.

[266:A] Original Weekly Journal, May 21, 1720.

[280:A] "This house was one of the last of the hundreds of Drury Taverns (for in that district it was included). Tradition formerly said it had, in the reign of Charles II. been much celebrated for the gaiety of its visitors. The rooms in which the concerts were performed and balls given, were at the top of the house: these were large, others smaller; the bar conveniently situated to see who went up stairs. All the premises, except the Tavern part, which dwindled into a public-house, were let to an organ-builder and harpsichord-maker."

European Magazine.

[336:A] *Vide* London Chronicle, vol. IX. p. 375.

[390:A] "If any Courtier bowed in a cringing manner, or used flattering expressions, he was either banished the Court, if the nature of his place admitted of it; or turned into ridicule, if his dignity exempted him from any severer punishment." Lampridius, Life of Alexander Severus.

CHAPTER. IV.
ANECDOTES OF ECCENTRICITY.

To particularise every species of Eccentricity which has distinguished this great community would be useless; but the whims of certain individuals of it ought to be noticed, in order that a just estimate may be formed of the grand whole. In the month of November 1700 an old gentleman was found lifeless on the floor of his apartment in Dartmouth-street by his landlady, who had been alarmed by hearing him fall. He died intestate, and worth 600*l. per annum*; but his manner of living was penurious to the most extravagant degree, allowing nature barely four-penny worth of boiled meat and broth *per* day. When he went from home he was under the necessity of hiring a boy for a penny to lead him across the Park, as he was near-sighted; but this was almost the only intercourse he had with mankind, except to receive his rents, which may be imagined from the state of his clothing as he lay dead: the body had seven shirts on it, each dreadfully soiled, and that next the skin actually decayed; and his other clothing was tied on with cords, that had even lacerated the flesh.

Eccentricity may exist in the brain of the most exalted character; the best intentions are often marked by it; therefore the reader must not suppose that censure is implied when good actions are classed under this head: he that deviates from the common path is eccentric; but, if his purposes are virtuous, the good man will forgive the deviation.

Some Professors of Religion are very apt to be eccentric in their conduct. Joseph Jacobs was the leader of a set of enthusiasts in 1702, who preached to his votaries at Turners-hall: he was originally a Linen-draper. "Observator" says, his congregation were "the remnant of the tribe of Ishmael; for their hand is against every body, and every body's hand against them. By their bristles (they suffered their hair to flourish luxuriantly) one would take them to be a herd of the Gaderines swine into which the Devil has newly entered, from whom at latter Lammas we shall have great cry and little wool. They are compounded of Philadelphians, Sweet-singers, Seekers, and Muggletonians. Their system of Divinity is a hodge-podge of Jacobs' putting together, and their philosophy is that of Jacob Behmen's. If their women do not backslide from the truth, it is their native virtue keeps them steadfast; for their Pastor by trade is authorised to examine their clouts. He that has the longest whiskers amongst them is by so much the better member; but Jacobs measures their profession by the Mustachio, and not by the ell and yard, as he used to do his linen. By their look you would take them to be of the Society of Bedlam; madmen we found them, and so we leave them."

This eccentric preacher died in June 1722. He retained the name of Whisker Jacobs to the day of his death. As he was singular in his life, so was he at his departure, having given orders that no mourning should be used at his interment in Bunhill-fields. Accordingly his executors gave the company white gloves and rings, but no scarfs or hatbands.

It would be extremely wrong not to include Dr. Sacheverell in the list. This gentleman contrived to turn his talents in eccentricity to some account, and was the cause of a wonderful acquisition of members to the class of oddities. I shall leave the Doctor's "birth, parentage, and education," to the biographers who have treated of the subject; and introduce him as a *singular* character, and a willing instrument in the hands of faction, and as one that contrived to confound the State, rouse the passions, and raise a mob wherever he chose to exhibit himself; nay, even to animate the Rev. Mr. Palmer, preacher at Whitehall, at the risk of suspension, to pray for him by name as a patient sufferer under the persecution of the House of Lords, who brought him to trial, Feb. 27, 1709-10, on charges of having maintained that the necessary means used to bring about the Revolution were odious and unjustifiable; that resistance to the Supreme Power was illegal under any pretence whatever; that it was the duty of superior pastors to thunder out their ecclesiastical anathema's against persons entitled to the benefit of the toleration, &c. &c.; which they decreed the Commons had substantiated, contents 69, non-contents 52. After this event he became the idol of the mob, and of several well-meaning but weak people. His vanity led him to make a kind of triumphal journey through the country, where he was generally received as a conqueror, and in some instances by Corporations and the Clergy with flags displayed, ringing of bells, and bonfires. However disgraceful such conduct, he furnished the industrious of many classes with the means of enriching themselves: the Printers and Publishers fattened on his Sermons and his Trial; the Engraver on his physiognomy; and even the Fan-maker sold his "Emblematical fans with the true effigies of the Rev. Dr. Henry Sacheverell done to the life, and several curious hieroglyphicks in honour of the Church of England finely painted and mounted on extraordinary genteel sticks." After this summary of the Doctor's exploits, who will deny his claim to eccentricity, or that he was a most unworthy son of the Church, a teacher of bigotry, not of peace? But he is forgotten; and but one small marble lozenge shews his present resting-place.

In 1711 Gustavus Parker entertained the publick with a specimen of his eccentricity, exhibited in a "Monthly Weather-paper," or baroscopical prognosticks of the description of Weather to happen a month *after* his publication. He even pronounced whether there would be warm or cold rain, or be clear, for the day and night, and from which point the wind would blow. Though Mr. Parker entered into a laboured explanation of the principles on which he founded his infallible judgment, they were confuted most completely by the observations of an individual, who placed the real state of the weather opposite the anticipated; from which I pronounce him no conjurer.

Politicks had arrived to a dreadful state of effervescence in 1713. Many authors exerted themselves to fan the flames, and but few endeavoured to extinguish them. One eccentric person ("which lived at the sign of the Queen's-arms *and Corn-cutter* in King-street, Westminster, where a blue sign-board is fixed to *the other* that shews what cures I perform, *viz.* the scurvy in the gums, or tooth-ache, likewise the piles and all casual sores, and fasteneth loose teeth, and causeth decayed gums to grow firm and well again") with more zeal than ability collected a *farrago* of scraps of religion and moral sayings, and connected them in a way peculiar to himself by fervent wishes and pious ejaculations; which he published twice a-week under the title of the "Balm of Gilead, or the Healer of Divisions, by Thomas Smith, Operator."—I consider this Thomas Smith a worthy predecessor of many an Itinerant Methodist.

The public-house is a hot-bed for vulgar eccentricity; and without doubt the following mad exploit of four men in January 1715-16 originated in one of them, which is thus described in the London Post of the 21st. They solemnly bound themselves to support each other in every difficulty and danger that might occur during an excursion up the Thames on the ice for four days, in which they determined to avoid every track made by man, and to explore a way for themselves. They set out provided with poles from the Old Swan near London-bridge; and two of them were seen to fall through air-holes opposite Somerset-house and Lambeth, but the others were never heard of.

I am rather at a loss under what title to place the ignorance and absurdity displayed in the ensuing paragraph, copied from the News Letter of Feb. 25, 1716; but, as superstition is closely allied to folly, and eccentricity is a species of folly, I believe this to be the proper one. "The Flying Horse, a noted victualling-house in Moor-fields, *next to that of the late Astrologer Trotter*, has been molested for several nights past in an *unaccountable manner*; abundance of stones, glass bottles, clay, &c. being thrown into the back side of the house, to the great *amazement and terror* of the family and guests. It is altogether unknown how it happened, though all the neighbouring houses were diligently searched, and men appointed in proper places to find the occasion."

The unknown author of the Advertisement which follows appears to have been nearly related to Thomas Smith the Corn-cutter, but far more enlightened. The motives that dictated it must be approved, however extraordinary such a production may appear in the Postman of July 31, 1716.

"Whoever you are to whose hands this comes, let the truth it contains abide upon your mind, as what is intended for your greatest benefit. The method taken I know is uncommon; yet, if there is the least probability of success, though it be only with a few, the design will be justified, as intending the glory of God in your salvation. Remember then that you were once told in this manner, that being zealous for names and parties is what will stand you in no stead at death, except you have the life in you that shall never die. Are you a Christian? or, have you only the name from education, as it is the professed Religion of your Country? If you can say on your conscience you have endeavoured to lay aside prejudice wherein you might have reason to suspect yourself of it, and, apprehending your lost condition without a Saviour as revealed in the Gospel, you have devoted yourself to God in him, and therefore hope you are a true Christian, it is well—give God the praise; but, if in your conscience you must say you have no more than the name, stay Man, Woman, whoever you be, consider, think before this go out of your mind or hand how you shall escape, if you neglect so great salvation."

The nobility and young men of fashion of most countries are rather eccentric in their amusements; and surely this observation may safely be applied to those of England in 1717, when a set of *escape graces* subscribed for a piece of plate, which was run for in Tyburn-road by six Asses rode by Chimney-sweepers; and two boys rode two Asses at Hampstead-heath for a *wooden spoon* attended by above 500 persons on horseback. Women running for Holland smocks was not uncommon; nay, a match was talked of for a race of women in hooped petticoats; and another actually took place in consequence of a wager of 1000*l.* between the Earl of Lichfield and Esquire Gage, that Gage's Chaise and pair would outrun the Earl's Chariot and four. The ground was from Tyburn to Hayes; and Gage lost through some accident. Vast sums were betted on all these eccentric operations.

In the month of February 1717-18, James Austin, inventor of the Persian Ink-powder, most extravagantly grateful to his customers, determined to do an act which renders him a fit subject for my groupe of oddities. He selected the Boar's-head in East-cheap for the reception of those persons, and provided for them a Pudding, to be boiled fourteen days, for which he allowed a chaldron of coals; and another baked, a cube of one foot; and nearly a whole Ox roasted. Such was the fare. The musick was commensurate with the vastness of the entertainment, at least in one particular; which was a drum, that had served as an alarm in some Turkish army, eighteen feet in length, and near four feet in diameter. Swift might have made good use of Austin in the travels of Lemuel Gulliver.

Mist's Journal notices the Austin feast a second time, and asserts that the copper for boiling the great pudding was then, April 19, erected at the Red-lion in Southwark Park, where crowds of people went to see it. Mist adds that the pudding would weigh 900lb.; and when boiled was to be conveyed to the *Swan Tavern*, Fish-street-hill, Monday, May 26, to the tune of "What lumps of pudding my mother gave me!"

Poor Austin boiled his pudding, and advertised that the company expected was so numerous, he should be under the necessity of carrying it to the Restoration-gardens in St. George's-fields, where he *attempted* to convey it, as appears from a second notice; but the rabble, attracted by the ridiculous cavalcade, broke through every restraint, and carried off banners, streamers, &c. &c. which he demanded should be restored by the 6th of June under pain of prosecution for robbery. He says nothing of the fate of his Pudding; I must therefore leave him, in order to pay attention to a fellow-labourer in the works of singularity—a poor Benedict, who declared in the Flying Post of July 8, 1718, "About two years ago I intermarried with the daughter of Ben Bound of Foster-lane, ironmonger, who agreed to give me 600*l*. Soon after he furnished me three rooms to the value of 50*l*., for which he pretended he gave 300*l*.; upon which I asked him for the remainder of the 600*l*.; but he answered, if I insisted upon any money, he would sue me for the goods. Whereupon I filed a bill in Chancery against him, and he owned in his answer he had given me the goods; but, being resolved to have them again at any rate, upon the 11th of June last he persuaded my wife to carry them away; and upon the 12th I was arrested in a sham action for 200*l*. at the suit of one Jeffery Sharpe (whom I never heard of before), and by 14 officers carried to prison; and in the mean time my house was ransacked; and, had it not been for an Attorney, I had not saved the value of one penny, most of my goods being carried away, and the rest packed up. And after they had kept my wife a fortnight, they were so barbarous to let her lie two nights upon chairs; so that she is returned to me again: and I hope if her father desist from giving her ill advice, and coveting the rest of my goods, she will still prove a good wife.

JOHN NEWALL."

A woman who lived in great apparent poverty died in March 1718 within the parish of St. Dunstan in the East. Those who prepared her for burial are said to have found 8000*l*. concealed in her bed.

The malicious Miser deserves a niche in this temple of worthies. Such was Mr. Elderton, a farmer of Bow, who went by the name of the old Farmer of Newgate; where he was confined, and even died, because he had determined not to pay the assessments in common with his neighbours[406:A].

Another worthy was Mr. Dyche, whose singularity is thus mentioned in the Whitehall Evening-Post for August 1619: "Yesterday died Mr. Dyche, late School-master to the Charity Children of St. Andrew Holborn. He was a strict Nonjuror, and formerly *amanuensis* to the famous Sir Roger L'Estrange.

It is said he wore a piece of the halter in which parson Paul was executed (in the rebellion of 1715, for carrying arms against the King) in his bosom; and some time before his death had made a solemn vow *not to shift his linen* till the Pretender was seated on the Throne of these Realms."

In the month of March 1720 an unknown lady died at her lodgings in James-street, Covent-garden. She is represented to have been a middle-sized person, with dark-brown hair and very beautiful features, and mistress of every accomplishment peculiar to ladies of the first fashion and respectability. Her age appeared to be between thirty and forty. Her circumstances were affluent, and she possessed the richest trinkets of her sex generally set with diamonds. A John Ward, Esq. of Hackney, published many particulars relating to her in the papers; and, amongst others, that a servant had been directed by her to deliver him a letter after her death; but as no servant appeared, he felt himself required to notice those circumstances, in order to acquaint her relations of her decease, which occurred suddenly after a masquerade, where she declared she had conversed with the King, and it was remembered that she had been seen in the private apartments of Queen Anne; though after the Queen's demise she had lived in obscurity. This unknown arrived in London from Mansfield in 1714, drawn by six horses. She frequently said that her father was a nobleman, but that her elder brother dying unmarried the title was extinct; adding that she had an uncle then living, whose title was his least recommendation.

It was conjectured that she might be the daughter of a Roman Catholick who had consigned her to a Convent, whence a brother had released her, and supported her in privacy. She was buried at St. Paul's, Covent-garden.

When some decay in the draw-bridge on London-bridge had rendered it necessary to prevent the passage of persons and vehicles, in order to its repair in April 1722; the silence and desolate appearance of a place so much frequented at all other times attracted the attention of some wealthy tradesmen, who entered into the whimsical resolution to have a table set in the midst of the street, where they sat drinking for an afternoon, that they might be enabled to say at a future period, "however crowded the bridge is at present, I have drank punch on it for great part of a day."

An extraordinary method was adopted by a Brewer's servant in February 1723 to prevent his liability for the payment of the debts of a Mrs. Brittain whom he intended to marry. The lady made her appearance at the door of St. Clement Danes habited in her shift; hence her enamorato conveyed the modest fair to a neighbouring Apothecary's, where she was completely equipped with clothing purchased by him; and in these Mrs. Brittain changed her name at the church.

Eccentricity is generally a source of ridicule, but rarely one of profit. An instance of the latter is recorded in the London Journal: a Mr. Morrisco, an eminent Weaver, and a man of vast possessions, resident in Spital-fields, had a bill drawn on him from abroad of 80,000*l.* which was held by an Ambassador at our Court, and sent for acceptance. When the old gentleman made his appearance, the messenger was appalled at his figure, which exhibited penury personified; he therefore hurried back to the Ambassador, full of doubts and fears whether it could be possible such a man should be capable of raising even 800*l.* The representative of Sovereignty, terrified at the idea of his probable loss, resolved to satisfy himself by personal inspection; which he had no sooner done than Morrisco divined his thoughts, and to ease them, and turn his doubts to present profit, he offered to pay the bill immediately for a valuable consideration; the offer was gladly accepted, and Morrisco fairly pocketed 4000*l.* the *produce of his shabby habiliments*.

The name of Don Saltero, the odd collector and exhibitor of natural and artificial curiosities at Chelsea, made its first appearance in the newspapers June 22, 1723, whence the following whimsical account of himself and his rarities are extracted:

> Sir, Fifty years since to Chelsea great
>
> From Rodnam on the Irish main
>
> I stroll'd, with maggots in my pate,
>
> Where much improv'd they still remain.
>
> Through various employs I've past:
>
> A scraper, vertuos', projector,
>
> Tooth-drawer, trimmer, and at last
>
> I'm now a gimcrack whim collector.
>
> Monsters of all sorts here are seen,
>
> Strange things in nature as they grew so;
>
> Some relicks of the Sheba Queen,
>
> And fragments of the fam'd Bob Cruso.
>
> Knick-knacks too dangle round the wall,
>
> Some in glass cases, some on shelf;
>
> But what's the rarest sight of all,
>
> Your humble servant shows himself.

On this my chiefest hope depends.

Now, if you will the cause espouse,

In Journals pray direct your friends

To my Museum Coffee-house;

And in requital for the timely favour,

I'll *gratis* bleed, draw teeth, and be your shaver;

}

Nay, that your pate may with my noddle tally,

And you shine bright as I do—marry, shall ye

Freely consult my revelation Molly;

Nor shall one jealous thought create a huff,

For she has taught me manners long enough.

DON SALTERO.

Chelsea Knackatory.

Several frolicsome gentlemen hired a hackney-coach in 1724, to which they affixed six horses; the coachman and postillion they habited as kennel-sweepers or scavengers; and they placed as many shoe-boys as could cling to the vehicle behind as footmen, with their stools on their heads and baskets of implements by their sides. Thus equipped they drove to the Ring in Hyde-park, and there entertained the company with this species of eccentricity.

There is a certain degree of whim in some of the wagers we find recorded in the newspapers, that, however absurd the bettors may appear, a smile is excited perforce.

In the above year two gentlemen, full of money and destitute of wit, had a dispute respecting the quantity that might be eaten at one meal. This ended in a bet of 5*l.* proposed by one of them, that himself and *another* would eat a bushel of tripe, and drink four bottles of wine, within an hour. The parties met at Islington, where the tripe was produced and the wine displayed; nothing remained but the introduction of the *another*; that *another*, gentle reader, proved a sharp-set Bear, who fully justified his friend's prognostick with the tripe diluted by three bottles of wine poured into it.

Applebee's Original Weekly Journal for November 19, 1726, has the following curious article, which fills another niche in our Pantheon of Eccentrics: "For the entertainment of our brother *dumplineers*, we shall inform them of a curiosity contrived for their accommodation at the Sun Tavern in

St. Paul's Church-yard; which is the invention of Mr. Johnston, the master of the house; being a larder erected in the middle of his yard, which stands upon four pedestals, in a perfect round twelve feet in circumference, in the lower part whereof is three round shelves with cylindrical doors to open and shut; the same is covered with a curious slab of black and white marble three feet in diameter, and a direct circular figure, from whence the four pedestals are carried up, between each of which are two sliding sashes with convex glasses: the four pillars are adorned with curious iron-work and other ornaments, as well for beauty as use, and a shelf runs round the inside for containing proper provent for the stomach. In the midst hangs a crown of iron painted and gilt, and the top rises into a dome twelve feet in height, in the same manner as that of St. Paul's, which is leaded over with four round or port holes covered with wire for the conveniency of admitting the air and keeping out the flies. On the top of the dome is a globe, upon which sits Bacchus astride upon a tun, to signify his Godship is willing to lay a good foundation, that he may be the better able to contain his liquor; on his head is the Sun dispersing his rays; from the four sides are four sliding shelves which draw out for the accommodation of such dumplineers as desire to drink their wine at the fountain-head, or next the cellar door. The whole is neatly painted and gilt."

There is sometimes a degree of eccentricity blended with revenge; an instance of which occurred in 1727. The pastor of the parish of St. Andrew Undershaft had differed with a female of his flock to a very violent degree; in consequence, the lady renounced his spiritual governance while living, and solemnly declared her corpse should not receive the rites of burial from his lips when dead. This resolution was communicated by the executors to the undertaker, who provided a Clergyman to officiate at the funeral. As the Priest of the parish had notice of this strange proceeding, he determined to prevent the intruded Priest from performing the ceremony; but the latter, equally tenacious, insisted on his right, in compliance with the lady's will. A violent dispute succeeded, which terminated by both parties reading the burial service.

After this shameful scene of impiety, the Parish Priest retired to the Vestry-room, and enquired of the Clerk whether he had provided him a ticket for hat-bands and gloves, as usual. The Clerk replying in a surly manner that he had not, the Priest wreaked dire vengeance on his body by a thorough beating[414A]. In short the offending Clerk by his

>Ecclesiastick

>Was beat with fist instead of a stick.

The St. James's Evening Post of January 1728 mentions a nameless oddity, who kept open house in his *own way* during the holidays at a Tavern near St.

James's-market: "He treats all the company that comes, provided they appear fit for a gentleman to keep company with; pays his reckoning twice a day, and thinks no expence too great that their eating and drinking can put him to. He never quits his room, or changes his linen. The house has already received some hundreds of pounds from him, and is likely to receive many more, if his constitution can but do its duty. He proposes to hold it for three months; and it is said, this is not the first time he has done so."

Abraham Simmonds, a tobacconist, who retired to enjoy a handsome independence at Lewisham, died in 1728. His widow and executrix found, to her utter dismay, upon opening his will, that he had directed his body to be buried in his own orchard, wrapped in a blanket, without any of the usual religious ceremonies; and that his favourite dog after his natural decease should be deposited in the same grave. The lady seems to have been a sagacious wife, and a good hand at a quibble. She strictly complied with the eccentric wishes of Mr. Simmonds; but, as that gentleman neglected to say his body must *remain* in the Orchard, she had it conveyed into a handsome coffin, and thence to the church-yard, where the Parish Priest performed the burial rites.

Orator Henley, who is said to have restored the antient eloquence of the pulpit, was frequently mentioned in the Newspapers *circa* 1724 as appointed to preach Charity Sermons. He appears however in 1726 to have entered into the true spirit of eccentricity, and frequently advertised in the following style:

"On Sunday July 31 the Theological Lectures of the Oratory begin in the French Chapel in Newport-market, on the most curious subjects in Divinity. They will be after the manner and of the extent of the Academical Lectures. The first will be on the Liturgy of the Oratory, without derogating from any other, at half an hour after three in the afternoon. Service and Sermon in the morning will be at half an hour after ten. The subjects will be always new, and treated in the most natural manner. On Wednesday next, at five in the evening, will be an Academical Lecture on Education antient and modern. The chairs that were forced back last Sunday by the crowd, if they would be pleased to come a very little sooner, would find the passage easy. As the town is pleased to approve of this undertaking, and the institutor neither does nor will act nor say any thing in it that is contrary to the laws of God and his country; he depends on the protection of both, and despises malice and calumny." One of the writers of the Weekly Journal says, the fame of Henley led him to visit the Oratory, and adds, "About the usual hour of the Orator's entering the public scene of action, a trap-door gave way behind the pulpit, as if forced open by some invisible hand; and at one large leap the Orator jumped to the desk, where he at once fell to work. I eyed the person of the Orator thoroughly, and could point out in every lineament of his face the features and muscles of a Jew, with a strong tincture of the Turk. But, to come to his oration, which turned on the important subject of Education antient and modern—I had entertained hopes of meeting with something curious at least, if not just, on the great theme he had made choice of; though, instead of it, I heard nothing but a few common sentiments, phrases, and notions, beat into the audience with hands, arms, legs, and head, as if people's understandings were to be courted and knocked down with blows, and gesture and grimace were to plead and atone for all other deficiencies." The price of admission was one shilling.

Mr. Henley issued his notice of intended lectures in November 1728 in the ensuing strange manner: "At the Oratory in Newport-market, to-morrow, at half an hour after ten, the Sermon will be on the Witch of Endor. At half an hour after five the Theological lecture will be on the Conversion and Original of the Scottish Nation, and of the Picts and Caledonians; St. Andrew's relicks and panegyrick, and the character and mission of the Apostles.

"On Wednesday at six, or near the matter, take your chance, will be a medley Oration on the History, Merits, and Praise of Confusion, and of Confounders in the road and out of the way.

"On Friday will be that on Dr. Faustus and Fortunatus and conjuration; after each the Chimes of the Times, No. 23 and 24. N. B. Whenever the prices of the seats are occasionally raised in the week-days, notice will be given of it in the prints. An account of the performances of the Oratory from the first to August last is published, with the discourse on Nonsense; and if any Bishop, Clergyman, or other subject of His Majesty, or the subject of any foreign Prince or state, can at my years, and in my circumstances and opportunities, without the least assistance or any patron in the world, parallel the study, choice, variety, and discharge, of the said performances of the Oratory by his own or any others, I will engage forthwith to quit the said Oratory.

J. HENLEY."

This eccentric gentleman, full of conceit and self-sufficiency, attracted the notice of the Grand Jury for the City and Liberty of Westminster January 9, 1725-9, who presented him thus:

"Whereas the Act, made in the first year of the reign of King William and Queen Mary, for exempting their Majesties' Protestant subjects dissenting from the Church of England from the penalties of certain laws, was wisely designed as an indulgence for the tender and scrupulous consciences of such Dissenters, and as a means to unite all the Protestant subjects in interest and affection: And whereas it is notorious, that John Henley, Clerk in Priest's orders according to the form of the Church of England, did about three years since hire a large room over the market-house in Newport-market within this City and Liberty of Westminster, and cause the said room to be registered in the court of the Archdeacon of Middlesex (pursuant to the said Act of Toleration) as a place for religious worship, to be performed therein by him the said John Henley, who pretended to dissent from the Church of England on account of Infant Baptism (although that has been the least of his exercises, nor are his audiences of that persuasion), and by his advertisements in the public newspapers invited all persons to come thither, and take seats for twelve-pence a-piece, promising them diversion under the titles of *Voluntaries, Chimes of the Times, Roundelays, College-bobs, Madrigals,* and *Operas,* &c.: And whereas it appears to us, by information upon oath, that the said John Henley, notwithstanding his professed dissention and separation from the Church of England, has usually appeared in the habit worn by Priests of the Church of England; and in that habit has for several months past upon one or more days in the week made use of the said room for purposes very different from those of religious worship; and that he has there discoursed on several subjects of burlesque and ridicule, and therein and in his comments upon the public newspapers, and in his weekly advertisements, has uttered several indecent, libertine, and obscene expressions, and made many base and malicious reflections upon the established Churches of England and Scotland, upon the Convocation, and almost all orders and degrees of men, and upon particular persons by name, and even those of the highest rank: And whereas it appears to us more particularly, by information upon oath, that he the said John Henley did, on the 12th day of December last, cause to be published in the Daily Post an advertisement, giving notice that on the evening of the next day he would pronounce King Lear's oration in an apology for madness, on which evening he did in the said room (called by him the Oratory) in the habit of a Clergyman of the Church of England repeat a speech out of the tragedy of King Lear, acting in such manner and with such gestures as are practised in the theatres; and that the said John Henley did, on the 17th day of the same month, cause to be published in the said Daily Post another advertisement, inviting such as went the following evening to the ball in the Haymarket to come first to his said room in their habits and masks for twelve-pence a-piece; and that according to such invitation several persons so dressed and masked did then and there appear, and were admitted upon paying the said moneys, for their seats:

"We the grand Jury for, &c. conceiving that this behaviour of the said John Henley is contrary to the intention of the said Act of Toleration, and tends to bring a disrepute upon the indulgence so charitably granted to truly scrupulous Dissenters, that it gives great offence to all serious Christians, is an outrage upon civil society, and of dangerous consequence to the State, and particularly that the said assemblies by him held as aforesaid are unlawful ones, his said room not being licensed for plays, interludes, or masquerades, do present the said John Henley, and his accomplices and assistants to us unknown, as guilty of unlawful assemblies, routs, and riots, &c. &c. &c."

Henley, actuated by the genuine spirit of perseverance and opposition, proceeded with his lectures. If *any effect* was observable from the presentment, it was that of threefold eccentricity and impropriety of subjects for his Orations. The bill of fare issued for Sunday September 28, 1729, contains a list of the fashions in dress of the time, and is therefore curious:

"At the Oratory, the corner of Lincoln's-Inn-fields near Clare-market, tomorrow, at half an hour after ten: 1, The postil will be on the turning of Lot's wife into a pillar of salt; 2, The Sermon will be on the necessary power and attractive force which Religion gives the spirit of man with God and good Spirits.

"II. At five: 1, The postill will be on this point, *In what language our Saviour will speak the last sentence on mankind*; 2, The lecture will be on Jesus Christ's sitting at the right-hand of God, *where that is*; the honours and lustre of his inauguration; the learning, criticism, and piety of that glorious article.

"The Monday's orations will shortly be resumed. On Wednesday the oration will be on the Skits of the Fashions, or a *live* gallery of family pictures in all ages; ruffs, muffs, puffs manifold; shoes, wedding-shoes, two-shoes, slip-shoes, peels, clocks, pantofles, buskins, pantaloons, garters, shoulder-knots, perriwigs, head-dresses, modesties, tuckers, farthingales, corkins, minikins, slammakins, ruffles, round-robbins, toilets, fans, patches; Dame, forsooth, Madam, My lady, the wit and beauty of my Grannum; Winifred, Joan, Bridget, compared with our Winny, Jenny, and Biddy; fine ladies and pretty gentlewomen; being a general view of the *beau monde* from before Noah's flood to the year 29. On Friday will be something better than last Tuesday. After each a bob at the times."

I believe the following curious advertisement to have been the production of the Lady Hamilton, widow of the Duke killed by Lord Mohun: "I Elizabeth duchess dowager of Hamilton acknowledge I have for several months been ill in my health, but was never speechless, as certain penny authors have printed; and so, to confute these said authors and their intelligence, it is thought by my most intimate friends, *it is the very last thing that will happen to me*. I am so good an Englishwoman that I would not have my countrymen imposed on by purchasing false authors; therefore, have ordered this to be printed, that they may know what papers to buy and believe, that are not to be bribed by those who may have private ends for false reports. The copy of this is left in the hands of Mr. Berington, to be shewn to any body who has a curiosity to see it signed by my own hand.

E. HAMILTON[423:A]."

Another, published in September 1732, was inclosed by a deep border of black, and is strongly demonstrative of religious eccentricity, or, if you please, religious frenzy.

"Just published, Divine Inspiration; or a Collection of Manifestations to make known the Visitation of the Lord, and the Coming of his Kingdom in great power and glory, according to the Scripture promise, by the preaching of the everlasting Gospel, as Rev. xix. &c.

"Also, that the righteousness of God in his express sovereign power, wisdom, and love, may be known in the Divine word, the Sent of God to manifest and execute Divine will both in mercy and judgment, the two great witnesses, the messengers of God in this approaching day of the Lord upon us.

"Lastly, this is the earnest prayer of them that have known and tasted the power of the Divine word, and who, as a testimony of their knowing God, in his out-speaking word immediately revealing, and from universal love and charity wishing true knowledge may descend, and increase and multiply in and upon man of every order and every degree, and to be the voice and word of God, do here give and set their hands, believing he that now speaks will come, and that suddenly, according as hath been the voice of the Spirit of the Holy Ghost, the Comforter in the Anointed, saying, So come, O Lord."

This strange effusion is signed by twelve persons, four of whom were women.

"By the mouth of Hannah Wharton at Birmingham and Worcester."

Master Henley thus informed the publick in October 1732: "Before any person casts an imputation on me, in reference to the Oratory, wherein I know no fault but one, that it is a pattern of the truest principles of Religion, with the most various and assiduous endeavour to merit, in the capacity of a scholar and a clergyman, that is, or ever was in this island, or in the world; before I am reflected upon for this, I would desire every man who educates a son to orders, and him who is so educated, to consider this case, and to make it his own.

"I waited some years ago on a certain Prelate with a solicitation of a pulpit in town, signifying my resolution to cultivate and exert the talent of preaching which God had given me, in the most complete and public manner. His answer was, that I might be of use; but, before he could do for me, he must have a *pledge* of my attachment to the government. I was an entire stranger to politicks; but gave him that *pledge*.

"A pledge demanded, given, and accepted for a consideration, is a contract for that consideration; the hinge of my interest and fortune very much turned upon it. It was the year 1721-2, a tender crisis; and, doubtless, he made a job of it to the Government. When I applied for the consideration, he shifted off. Had he any possible exception to my intellectual or moral qualifications (though nothing can be more immoral, or sooner make the world Atheists than a perfidious prelate), he should, before he drew me in, have told me, that if he met with any such exception, he would not do what I solicited; and that he would take time to examine. This would have been fair. He assigned no exception at all during a whole year, till I had sacrificed my interest to him on his own demand; and it is easy to frame exceptions, if a person be inclined to break his word. My judgment is, he and his clergy even envied me in the pulpit, and were jealous of my advancement, timorous that at Court there might be a patron, or a patroness of learning, and apprehensive that I might outstrip them there. Was I on my death-bed, I would take the Sacrament, that I know the former part, and believe the latter part (without the least vanity for so poor a triumph as excelling them would be) of this advertisement to be a matter of fact.

J. HENLEY."

A *Miss* Jennings, or rather perhaps *Mrs*. Jennings, died in November 1736, who is said to have laid strong claims to eccentricity. This lady breathed her last at the *Oxford-arms Inn*, Warwick-lane; and was buried at Christ-church, Newgate-street; but the singularity of her conduct consisted in a predilection for *Inns*; she made them in short her constant residence, whether in the country or in London, where she had her steward, two female servants, a coachman and footman; and, though she sometimes remained several months stationary, her bills were regularly paid every night. At the same time her host was kept in utter ignorance of her name. Mrs. Jennings left a fortune of 80,000*l*. to five children, her first cousins; and appointed ——Jennings, Esq. of Northaw, her executor.

A Chair-woman, named Frances White, was interred at St. Margaret's, Westminster, in 1736; but the *singularity* of the circumstance is, that she should have been deposited before the Altar of the Church, which she thus accomplished: In the course of her pursuits she was observed to be remarkably assiduous and industrious, and often asked charitable assistance: this she frequently received, and so carefully preserved that her sister gained a bequest of 1150*l*. on the easy condition of procuring a grave for her body *within* the church, and affording it a handsome funeral. The above sum had been concealed in various *hiding-places* contrived in her chamber.

A writer in the Weekly Miscellany for August 7, 1736, pertinently observed, that "the attention of the good people of England is very frequently ingrossed by the bold pretensions of persons starting up from time to time in several sciences, but more particularly in those of Divinity and Physick; and with the more reason of hoping to succeed in their views, as the soul, in which the one is concerned, and the body, in which the other, are the two grand subjects which engage the human mind; and each of these pretenders respectively becomes in vogue for a certain period, and then generally dies away in a silence proportioned to the noise they once made. The Stroking Doctor in the reign of Charles II.; the French Prophets in the reign of Queen Anne; the Quicksilver lunacy lately; the itinerant preaching Quakeress since; and Mr. Ward's pill and drop, not yet quite gone off from its vogue—are signal instances of the truth of our observation. So it may be observed, that the Quicksilver fashion seems to have been beat out of doors by the pill and drop; and now the vogue of the pill and drop, which seem to owe their success to their violent operation in desperate cases, appears in a fair way of subsiding to a new object of the public attention, which really seems (beyond all that we have named) to deserve it, as it is attended with plain and unartificial fact, as it is neither violent or dangerous in the operation, and carries in every act the clearest demonstration along with it.—What we mean is the famous female Bone-setter of Epsom, who must be allowed as much to excel the others, as certainty does imagination, as simplicity does artifice, and as seeing and feeling do the other senses.

"This person, we are told, is daughter of one Wallin, a bone-setter of Hindon, Wilts, and sister of that Polly Peachem whom a gentleman of fortune married. Upon some family quarrel she left her father, and wandered up and down the country in a very miserable manner, calling herself *Crazy Sally*; and often, as it is presumed for grief, giving way to a practice that made her appear to have too good a title to the name. Arriving at last at Epsom, she has performed such wonderful cures, that we are told the people thereabout intend a subscription for 300*l.* a year to keep her among them."

Many of those cures are then described, which seem well attested, and are really surprising. "In fine, the concourse of people to Epsom on this occasion is incredible; and it is supposed she gets near 20 guineas a day, as she executes what she does in a very quick manner. She has strength enough to put in any mans shoulder without assistance; and this her strength makes the following story, which may be depended upon, the more credible.

"An impostor came to her, sent, as it is supposed, by some Surgeons, on purpose to try her skill, with his head bound up; and pretended that his wrist was put out; which, upon examination, she found to be false; but, to be even with him, she gave it a wrench, and really put it out, and bade him go to the fools who sent him, and get it *sett again*; or, if he would come to her that day month, she would do it herself."

This strange woman utterly ruined herself by giving way to that eccentricity, which too frequently in one way or other marks all our characters. The object of it was a Mr. Hill Mapp, on whom she fixed her affections, and to whom she was determined at all events to be married, though every effort was made by her friends to prevent the match. On the day appointed for the ceremony, Sir James Edwards, of Walton-upon-Thames, waited on her with the daughter of Mr. Glass, an Attorney, a poor afflicted child whose neck was dislocated and supported by steel instruments. Miss Wallin saw the girl, and said she could restore the parts, but would do nothing till she became Mrs. Mapp. A gentleman present, finding her resolute, lent her his chariot to convey her to Ewell, where she expected to obtain a conveyance to London with her intended husband, though in that expectation she was disappointed. "As she was going to Ewell, Mr. Walker, brazier, of Cheapside, met her, and returned with her to the Inn. He was carrying down his daughter to her, a girl about 12 years of age, whose case was as follows: the vertebræ, instead of descending regularly from the neck, deviated to the right scapula, whence it returned towards the left side, till it came within a little of the hip-bone, thence returning to the locus, it descended regularly upon the whole, forming a serpentine figure. Miss Wallin set her strait, made the back perfect, and raised the girl two inches. While this was doing, Sir James Edwards's chariot with two gentlemen in it, came to beg her to come back to Epsom, suspecting she might not return again; but all their persuasions availed nothing, and the best terms they could make with her were, that she should not go to London to be married, but have the chariot and go to Headley, about three miles from Epsom. As the coachman was driving her by Epsom, she was told that the Minister of Headley was suspended for marrying Mr. C. whereupon the coachman said he would carry her no further, unless it was to Epsom. She then alighted, and went into a cottage on the side of the town; presently after which, information being given that she was there, Mrs. Shaw and several other ladies of that place went to her on foot to importune her to return; but, to avoid any farther solicitation, she protested she would never come nigh the town, if they opposed her marriage any longer; and then walked on towards Banstead. Sir James Edwards, being informed how much she was affronted by his coachman, immediately ordered a pair of his horses to be put to a four-wheeled chaise, and sent them with another driver to offer their service to convey her where she pleased. Mr. Bridgwater in his chaise, and several other people on horseback, followed her also, and overtook her when she had walked about a mile over the Downs towards Banstead, where she had determined to be married. When she came there, the Minister having no licences, she returned to her first resolution of going to London; but, the horses having travelled that morning from Walton, and being harassed about without any refreshment, the coachman was afraid to venture so far as London with them, and desired to be excused; upon which Mr. Bridgwater, in regard to the child Sir James Edwards had brought, and other unhappy creatures who were in Epsom waiting for their cure, brought her in his chariot to London, saw her married, and conveyed her back again immediately after, being fully resolved to see her perform her promise." Mrs. Mapp was buried at the expence of the parish of St. Giles in 1737!!

The methods adopted by Lord and Lady Vane to render themselves conspicuous in the annals of their Country were so extremely eccentric, and are so well known, that their shades would feel indignant should I refuse the Viscount's advertisement a niche in this odd catalogue of worthies. His Lordship thus introduced himself to public notice January 24, 1737:

"Whereas Frances, wife of the right honourable the Lord Viscount Vane, has for some months past absented herself from her husband, and the rest of her friends, I do hereby promise to any person or persons who shall discover where the said lady Vane is concealed, to me or to Francis Hawes, Esq. her father, so that either of us may come to the speech of her, the sum of 100*l.* as a reward to be paid by me on demand at my lodgings in Piccadilly. I do also promise the name of the person, who shall make such discovery, shall be concealed, if desired. Any person concealing or lodging her after this advertisement, will be prosecuted with the utmost rigour. Or, if her Ladyship will return to me, she may depend upon being kindly received. She is about 22 years of age, tall, well-shaped, has light brown hair, is fair-complexioned, and has her upper teeth placed in an irregular manner. She had on when she absented a red damask French sacque, and was attended by a French woman, who speaks very bad English.

VANE."

The variety produced under this head is already so great that I shall desist, lest I tire my readers: besides, it will be difficult to select instances nearer our present time without offending individuals or their relatives.

FOOTNOTES:

[406:A] Original Weekly Journal, Dec. 6, 1718.

[414:A] This affair is mentioned in all the Newspapers of the day.

[423:A] Evening Post, May 23, 1730.

END OF THE FIRST VOLUME.

www.ingramcontent.com/pod-product-compliance
Ingram Content Group UK Ltd.
Pitfield, Milton Keynes, MK11 3LW, UK
UKHW031348260325
456749UK00003B/557